Contemporary Chinese Civil and Commercial Law

Tao Huang · Weiping He

Politics Meets Markets

Laws and Regulations of China's Financial Markets

Springer

Tao Huang
Guanghua Law School
Zhejiang University
Zhejiang, China

Weiping He
Monash Law Faculty
Monash University
Melbourne, VIC, Australia

ISSN 2524-6194 ISSN 2524-6208 (electronic)
Contemporary Chinese Civil and Commercial Law
ISBN 978-981-97-9175-0 ISBN 978-981-97-9176-7 (eBook)
https://doi.org/10.1007/978-981-97-9176-7

This Springer imprint is published by the registered company Springer Nature Singapore Pte Ltd.
The registered company address is: 152 Beach Road, #21-01/04 Gateway East, Singapore 189721, Singapore

Acknowledgements

As a result of our collaborative efforts, this book on the studies of the contemporary China's financial markets and its law is both a planned and unplanned outcome.

At the beginning of our collaboration a few years ago, we decided to contribute to academia with a book on Chinese financial law. This work was not meant to merely introduce what the legal framework of China's financial market looks like to the readers outside China, nor was it intended to explain to Chinese readers how China's financial market laws differ from those abroad (although, given that the two of us are based in different jurisdictions, this approach might seem natural). Instead, our plan was to use a universal language and theory, understandable to international audience, to explain the nature and nuances of institutions and their interactions underpinning China's financial markets. Our aim goes beyond answering "what it is" or "why it is so". Specifically, we chose political institutions as the core thread to "tell the story", as this was the distinctly "local characteristics" of China's financial markets within the global financial system. We believe we have achieved this goal.

At the same time, the specific content of this book was not something that could be pre-planned. The reason is simple: the evolution of China's financial market institutions over the past few years has exceeded expectations. This is not something any author or any academic could have envisaged or anticipated. The changes in China's financial markets are not only reflected in the rapid expansion of the markets themselves but also in the structural changes of the underlying legal system, with the avalanche of disputes. As a result, the writing process of this book often felt like "crossing the river by feeling the stones" (borrowing Deng Xiaoping's phrase).

The completion of this book benefited from the support and assistance of our institutions and partners. To this end, we extend our gratitude to Shanghai Jiao Tong University and Zhejiang University, where Huang Tao worked successively, and to Monash University, where He Weiping is based. We also wish to thank our academic peers who offered critiques through the writing process, and after the completion of draft chapters of this book. The list of contributors would likely be too long to enumerate here, so we would thank them in person after the publication of this book. In particular, we are grateful to Dr. Yuan Zhao, who has since left academia and who provided excellent research assistance and contributions at the preliminary stages of this book.

Lastly, it is perhaps most important for the co-authors to take this opportunity to thank each other. Despite residing in different countries and teaching the laws of our respective jurisdictions, we attempted to produce the works that observe and explain the evolution of China's financial market legal system with a degree of objectivity and free from the constraints of particular ideological perspective.

December 2024

Tao Huang
Weiping He

Contents

Chapter 1
Introduction

There is a consensus in the field of economics on the causal relationship between financial development and economic growth, namely: a significant reason for a country's wealth is having developed financial markets (including the banking system and securities market).

However, in stark contrast to the above consensus, when scholars attempt to explain why the level of development of financial markets varies so greatly among different countries, different viewpoints emerge. Broadly speaking, there are two main perspectives on this issue: the legal origins view and the political institutions view.

Represented by LLSV, the legal origins view holds that the level of financial market development in a country largely depends on the legal system it belongs to. Specifically, countries that follow the Anglo-American common law legal tradition have the most developed financial market systems (intuitively, internationally recognized financial centers like the US, UK, Hong Kong, and Singapore, which are all based in Anglo-American common law legal systems, confers this view). The reason is that countries with common law systems provide better protection for minority shareholders, thus having a larger financial system than those with civil law traditions.

On the other hand, scholars supporting the political institutions view argue that legal origin is not the primary influence on a country's financial development. Instead, the legal systems affecting financial development are products of political activities and political systems. The logic behind this is: without a state that ensures the enforcement of financial contracts, the development of the banking system and securities market will be greatly hindered. Unless there is a self-enforcing system to constrain the state's authority and discretionary power, the state would have strong incentives to sacrifice financial market development to maintain its political position when regulating financial markets. The long-term decline of financial markets in Latin America compared to North America over the past century supports the political institutions view.

T. Huang and W. He, *Politics Meets Markets*, Contemporary Chinese Civil and Commercial Law, https://doi.org/10.1007/978-981-97-9176-7_1

When discussing China's financial markets, we inevitably observe some unique phenomena. For example, after about forty years of market-oriented reforms, China's financial market is undeniably significant globally: the total assets of the national financial industry exceed 400 trillion yuan, and five banks and insurance institutions have become globally systemically important financial institutions.[1] In the global stock exchange rankings, the Shanghai and Shenzhen stock exchanges have consistently ranked among the top ten,[2] and currently, three of the world's ten largest banks by market capitalization are Chinese.[3] However, China's financial markets have always been criticized for deficiencies, with scandals in the banking system and securities market occurring from time to time, and investor protection has been a significant problem.

If we view China in the light of the aforementioned academic viewpoints, it would be rather problematic: on one hand, the history of the development of China's financial markets since 1979 is also a history of the development of China's legal system. The varied development of the financial markets at different times reflects the evolving state of financial market laws and regulation, showcasing both advancements and setbacks. On the other hand, the introduction and enforcement of China's financial markets rules are greatly influenced by factors outside the arena of law. The factors, of political nature, include not only specific political interests in decision-making or enforcement but also structural constraints as result of the political system.

No country can avoid the influence of politics on the formulation and enforcement of laws. In China, this influence is highly unique and characteristic, particularly in the field of financial markets. On one hand, China's financial market is not the spontaneous order described by Hayek[4]; it is a product shaped by political forces. The most typical example was the establishment of China's two stock exchanges in Shanghai and Shenzhen by the municipal governments around 1990. On the other hand, unlike former socialist countries which were part of the Soviet Union, China's political system has not westernized. This has created a unique institutional combination in the Chinese financial markets, resulting in many characteristics not observed in other financial markets.

Therefore, the authors of this book attempt to explore the unique institutional factors influencing China's financial markets and the financial markets legal system. These factors are distinctly characteristic of Chinese, including but not limited to the Communist Party of China ('Party') factor, the courts, and the interactions between

---

[1] The State Council, 2022, Report on the Financial Work Situation by the State Council, www.npc.gov.cn/npc/c2/c30834/202210/t20221029_320028.html.

[2] Visual Capitalist, Mapped: The Largest Stock Exchanges in the World, https://www.visualcapitalist.com/largest-stock-exchanges-in-the-world/.

[3] GlobalData, Top 10 Banks in the World by Market Capitalization, https://www.globaldata.com/companies/top-companies-by-sector/financial-services/global-banks-by-market-cap/.

[4] F. A. Hayek, Law, 2022, Routledge, Legislation and Liberty, Volume 1: Rules and Order.

different institutions within the administration. These factors may also exist in developed financial markets, but the uniqueness of the Chinese story lies in the relationship between political factors and the financial markets and the legal system.

From our perspective, political factors are certainly very important for China's financial markets, but the authors' findings do not simply side with either of the two aforementioned scholarly views. Through their investigations, the authors attempt to explore the relationships among politics, law, and financial markets in China, particularly the influence of China's political system on the formation, development, and enforcement of financial markets laws and elucidate the nature of these interactions. This book aims to present the readers with the current state of China's financial markets laws in action, rather than merely "introducing" or "explaining" China's financial markets rules on paper.

The book is divided into eight chapters. Chapter 2 discusses the core Party factors; Chap. 3 delves into the administrative system and their effects on the development of the China's financial market laws. Chapters 4–6 observe some financial markets disputes from different angles. Chapters 7 and 8, set against the backdrop of the recent rise of financial technology, explore the prospects for repositioning of the state regulatory power vis-a-via the financial markets.

The focus of Chap. 2 is the core element of China's political system: the Party. We will examine the role the Party has played in the governance of financial markets and the development of the relevant laws over the past few decades, including legislative, administrative enforcement, and judicial activities. Our findings reveal: since the introduction of Deng's opening-up policy, the Party has played multiple de facto roles in the financial markets: a lawmaker, a regulator, and an adjudicator. From the top, the Party designs and guides the development of the financial law regime, and determines the contours of the regime while strengthening the legitimacy and legality of the regime. In detail, the Party supplements and complements the institutional structure in China: the legislature, the regulatory authorities, and the judiciary in the financial markets which are ostensibly not so dissimilar to that in the West. Over time, especially under Xi, the Party's role has become increasingly dominant and ubiquitous, which is reflective of ever increasingly blurring demarcation between the Party and the State, as well as the ascendency of the Party over the State. It seems to be increasingly the case that the Party is willing to step up in the position of the State. On one account, China's experience provides a contrasting example to the typical governance regimes employed in Western jurisdictions.

By exploring the power dynamics and conflicts of interest among different regulatory bodies, Chap. 3 will examine the changes in the legal system of China's asset management industry in recent years. This case study will illustrate the structural obstacles, imbedded in the political system, that were encountered in the reforms of the financial markets law system, as well as the internal and external environment necessary to overcome these obstacles.

China is aiming to reform its financial regulatory structure by adopting a function-based structure. This involves the merging of regulators and the introduction of new laws and regulation. At the heart of it, the reforms would require a redistribution of the regulatory powers of the regulators. Through the lens of asset management product regulation, this chapter outlines the financial regulatory structure resulting from the 2018 reforms. One key point that can be discerned is that China's regulatory structure did not adequately protect the interests of investors. This inadequacy not only provided fertile ground for investors to lose their savings through the unscrupulous and inappropriate practices of bad actors in relation to asset management products, it also heightened the possibilities for systemic financial risks and financial instability. The chapter concludes that without redistributing the powers of the regulators, the 2018 reforms will have a limited impact on the manner in which the financial system is regulated.

Chapter 4 will delve into issues within the judicial realm, examining the unique relationship between the political-legal system and their effects on the development and the regulation of financial markets. Here, we will address an intriguing phenomenon: during the early days of rapid development of the Chinese securities market, courts did not play an active role in investor protection. So, what kind of mechanisms were in place to substitute for the courts' functions?

China's securities markets have experienced rapid growth in the past two decades. The Shanghai Stock Exchange, for example, was ranked the fourth-largest stock exchange in the world as of end of June 2023.[5] China's judiciary has been absent in protecting the interest of investors in its securities markets. This therefore raises the obvious question of who plays the role in protecting Chinese investors in this fast-growing and potentially volatile market. This chapter finds the Chinese state, by deploying various political resources, plays a direct role that is often more significant than that played by the judiciary in protecting the interest of investors. China's capital markets are reflective of its unique historical and contemporary conditions. The establishment and development of China's securities markets are made possible under the direction of the state.

Chapter 5 will focus on a relatively micro-level phenomenon with significant macro-level implications: the frequent use of the term "financial security" by the courts when exercising judicial power. Notably, "financial security" lacks a clear definition in any Chinese legal texts and is more appropriately defined in the political discourse. What, then, is the purpose behind courts employing this term? Our empirical research aims to uncover the underlying motivations. In the past few years, the term financial security has been increasingly referred to by politicians in China's public discourse. This term was meant to broadly denote national security considerations in relation to financial markets. This chapter draws on and analyses a recent study of 242 Chinese court decisions undertaken by the authors and explores the nature and the extent of the term 'financial security' as used in judicial decisions in China. Our research demonstrates that the judiciary makes frequent use of this term even though it is a term which remains to be defined in legislation and regulation. This chapter offers a means of categorising the manner in which the term financial security is deployed, which may assist in a better understanding of the Chinese courts' judgments in the contemporary context as well as in the future. It also offers an

[5] Visual Capitalist, Mapped: The Largest Stock Exchanges in the Worldhttps://www.visualcapitalist.com/largest-stock-exchanges-in-the-world/.

account of the thinking and motivation behind legal reasoning that assists in gaining an insight into the use and implications of financial security that appear to underpin these decisions. The adoption of the term financial security, similar to the Greek myth of the Delphic Oracles, is indicative of the role played by the courts in the light of the Chinese political system.

In Chap. 6, the authors note that Chinese courts often refuse to accept certain financial disputes for various reasons, even though the formal litigation rules do not permit such refusals, which in turn, necessitates an analysis of China's judicial system within the broader political context to provide a comprehensive explanation. In China, courts may refuse to accept certain legal actions involving financial matters without any solid or explicit legal grounds. An analysis of such a phenomenon should help scholars to understand the functioning logic of China's judicial power. This chapter suggests that there are a number of reasons behind the filtration system, including a lack of applicable legal rules, a weak ability of the courts to understand complicated financial matters, the background of the economic system transition, the political consideration of 'maintaining social stability' and judiciary self-interest. Filtration has inevitably had a negative effect on China's financial markets, and reform is thus necessary.

Chapter 7 shifts the focus to the role of big tech in the context of financial markets following the rise of fintech. Specifically, it examines whether big tech has the potential to undermine the state power within the financial markets. This ongoing and open-ended question prompts the authors to reflect on the relationship between financial markets and the laws and the state power. In the past decades, the rise of Bigtech in finance has taken place at a time of declining public trust in governments and traditional financial institutions. In addition to the changes they brought to finance, the chapter outlines that Bigtech, leveraging on technological advances, challenge the *status quo* financial law and regulation, thus the financial systems. Technology has the potential to fill the void of trust left by *status quo* financial system. The chapter in turn raises the question as to whether the functions or the roles of the State in financial markets perhaps should be reconsidered and the possibility that technology may provide a means to fill the void of trust left by the governments and financial institutions.

Chapter 8 can be seen as a continuation of the sixth, but with a more sharpened focus: the rise of internet equity crowdfunding. While many countries have actively integrated this new form of financing into their legal frameworks, China's new Securities Law of 2020 rejected similar reforms. Whether the legal system embraces equity crowdfunding is a matter of different policy objectives. This policy choice made by the Chinese authorities was largely driven by political factors. Along with the fast development of internet technology, a new financing model—equity crowdfunding—has been rising rapidly in recent years. Against this background, it has become an important global topic in the field of securities law as to how to balance the objective of investor protection and that of capital formation. By referencing to the JOBS Act in the US, it is suggested in this chapter that modern securities law should respond to the demand of equity crowd-funding development. Besides broadening the scope of the applicability of the exemption rules, securities law has evolved beyond the traditional division between public and private offerings by introducing a new equity crowd-funding exemption system.

Overall, the authors do not intend to provide a panoramic view of the legal system of China's financial markets. Instead, by identifying the political factors that either promote or hinder the development of financial markets and the laws, the aim is to interpret the nature and the interactions among financial markets, financial markets laws, and political systems. Returning to the earlier discussion on the legal origin and the political institutions theories, the last thirty years of China's financial market legal system offer us the following insights: the protection of investors' rights, especially those of small and medium investors, highlighted by the theory of legal origin, is crucial and naturally should be a key focus of legal reforms. On the other hand, by looking beyond the legal rules and after analyzing the underlying political factors and their mechanisms, we can better grasp the driving forces behind the evolution and development of China's financial markets and its legal system.

Chapter 2
The Party State or the Party is the State? The Communist Party of China in the Development of China's Financial Law Regime

Abstract Since the introduction of Deng's opening-up policy, the Communist Party of China (CPC) has played multiple de facto roles in the financial markets: a lawmaker, a regulator, and an adjudicator. From the top, the CPC designs and guides the development of the financial markets law regime, and determines the contours of the regime. In detail, the CPC supplements and complements the institutional structure in China, which is made up of the legislature, the regulators, and the judiciary, and which in itself is ostensibly not so dissimilar to that in the West. Over time, especially under Xi, the CPC's role has become increasingly dominant and ubiquitous, which is reflective of ever increasingly blurring demarcation between the Party and the State, as well as the ascendency of the Party over the State. On one account, China's experience provides a contrasting example to the typical regulatory regimes employed in Western jurisdictions.

1 Introduction

In the past four decades, financial market activities have become increasingly crossing national boundaries.[1] Yet the differences among jurisdictions are striking: even jurisdictions with similar circumstances of cultural and economic development could have 'diametrically opposed views on the same issues'.[2] China has developed a financial markets law regime which is seemingly not too dissimilar to that in the West over the past four decades. For example, Shanghai, Beijing, and Shenzhen are

---

[1] See Eric Helleiner, Explaining the Globalization of Financial Markets: Bringing States Back In' (1995) 2(2) *Review of International Political Economy* 315, 315–341.

[2] See Philip Wood, *Maps of World Financial Law* (Sweet and Maxwell, 6th ed, 2008) 11 (preface).

In this article, this term 'financial regime' is used broadly to include all institutions and other infrastructures in the financial markets.

T. Huang and W. He, *Politics Meets Markets*, Contemporary Chinese Civil and Commercial Law, https://doi.org/10.1007/978-981-97-9176-7_2

now considered three of the ten largest globe financial centres.[3] By market capitalization of listed companies, Shanghai and Shenzhen stock exchanges are two of the top ten stock exchange operators globally as of August 2022.[4] Also by the market capitalization, three Chinese banks are ranked as three of the largest banks on this planet.[5] Since 2016, the RMB, the Chinese currency has also been included in the IMF's SDR basket, and weighed in the third place after USD and EUR, and ahead of JPY and GBP.[6] In March 2023, the National People's Congress in China passed the *Reform Plans for the Party and the State Institutions*, under which the Central Financial Commission and the Central Financial Work Commission, which serve as commissions of the Central Committee of the CPC have been established.

In understanding the dynamics of the financial markets law regime in China and the current regulatory landscape, the Communist Party of China (the CPC)[7] is undoubtedly the most striking local factor in terms of 'local knowledge'.[8] The increasingly paramount role of the CPC has been known and recognized, but not fully understood.[9]

Given the nature of the one-party state, the current financial markets law regime in China embodies President Xi's political ambitions: that 'the Party leadership is the fundamentals of a socialist legal system and is the cornerstone of the principle of the rule by law governance. The Party leadership should shine through all corners and all aspects of governance of the nation. 'The Party the leader', 'The People the masters of the nation', and 'Rule by law' are three in one'.[10] Furthermore, the governance of the financial markets is subject to the maxim that 'the Party leads finance',[11] which in more concrete terms means 'strengthening the Party leadership in the financial markets, improving the mechanisms of the Party leading the financial markets, and improving the institutionalisation of such mechanisms.'[12]

---

[3] GFCI 32 Rank, https://www.longfinance.net/programmes/financial-centre-futures/global-financial-centres-index/gfci-32-explore-the-data/gfci-32-rank/.

[4] Largest stock exchange operators worldwide as of August 2022, by market capitalization of listed companies, https://www.statista.com/statistics/270126/largest-stock-exchange-operators-by-market-capitalization-of-listed-companies/.

[5] Largest banks and bank holding companies by market cap, https://companiesmarketcap.com/banks/largest-banks-by-market-cap/.

[6] IMF, RMB inclusion in the SDR Basket, https://datahelp.imf.org/knowledgebase/articles/1081105-rmb-inclusion-in-the-sdr-basket.

[7] The Communist Party of China is officially abbreviated as CPC. See *Communist Party of China News Network* (Web Page). http://cpc.people.com.cn/.

[8] From the perspective of anthropology, local knowledge gives emphasis to "cultural traditions and historical phases" in understanding facts and the law. Clifford Geertz, 'Local Knowledge: Further Essays in Interpretive Anthropology' (Basic Books, 1985) 234.

[9] There has been criticism that the CPC's role was overlooked or "hidden" in Chinese governance issues. See Holly Snape & Weinan Wang, 'Finding a Place for the Party: Debunking the "Party-State" and Rethinking the State-Society Relationship in China's One-Party System' (2020) 5(4) *Journal of Chinese Governance* 477, 477–502.

[10] Xi Jinping, 'Promote Socialist Rule of Law' (2015) 1 *Qiushi*.

[11] The term finance should be interpreted broadly to include every aspect of the financial markets.

[12] See 'During the 40th Collective Learning Session of the Central Political Bureau of the CPC, Xi Jinping Stressed the Importance of Financial Vitality for Economic Vitality, the Importance of

From the perspective of politics, the role of the CPC leads to a power structure in the Chinese society which is in stark contrast to that of democracies. From a legal perspective, the transformation of the CPC from a revolutionary party to a governing party meant that it has transitioned from the position of an outsider in the state to that of an insider.[13] This process has been accompanied by the increasing integration of the party machinery with that of the state. The CPC should not be narrowly viewed as a political party of ideology or as a governing party. Understanding the role of the CPC and its policies and mechanisms is the crucial first step towards understanding the financial markets law regime of China.[14] Recognition of the CPC's particular role in the development of the financial law regime provides important evidence of China as a unique model of economic, social and legal development.

From the outset, it should be acknowledged that China has a different culture and is at a different stage of economic development to that of Western countries. While political parties are common in various jurisdictions, the role of the CPC in the financial markets law regime in China is different to that of parties in a competitive party-political system such as the UK or the US. The CPC's control of the financial markets has been long recognised.[15] In a systematic manner, this chapter delineates and evaluates the role of the CPC in the development of the financial markets in the past four decades in China, as a de facto law maker, a de facto regulator as well as a de facto adjudicator. More importantly, the chapter highlights and analyses the discernible changes under Xi which have deviated from the path that China had been travelling in the previous three decades.

The role of the CPC in Chinese society has evolved and is evolving. What is relevant for the purposes and the development of the financial markets law regime in China is the role of the CPC after the introduction of Deng's Opening-up Policy. In the early days after the introduction of this policy, Deng advocated for the principle of 'separation of the Party and the Government' (the Separation principle') which can be traced back to Deng's 1978 speech titled *Emancipate the Mind, Seek Truth from Facts and Look Forward in Unity* at the 3rd Plenary Session of the 11th CPC

Financial Stability for Economic Stability, and the Importance of Carrying out Good Financial Work and Maintaining Financial Security', *People's Daily* (27 April 2017).

[13] Simply resorting to the state-society lens would prove inadequate to answer the question of how the contemporary Chinese financial markets law regime emerged and evolved. The CPC's role must be considered and analysed in detail.See Lin Shangli, 'Centralization and Decentralization: the Power Relationship between the Party, the State and Society and the Changes Thereof' (2002) 1 *Fudan Political Science Review* 152. From the perspective of economics, the CPC is not separate from the state, but intertwined with the state itself.See Yao Yang, Xi Tianyang, *China's New Narrative: An Analysis of the Operating Mechanism of the Political and Economic System with Chinese Characteristics* (Truth & Wisdom Press, 1st ed, 2018) 10.

[14] See Qiang Shigong, 'Constitutionalism with Chinese Characteristics? Backer's Study on China's "Single Party Constitutional State" System' (2012) 5 *Peking University Law Journal* 952.

[15] See Sebastian Heilmann, Regulatory Innovation by Leninist Means: Communist Party Supervision in China's Financial Industry, The China Quarterly, 21 March 2005. The judicial reforms under Xi have elevated the power of the Party in the judicial systems. See Qianfan Zhang (2021) The Communist Party Leadership and Rule of Law: A Tale of Two Reforms, Journal of Contemporary China, 30:130, 578–595.

Central Committee.[16] At the time, Deng was concerned with the practice of the Party's blanket interventions in government affairs. At the Meeting of the Political Bureau of the CPC Central Committee in 1980, the Separation principle was put forward again by Deng.[17] While the Separation principle was repeatedly referred to by Deng in his speeches,[18] unfortunately the proposed reform measures[19] were not adopted in the early 1980s.[20]

The Separation principle gradually faded out from public discourse after the late 1980s, largely due to the political turmoil surrounding the Tiananmen Square Massacre.[21] The Party's role in the Chinese society under the Separation principle was instead being reconsidered and the interactions of the Party and Government were being re-assessed.[22] The official attitude was not clear until 2017. In 2017, Wang Qishan, a member of the Standing Committee of the Political Bureau of the CPC Central Committee stated that 'under the leadership of the Party, there is no separation of the Party and the Government, only the separation of work between

---

[16] Deng Xiaoping, 'Emancipate the Mind, Seek Truth from Facts and Look Forward in Unity' (Speech, 3rd Plenary Session of the 11th CPC Central Committee, 13 December 1978). http://www.people.com.cn/item/sj/sdldr/dxp/B101.html.

[17] Deng Xiaoping, 'Reform of the Leadership System of the Party and the State' (Speech, Enlarged Meeting of the Political Bureau of the CPC Central Committee, 18 August 1980), in *Selection and Compilation of Important Documents since the Third Plenary Session of the CPC Central Committee* (People's Publishing House, 1982).

[18] See, eg, 'Talks during Listening to Reports on the Economic Situation' (10 June), 'Establishing the Concept of a Legal System among All the People' (28 June), 'Issues on Political System Reform' (A Collection of Four Talks) (September–November), in *Selected Works of Deng Xiaoping* (People's Publishing House, 1993) vol 3.

[19] The reforms proposed by Deng in his speech 'Reform of the Leadership System of the Party And the State' include: amending the constitution, improving the People's Congress system and preventing over-concentration of power; streamlining the party and government institutions and personnel; establishing a powerful top-down work system from the State Council to local governments at all levels, so that the work within the scope of government functions and powers shall be discussed, decided and issued by the State Council and local governments rather than the Party Central Committee and local Party committees; for enterprises and institutions, promoting and improving the 'workers' congress', and for factories, gradually transforming the responsibility system of factory directors and managers under the leadership of the Party committee, etc.

[20] In 1987, the then President Zhao Ziyang referred to this principle in his speech at the 13th CPC National Congress titled *Advance along the Socialist Road with Chinese Characteristics*. Again, no concrete measures were adopted. *Advance along the Socialist Road with Chinese Characteristics* (Report, 13th National Congress of the Communist Party of China, 25 October 1987). http://www.gov.cn/test/2008-07/01/content_1032279_2.htm.

[21] 'Under the influence of the political turmoil of the mid to late 1980s, reform of the political system centred on the reform of party-government relations also entered a period of adjustment.' 'Political turmoil in the mid to late 1980s' the official term used by the mainland for the Tiananmen protests. See Huang Long, 'The History, Core and Solution of China's Party-Government Relations since the Founding of New China: Also on Three Models of Party-Government Relations' (2020) 12 *The South Journal* 21, 3.

[22] Ibid; Liu Jie, 'The Changing Course of CCP-Government Relations and Governance Reform' (2011) 12 *Journal of Social Sciences* 4.

the Party and the Government,.'[23] In 2018 the emphasis was given to overall Party leadership in Chinese society and Party leadership at various levels of government.[24]

On the other hand, over time, in the corporate China, the CPC has become much more visible and prominent. In 2005, the role of the CPC was introduced formally into the *Company Law*.[25] In 2012, the CPC Committee issued a plethora of proposals with the purpose of establishing the Party leadership as well as the Party membership mechanisms, promoting the reach of the Party in non-public enterprises, exploring effective ways for the Party and its members to play their roles in those enterprises, strengthening the team-building of the Party members, etc.[26] Under Article 5 of the CSRC's 2018 *Code of Corporate Governance of Listed Companies*,[27] listed companies shall set up a Party Committee to carry out the activities of the Party, and shall provide necessary conditions for the activities of the Party Committee. Furthermore, state-controlled listed companies shall include provisions concerning Party-building activities in their constitutions.

Against the backdrop of the overarching role played by the CPC in the Chinese society, after examining aspects of the development of the financial markets law regime over the past four decades, this chapter articulates and theorises the role of the CPC, as a law maker, a regulator, and as an adjudicator. The CPC is not only a leader in an abstract sense, but a key interested party in all aspects of the financial markets law regime. Furthermore, the sense of 'the Party is the State' now looms large in the financial markets law regime. Once not so visible hand of the CPC has become increasingly visible and ubiquitous if not dominant. In doing so, the chapter aims to demystify and rationalise the interactions of the CPC with other organs of the state, therefore shed light on nature and dynamics of the development of the financial law regime in China. In conclusion, examining against the Coasian transaction costs theory, while acknowledging the CPC has played an important role in the markets, the authors point out that there are boundaries or limitations to such a role. The authors intend to observe and undertake analysis objectively to the best of their ability.

---

[23] 'Accurately Grasp the Concept of "Division of Labour across the Party and Government"', *People's Daily Online* (10 April 2017). 'Two Sessions' refers to the annual Plenary Sessions of the National People's Congress and the National Committee of the Chinese People's Political Consultative Conference in 2017.

[24] *Decision of the CPC Central Committee on Deepening the Reform of the Party and State Institutions* (adopted at the 3rd Plenary Session of the 19th CPC Central Committee, 28 Feb 2018).

[25] *Company Law of the People's Republic of China 2005* (Standing Committee of the National People's Congress, Order No 42, 1 June 2016). (Before the 2005 Amendment).

Article 17: The grassroots organisations of the Communist Party of China in a company shall carry out their activities according to the Constitution of the Communist Party of China.

(After the 2005 Amendment).

Article 19: The Chinese Communist Party may, according to the Constitution of the Chinese Communist Party, establish its branches in companies to carry out activities of the Chinese Communist Party. The company shall provide necessary conditions to facilitate the activities of the Party.

[26] *Opinions on Strengthening and Improving Party-Building in Non-Public Enterprises (Trial Implementation)* (General Office of the CPC Central Committee, 2012).

[27] China Securities Regulatory Commission, *Announcement No. 29* (2018).

2 The Roles that the CPC Plays in the Financial Markets

2.1 The CPC as De Facto Law Maker in the Financial Markets

The role of the CPC as a de facto law maker in promulgating rules for the financial markets is multi-faceted. Although the CPC is not the formal body of law-making pursuant to the *Legislation Law*, institutional arrangements among the government and the regulatory bodies determine that legislative work is led by the Party. At all levels of government, the CPC acts as the integral part of law-making activities.

During the forty years following Deng's opening-up reforms, it is clear that legislative bodies implemented the Party's policies and decisions with respect to the financial markets.[28] While it was acknowledged that this phase of law-making was focused on structural issues of the markets instead of specifics, these laws were able to set out rules for the nascent markets.[29] In recent years, the most significant reforms in

[28] For instance, in 1995, the National People's Congress and its Standing Committee introduced six basic laws concerning the financial sector(i.e. the 'five laws and one decision') including *Law on the People's Bank of China, Law on Commercial Banks, Guarantee Law, Negotiable Instruments Law, Insurance law* and *Decision of the Standing Committee of the National People's Congress on Punishment of Crimes of Disrupting Financial Order*. There is no surprise that 1995 is also known as 'the year of financial legislation' [Wu Zhipan, Ten Years of a Financial Legal System] (2005) 13 *China Finance* 11, 11. This unprecedented legislative intensity is the legislative body's direct response to the policy goals put forward by the 14th National Congress of the CPC, i.e. 'establishing a socialist market economy', and more specific directions from the 3rd Plenary Session of the 14th CPC Central Committee, i.e. 'making the People's Bank of China into a genuine central bank', 'gradually transforming specialized banks into commercial banks', 'establishing policy banks' See [Decision of the Central Committee of the Communist Party of China on Some Issues concerning the Establishment of the Socialist Market Economy] (People's Republic of China) 3rd Plenary Session, 14th CPC Central Committee, 14 November 1993. http://www.people.com.cn/item/20years/newfiles/b1080.html. At the same time, the promulgation of the six basic laws was also considered a response to the State Council's directives 'urging the promulgating of the Banking Law of the People's Republic of China, Law on the People's Bank of China, Negotiable Instruments Law, Insurance Law and other draft laws, and their submission to the National People's Congress". [Decision of the State Council on Reform of the Financial System] (People's Republic of China) State Council, Order No 91, 25 December 1993. As a result of the CPC's policies, the basic laws and key infrastructure of the financial markets were introduced and implemented within the relatively short time span of four years Together with the *Regulation on Foreign Exchange Administration* 1996, the *Securities Law* 1998, the *Interim Provisions on the Administration of Futures Trading* 1999.

[29] In the early stage of establishing a legal system after the Reform and Opening Up, the legislative work then often emphasised 'generality over specificity' due to the lack of practical experience in legislating activities. See Xin Chunying, 'Strive to Carry out Legislating Activities in Order to Form and Improve the Socialist Legal System with Chinese Characteristics' (Web Page). http://www.npc.gov.cn/npc/c10134/201008/15966d4479bc400d8c9db90f7dbe7f75.shtml. The challenge of market economy reform to China's financial market largely derives from whether the problem of 'soft financial constraint' under the planned system can be overcome, which depends on the transformation and improvement of the legal system. See Zhou Xiaochuan, 'Improve the Legal System, Perfect the Financial Ecology' (2005) 3 *Caijing*. Such scale and speed of law-making is

the financial markets is the introduction of the IPO Registration System ('the IPO Registration Reforms').[30] The IPO Registration Reforms were a direct result of the decision made at the 3rd Plenary Session of the 18th Central Committee of the CPC in 2013 with a view to 'improving the multi-level capital market system, and promoting the reform of the stock issuance registration system'.[31] To give effect to the decision, the *Securities Laws* was set to be accordingly amended.[32]

Since then, the proposed amendment to the *Securities Law* was paused[33] until the 6th meeting of the CPC Central Committee which took place in January 2019. At this meeting, two directives were passed.[34] The IPO Registration Reforms were then relaunched and back on the agenda of the government and regulatory authorities. It was decided that the STAR market at the Shanghai Stock Exchange will pilot such reforms. Finally, at the legislative level, the *Securities Law* was amended on 28 December 2019, which paved the way for the implementation of the IPO Registration Reforms. The conclusion thus could be reached that the CPC initiated, and then re-vitalized the stalled the IPO Registration Reforms.

---

historically comparable to the New Deal implemented by President Roosevelt in 1933, which led to the introduction of a series of major laws and regulations, including the *Banking Act of 1933*, the *Securities Act of 1933*, and the *Securities Exchange Act of 1934*.

[30] The significance lies in the fundamental differences between the proposed registration mechanism and the traditional 'approval' mechanism: see Cao Fengqi, 'Promoting the Reformation of Stock Issuance Registration System' (2014) 2 *Nankai Journal (Philosophy, Literature and Social Science Edition)* 118; Jiang Daxing, 'The "Power-Heavy" Securities Regulatory Commission in Retirement: The Registration System Reform and the Reorganization of Securities Regulatory Power' (2014) 2 *Law Review* 39.

[31] Decision of the CPC Central Committee on Several Major Issues concerning Comprehensively Deepening Reform (People's Republic of China) 3rd Plenary Session, 18th CPC Central Committee, 12 November 2013.

[32] See 'Incorporating the Securities Law into the Legislative Amendment Plan of the Standing Committee of the National People's Congress', *Economic Information Daily* (9 September 2013).

[33] The legislative work plan of the Standing Committee of the National People's Congress in 2018 included the *Securities Law (Amendment)* in the list of items for preliminary review. Since the start of the amendment work in 2013, the *Securities Law (Amendment)* was included in the 'bills for continued review' in the legislative plan for four consecutive years from 2014 to 2017. See '2018 Legislative Work Plan of the Standing Committee of the National People's Congress', *National People's Congress* (Web Page, 27 April 2018). http://www.npc.gov.cn/npc/c30834/201804/1c1b9070eb574282b8ef6d2f33615383.shtml.

[34] Namely, the *Overall Implementation Plan for the Establishment of the STAR Market and the Launch of the Pilot Program of the Registration System at the Shanghai Stock Exchange*, and the *Implementation Opinions on the Establishment of the STAR Market and the Launch of the Pilot Program of the Registration System at the Shanghai Stock Exchange*, It was made clear that 'the establishment of the STAR Market and the pilot program of the IPO registration system at the Shanghai Stock Exchange is an important measure to implement the "innovation-driven development" strategy and to deepen the reforms of the capital markets … We should steadily pilot the IPO registration system, comprehensively promote systemic reforms in the areas of listing, disclosure, trading and delisting, and establish and improve the stock IPO system centred on information disclosure.' See 'Xi Jinping Chaired the 6th Meeting of the Central Comprehensively Deepening Reforms Commission', *People's Daily* (23 January 2019).

Combatting misconduct in financial markets also provides a good illustration where the CPC plays a pivotal role. In order to address crimes such as falsifying financial accounts, the 24th session of the Standing Committee of the 13th National People's Congress passed the *Amendment (XI) to the Criminal Law.* It was a response to Xi's speech on 22 February 2020,[35] and Xi's reiteration of 'cracking down on illegal activities in the securities markets at another meeting on 30 July 2020.'[36] The promulgation of *Amendment (XI) to the Criminal Law* reflects the priority of CPC decisions on the capital markets, and its firm determination of a 'zero tolerance' approach in cracking down on misconduct in the securities and futures markets'[37] It also highlights the CPC's leadership in and the driving force behind the development of such rules governing financial markets.

For a long time, making rules concerning the financial markets was considered the exclusive power and responsibility of the central CPC. According to s 8(9) of the *Legislation Law*, the National People's Congress and its Standing Committee have the power to enact laws concerning the economy, tax, customs, finance and trade. In practice, as illustrated, this has translated into the central CPC's power and jurisdiction to lead and orchestrate authorities at the central level to introduce relevant rules and practices. Therefore, there was no official mandate for the local People's Congresses and their committees to make rules for localities, and local authorities tend to skirt around the issue.[38]

This situation has changed in recent years. Since 2016, local governments such as Shandong, Shanghai, Zhejiang and Sichuan have issued guidelines on promulgating rules concerning local financial markets, under which local governments are allowed to assume some regulatory responsibilities and exercise powers to mitigate financial risks. To some extent, this re-distributes legislative and regulatory powers between the central and local authorities.[39] These changes were derived from the CPC's policy on financial markets, which was first noted in 2013 in which the notion of 'defining the responsibilities of the central and local governments in financial

---

[35] *Solving the Problem of Low Cost of Misconduct in the Financial Sector, Especially in the Stock Markets.*

See 'Xi Jinping Chaired the 13th Collective Learning Session of the Central Political Bureau of the CPC and Made a Speech', *Chinese Government* (23 February 2019). http://www.gov.cn/xinwen/2019-02/23/content_5367953.htm.

[36] See 'The Central Political Bureau of the CPC Held a Meeting, and Xi Jinping, General Secretary of the CPC Central Committee, Chaired the Meeting', *Xinhua* (30 July 2019). http://www.xinhuanet.com/politics/2019-07/30/c_1124817133.htm.

[37] See 'The CSRC Held a Symposium on the Publicity and Implementation of *Amendment (XI) to the Criminal Law of the People's Republic of China*', *China Securities Regulatory Commission* (26 February 2021). http://www.csrc.gov.cn/newsite/zjhxwfb/xwdd/202102/t20210226_393226.html.

[38] For example, while introducing the *Regulations of Shanghai Municipality on Promoting the Construction of the International Financial Center* in 2009, the Standing Committee of the Shanghai Municipal People's Congress used language such as 'encourage', 'instruct', and 'facilitate'.

[39] See Weiping He, 'The Regulation of the Financial Sector in China: A Tale of Two Governments' (2018) 18(2) *Journal of Corporate Law Studies* 339.

regulation and risk mitigation' was presented.[40] The change was later interpreted as suggesting that 'local governments should take on the responsibility of risk mitigation in localities in accordance with the rules of the central government, on the understanding that financial markets management is mainly the responsibility of the central government',[41] with the purpose of 'improving the distribution of responsibilities between the central and local governments in financial regulation and giving local governments responsibilities regarding financial regulation'.[42]

What is also notable is that when making rules, the authorities would often refer to the fact that such rules are in fact CPC policies. For example, in April 2016, the General Office of the State Council issued a plan,[43] the purpose of which was said 'to implement the decisions and arrangements of the Central Committee of the CPC and the State Council'. Similarly, in September 2017, the General Office of the State Council issued its an Opinion[44] in which it stated the Opinion was 'reviewed by the CPC Central Leading Group for Comprehensively Deepening Reforms and approved by the State Council'. Such an approach is not exclusive to the General Office of the State Council and has been adopted by other authorities.[45]

All these examples above illustrate that the CPC is the driving force in the passage of key legislation. In addition, as de facto law-maker, the CPC also acts to enact laws directly.[46] Especially in relation to issues concerning the financial markets as a whole,

[40] See 'National Financial Work Conference Is Held in Beijing', *Chinese Government* (15 July 2017). http://www.gov.cn/xinwen/2017-07/15/content_5210774.htm.

[41] See at the 2017 National Finance Work Meeting: 'National Financial Work Conference Is Held in Beijing', *Chinese Government* (15 July 2017). http://www.gov.cn/xinwen/2017-07/15/content_5210774.htm.

[42] The *Several Opinions of the CPC Central Committee and the State Council on Serving the Real Economy, Preventing and Controlling Financial Risks and Deepening Financial Reform* ZF [2017] 23.

[43] GBF [2016] 21.

[44] *Opinions on Improving the Regulatory Systems and Mechanisms of Combating Money Laundering, Financing of Terrorism, and Tax Evasion (the Opinions)*GBH [2017] 84.

[45] For example, in July 2015, the People's Bank of China together with nine other government departments issued the Guiding Opinions on Promoting the Sound Development of Internet Finance (the Guiding Opinions) in which it was stated that the introduction of the Guiding Opinions was 'with the consent of the Central Committee of the CPC and the State Council'. Similarly, in issuing the Relevant Measures for Further Opening Up the Financial Industry (the Measures), the Office of the Financial Stability and Development Commission under the State Council stated that the Measures were 'to implement the decisions and arrangements of the Central Committee of the Party and the State Council on further opening up'.

[46] The joint issuance of documents by the Party and the government is a system that was implemented after 1949. From the issuing bodies' perspective, this includes joint issuance by the CPC Central Committee and the State Council, joint issuance by the general office of the CPC Central Committee and the general office of the State Council, and joint issuance by the functional departments of the CPC Central Committee and the ministries and commissions of the State Council. For studies on the legal status and standardisation of joint issuance of documents by the party and the government, see Feng Lixia, 'Institutional Logic and Standardization of the Joint Issuance of Documents by the Party and the Government' (2021) 1 *Chinese Journal of Law* 3.

the CPC often acts together with the State Council to promulgate rules.[47] The rules were all concerned with the key policy issues for the CPC and the government in relation to the financial markets at the time, and were all introduced by and in the name of the CPC and the government.

Furthermore, based on the purview of their powers, the CPC offices also act with the government on specific issues.[48] In particular, the mitigation of financial risks, and therefore maintaining the stability of the financial markets, is the key issue for the CPC. The presence of the CPC can often be observed in directives combatting financial risks. For example, in April 2016, the Propaganda Department of the CPC and the Office of the Stability Working Group, together with the PBoC, the Supreme People's Court and the Supreme People's Procuratorate issued two directives,[49]and together with the State Administration for Industry and Commerce, the Supreme People's Court and the Supreme People's Procuratorate one directive.[50] Together with the China Securities Regulatory Commission, in March 2018, the Office of the

---

[47] Such as the *Notice of the Central Committee of the CPC and the State Council on Deepening Financial Reforms and Preventing Financial Risks* which was issued in December 1997, the *Opinions of the Central Committee of the CPC and the State Council on Deepening the Reforms of the Investment and Financial System* in July 2016, the *Several Opinions of the CPC Central Committee and the State Council on Serving the Real Economy, Preventing and Controlling Financial Risks and Deepening Financial Reforms* in 2017 and the *Guiding Opinions of the Central Committee of the CPC and the State Council on Improving the Management of State Financial Capital* in June 2018.

[48] For example, the General Office of the Central Committee of the CPC together with the General Office of the State Council issued the *Provisions on Party Organ and Government Personnel's Personal Investment in Securities* in April 2001, and *Several Opinions on Strengthening Financial Services for Private Enterprises* in April 2019. These two offices also collectively introduced rules on the management of the regulators of financial markets, such as the Provisions on the Functions, Structure and Staffing of the China Banking and Insurance Regulatory Commission in August 2018 and Provisions on the Functions, Organizational Structure and Staffing of the People's Bank of China in January 2019.According to the principle of "the party governs the institutional organisation" specified in Article 3 of the *Regulations on the CPC's Institutional Organization*, the reform of Party and state institutions, the adjustment of systems, mechanisms and responsibilities, and the organising structure, staffing, allocation and adjustment of leadership positions of various organs (including organs of the Party, the National People's Congress, administrative organs, CPPCC organs, supervisory organs, judicial organs, procuratorial organs, organs of democratic parties and mass organizations) and public institutions are all subject to the *Regulations*. The CPC Central Committee has established the Central Institutional Organization Commission as the decision-making, deliberation and coordination body of the CPC Central Committee. The Office of the Central Institutional Organization Commission (the State Commission Office for Public Sector Reform) is a permanent office under the leadership of the Central Institutional Organization Commission, which is responsible for the reform of the national administrative system and its institutions as well as the daily management of institutional organisation. It is an organ of both the CPC Central Committee and the State Council.

[49] The *Implementation Plan for Special Overhaul of the Risks of Non-Bank Payment Institutions* YF [2016] 112. and the *Implementation Plan for the Special Rectification of Risks in Conducting Asset Management through the Internet and Engaging in Financial Business in a Crossover Manner.*

[50] The *Implementation Plan for the Special Rectification of Risks in Internet Financial Advertisements and Financial Activities Conducted in the Name of Investment and Wealth Management* GSB Z [2016] 61.

Central Cyberspace Affairs Commission of the CPC issued further guidance.[51] The CPC collaborates closely with the other arms of the state. The CPC's ever present on all key directives.

In summary, the CPC plays a key role of a de facto law maker in drafting and promulgating rules governing the financial markets. Its role is not confined to broad issues concerning the markets but also specific matters such as mitigating financial risks. Such a role was neither articulated in the *Constitution of the People's Republic of China* nor in the *Legislation Law.* While in the past the presence of the CPC was largely felt at the policy level, recently it could be also observed that the CPC has been featured prominently in legislation. For example, in the draft *Law of People's Bank of China* which was circulated for consultation in March 2020, the standard catch-all provision 'subject to the State Council' has been changed to 'subject to the Central CPC and the State Council'. The CPC dominates not only in form but also in substance. Most recently, the draft version of the *Financial Stability Law* which was circulated for consultation in April 2022 for the first time, contrasting to the previous legislative effort, articulated and embraced the leadership of the CPC as one of the principles.

2.2 The CPC as De Facto Regulator in the Financial Markets

In addition to the commonly recognised 'one bank two commissions'[52] regulatory institutional structure in China's financial markets, the CPC also plays the role of a *de-facto* regulator. Of course, the role of the CPC as a regulator does not necessarily mean that it employs day-to-day regulatory tools as a regulator in a general sense. The CPC rather plays such a key regulatory role through its unique position in the overall political and administrative institutional structure in China: it occupies the apex position in such a structure.

Between 1998 and 2003, the CPC established the (Central) Financial Work Commission. Based on the descriptions of the responsibilities of the Financial Work Commission,[53] it would appear that the focus of the Financial Work Commission

[51] *Guiding Opinions on Promoting Capital Markets in Serving Cyberspace Power Building* ZWBFW [2018] 3.

[52] 'One Bank Two Commissions' refers to China's institutional financial regulatory bodies at the central level, which consist of the People's Bank of China, the China Banking and Insurance Regulatory Commission, and the China Securities Regulatory Commission. See *Decision of the 1st Session of the 13th National People's Congress on the State Council Institutional Reform Proposal* (National People's Congress, 17 March 2018) ch 2 art 3.

[53] The responsibilities of the Financial Work Commission were 1) to enable the CPC to lead in the financial sector 2) to implement the CPC's policy and the State Council's directives in the financial sector, 3) to assist the Department of Organization of the CPC to manage officials in the financial sector, 4) to monitor the CPC officials in the financial sector, 5) to coordinate the CPC committees in financial institutions and local governments.

See *Circular of the CPC Central Committee on Perfecting the Party's Leadership in the Financial System and Strengthening and Improving the Party's Work on the Financial System* (19 May 1998).

was on the CPC's leadership. In fact, the regulations issued in the past indicate that the CPC exerts its powers and authority over specific matters.

First of all, what is often witnessed is that the CPC's policies are taken to be the basis for the introduction of specific rules. For example, in March 1997, the PBoC issued a notice[54] in which it was clearly explained that the notice was based on the work of the Central Political and Legal Affairs Commission of the CPC,[55] which was appended to the notice. Another example is that in December 2016, the National Development and Reform Commission and the China Securities Regulatory Commission issued a further notice,[56] in which it was stated that the object of the notice was 'in order to implement the tenets of' the two documents issued by the CPC and the State Council respectively.[57]

Reforms in the financial sector since the introduction of Deng's Opening-up policy have also evidenced the CPC's role as a de facto regulator, and the changing boundaries of the regulatory powers between the central and local governments are a result of the CPC's policies. In 1998, as a direct result of one of the *Major decisions of the Central Committee of the CPC and the State Council*,[58] the PBoC was able to abolish the 'one province one branch' policy in order to curtail local government intervention in its lending activities, instead set up nine branches across provinces. Another illustration, the reforms initiated in 2017 to increase the responsibilities of local governments in financial regulation were also prompted by the CPC. The

After the *Circular of the CPC Central Committee on Issues Pertaining to the Adjustment of the Party's Leadership in Financial Regulatory Institutions* (ZF [2003] Order No 5) was issued in 2003, the Central Financial Work Commission was dismissed and their responsibilities were transferred to the Party Committee of the 'one bank, three commissions'. See People's Bank of China, *A Brief History of Financial Development under the Leadership of the Communist Party of China* (China Financial Publishing House, 1st ed, 2012) 326.

54 The *Notice on Implementing the Opinions of the Central Political and Legal Affairs Commission of the CPC on the Freezing and Deduction of Bank Deposits by Judicial Authorities (the Notice)* YF [1997] 94.

55 *Opinions on the Freezing and Deduction of Bank Deposits by Judicial Authorities.*

56 *Notice on Promoting the Work concerning the Asset Securitization of Public–Private-Partnership (PPP) Projects in the Traditional Infrastructure Field* FGTZ [2016] 2698.

57 *Opinions of the Central Committee of the Communist Party of China and the State Council on Deepening the Reforms of the Investment and Financial System*'. Similarly, in April 2018, the PBOC, the China Banking and Insurance Regulatory Commission, the China Securities Regulatory Commission, and the State Administration of Foreign Exchange issued *Guiding Opinions on Regulating the Asset Management Business of Financial Institutions YF [2018] 106.*, which was drafted 'in accordance with the decisions of the CPC and the State Council' and to respond to the CPC and the State Council's decisions to 'serve the real economy, prevent and control financial risks, and deepen financial reform'.

58 See *Circular of the State Council on Approving and Transmitting the Implementation Plan of the Provincial Institutional Reform of the People's Bank of China* (GF [1998] 33).

responsibilities of local governments in financial regulation were redrawn and delineated.[59] As a result, local governments have officially taken on the role and renamed their Financial Services Office to Financial Supervision and Administration Bureau.

It is also observed that not only the CPC itself, but also the various departments within the CPC, directly or indirectly, take part in regulatory activities in financial markets. For example, in combating financial risks associated with internet-based activities, the CPC's Department for Stability and local CPC committees collectively shoulder the responsibility to prevent and deal with mass incidents caused by systemic financial risks.[60] The CPC's Department of Propaganda is focused on disseminating news in an attempt to guide public opinions and mitigate financial risks.[61]

On some occasions the voice of the CPC's departments has been decisive, resolute, and would have the final say on matters. For example, there have been multiple regulators in the fund management sector. There was no clear demarcation between the CSRC and the National Development and Reform Commission when it came to the matter on regulation of private securities funds. In 2011, the National Development and Reform Commission issued two notices[62] under which private securities funds are required to register with the National Development and Reform Commission. This overlaps with the CSRC's power to regulate securities markets which was mandated by the *Securities Law*. In order to resolve this overlap, in June 2013, the Office of the CPC's Public Sector Reforms Committee determined that the CSRC is said to be 'responsible for the supervision and administration of private equity funds,[63] and the NDRC is said to be facilitating i.e. to 'organize the formulation of policies and measures to promote the development of private equity funds, and

---

[59] *Several Opinions of the CPC Central Committee and the State Council on Serving the Real Economy, Preventing and Controlling Financial Risks and Deepening Financial Reform.* The specific expression of the document is 'We will ameliorate the distribution of responsibilities between central and local financial supervision and give local governments financial supervision responsibilities. Small loan companies, financing guarantee companies, regional equity markets, pawnbrokers, financial leasing companies, commercial factoring companies and local asset management companies will be supervised by local financial supervisory departments. We will strengthen the supervision of local financial supervisory departments over investment companies, farmers' professional cooperatives that carry out mutual credit assistance, social crowdfunding institutions and various local trading places within their jurisdiction.'.

[60] The *Circular of the General Office of the State Council on Printing and Distributing the Implementation Plan for the Special Rectification of Internet Financial Risks* (GBF [2016] 21, also see n 29) require that 'Local police organs, under the leadership of local Party committees and governments, shall work together with relevant departments to prevent and deal with mass incidents and maintain social stability. The National Public Complaints and Proposals Administration is responsible for the reception and acceptance of petitioners' relevant complaints. The Central Office for Maintaining Stability, the Supreme People's Court and the Supreme People's Procuratorate shall cooperate in the relevant works.'.

[61] See *Circular of the General Office of the State Council on Printing and Distributing the Implementation Plan for the Special Rectification of Internet Financial Risks* (GBF [2016] 21).

[62] *Notice on Further Regulating the Development and Filing Management of Equity Investment Enterprises in Pilot Areas* FGBCJ [2011] 253. the *Notice on Facilitating Orderly Development of Equity Investment Enterprises* FGBCJ [2011] 2864.

[63] The *Notice on the Distribution of Responsibilities for Private Securities Fund Management.*

work with relevant departments to study and formulate the standards and norms of government contribution to private equity funds'.[64]

The other factor which needs to be taken into consideration is that state-owned or controlled financial institutions are the pillars of the financial sector. Therefore, senior personnel in these institutions are accountable to the regulatory bodies as well as the CPC. This leads to the introduction of a set of CPC rules especially designed for the management such personnel.[65] While the rules are largely overlapping with relevant rules issued by regulatory bodies,[66] the CPC rules shows that the CPC, as a party, is self -regulating and that these senior personnel would be faced with party disciplinary actions in the event of breach.[67]

As most recently, on 24 July 2021, the CPC central together with the State Council directed that companies that engaged in educational training are prohibited from listing or being listed on the stock exchange.[68] Although not in the form of enacted laws or regulatory rules, such a directive had a global impact at the time. As a result, the stock of some Chinese companies such as New Oriental Education & Technology Group Inc, and TAL Education Group listed in the US plummeted.[69]

The examples discussed above demonstrate that when it comes to regulation and supervision of financial markets, the CPC is not a de jure regulator, but acts beyond the scope of a de jure regulator to some extent. The CPC 'leads', 'supports', and

---

[64] See 'Office of the Central Institutional Organization Commission Defines the Division of Responsibilities for Private Equity Fund Management', *CPC* (2 July 2013). http://cpc.people.com.cn/n/2013/0702/c164113-22040815.html. In fact, the power struggle between the CSRC and the NDRC on regulating private securities investment funds shows that the regulatory structure in China is still based on institutions instead of functions Such a regulatory structure allows the CPC to carry higher political authority and act as an arbiter when there is a dispute or conflict among regulatory bodies. For discussion on functional market and institutional supervision in China's financial realm, see Huang Tao, 'The Legal Path of China's Financial Market from "Institutional Supervision" to "Functional Supervision": Focusing on the Improvement of the Rules for Supervising Financial Products' (2011) 7 *Law Science* 105.

[65] For example, the Office of the CPC Central issued *Interim Provisions on the Administration of Leaders of Financial Enterprises under Central Management,* in which it was explicitly stated that the basis for promulgation of the *Interim Provisions* is the *Constitution of the Communist Party of China,* and other relevant laws.The *Interim Provisions* sets out detailed rules on matters concerning organisational structure, appointments and qualifications, selections, appraisals, salaries and bonuses, supervision, and training.

[66] The most relevant rules governing the supervision of high-level officials is the *Measures for the Administration of the Office-holding Qualifications of the Directors (Council Members) and Senior Managers of Banking Financial Institutions.*

[67] See Song Degong, Zhang Wenxian, *Laws and Regulations within the Party* (Higher Education Press, 1st ed, 2020) 24–6.

[68] Ministry of Education of the PRC, the General Office of the Central Committee of the Communist Party of China and the General Office of the State Council issued the "Opinions on Further Reducing the Homework Burden and Off-campus Training Burden of Students in Compulsory Education" https://www-moe-gov-cn.translate.goog/jyb_xxgk/moe_1777/moe_1778/202107/t20210724_546576.html?_x_tr_sch=http&_x_tr_sl=zh-CN&_x_tr_tl=en&_x_tr_hl=en&_x_tr_pto=sc.

[69] Reuters, Beijing tutoring crackdown slams U.S.-listed Chinese stocks, 24 July 2021.

'supplements' the regulatory bodies exercising their powers.[70] Therefore, the CPC is not only devising policies in the financial sector but is also an integral part of carrying out these policies.

2.3 The CPC as De Facto Adjudicator[71] in the Financial Markets

The judiciary in China is led and controlled[72] by the CPC. While the *Constitution* states the independence of the judiciary, such independence should be understood in the context of the leadership of the CPC, where the judiciary adjudicates individual cases free of interferences.[73] Similar to acting as a lawmaker and a regulator when it comes to the financial sector, the CPC also acts as an adjudicator. This does not mean that the CPC exercises the powers of the judiciary, or directly adjudicates individual cases, but that the CPC acts to direct judicial policies concerning the financial sector.

In recent years, the most influential reforms in the judiciary concerning the financial sector is the establishment of the financial courts, which is derived from the CPC Central's policy.[74] The President of the Supreme People's Court stated that the

[70] The party's deep involvement in financial supervision is likely to trigger discussions on the relationship between the Party and the government. Some political scholars believe that, unlike the separation of the Party and the government emphasized in the early stage of Reform and Opening Up, the new historical period envisions the ideal state of the institutional arrangement of the relationship between the Party and the government as the coordination and coupling between the Party and the state in systems, functions and political processes, rather than the simple separation of the Party and the government. See Lin Shangli, *The Communist Party of China and State Building* (Tianjin Renmin Chubanshe, 2nd ed, 2017) 259.

[71] The authors do not mean that the CPC adjudicates individual cases. As a de facto adjudicator, as our analysis will show that, the CPC has the power to dictate and determine the trajectory of the policies concerning the judiciary.

[72] While the Constitution and other laws require the courts to exercise judicial powers independently, the control of the courts by the CPC is primarily exercised through personnel system. Key personnel has to be nominated by the CPC. The courts are under the leadership of the CPC's Central Political and Legal Affairs Commission. In recent years, the Chief Justice of the Supreme Court reports to the Politburo Standing Committee of the Chinese Communist Party. See the Politburo Standing Committee of the Chinese Communist Party Hears the Working Report of the Chief Justice of the Supreme Court https://www.chinacourt.org/article/detail/2022/01/id/6469631.shtml.

[73] See 'Stand Firmly against the Influence of Erroneous Western Thoughts such as "Judicial Independence"', *China Court* (15 January 2017). https://www.chinacourt.org/article/detail/2017/01/id/2512852.shtml.

[74] The passage of the *Decision on Forming the Shanghai Financial Court* and the *Decision on Forming the Beijing Financial Court* took place at the 1st and the 17th meetings of the CPC Central Commission for Comprehensively Deepening Reforms Committee on 28 March 2018, and 30 December 2020 respectively. See 'Xi Jinping Chaired the 1st Meeting of the Central Commission for Comprehensively Deepening Reform', *Chinese Government* (28 March 2018). http://www.gov.cn/xinwen/2018-03/28/content_5278124.htm.

establishment of the Shanghai Financial Court is a result of 'adhering to the guidance of Xi Jinping's socialist ideology with Chinese characteristics in the new era', and carrying out the spirits of the CPC meeting resolutions and the State Council's directive.[75]

In China, the Supreme People's Court exercises its powers to issue various types of directives to signal judicial policies.[76] It is observed that often after the CPC Central makes decisions on certain matters, publicised or not, the Supreme People's Court also issues directives which correspond to those decisions and which have the effect of transforming the CPC's policies to judicial policies. For example, in response to the 1997 South Asia Financial Crisis, the CPC Central and the State Council issued the *Notice on Deepening Financial Reform, Rectifying the Financial Order and Preventing Financial Risks*,[77] and the Supreme People's Court also released a notice in response.[78]

In 2009, in the face of an escalating number of cases dealing with non-performing assets in the financial sector, the Supreme People's Court issued a directive,[79] the purposes of which were to 'implement the spirit of the CPC's Central Committee on studying and solving the problem of the loss of state-owned assets in the process of the assignment of distressed claims involving financial institutions'. The directive also identified parties to the meeting which include the CPC's Central Political and Legal Affairs Commission.[80]

Therefore, as part of the state, the judiciary, and in particular, the Supreme People's Court, responds to the CPC's policies with detailed directives and takes an active

---

[75] See Zhou Qiang, 'Notes to the *Decision on the Establishment of a Financial Court in Shanghai (Draft)*: On the 2nd Meeting of the Standing Committee of the 13th National People's Congress', *National People's Congress* (27April 2018). http://www.npc.gov.cn/npc/c30834/201804/7375fa32c7a64df4889be81b1d58cce5.shtml.

[76] See Huang Tao, 'The Judicial Document of Chinese Supreme People's Court: Status, Problems and Prospects' (2012) 4 *Legal Forum* 124.

[77] ZF [1997] 19.

[78] *Notice of the People's Court on the Implementation of Relevant Issues in ZF [1997] Order No 19* FF [1998] 2.

[79] *Minutes Summary on the Meeting on Hearing Cases about Transferring Non-Performing Creditor Rights of Financial Institutions* FF [2009] 19.

[80] Similarly, after the CPC convenes meetings, the Supreme People's Court would also issue judicial documents accordingly. For example, after the CPC's 2012's 4th National Financial Work Conference, the Supreme People's Court promulgated the Guiding Opinions on Provision by People's Courts of Judicial Guarantee for Preventing and Defusing Financial Risks and Promoting Financial Reform and Development in which it stated 'regulating financial orders, preventing financial risks, promoting financial reforms, supporting financial innovation and maintaining financial security are not only the main tasks of financial reforms and development for the next period, but also an important aspect of the People's Courts safeguarding the country's comprehensive promotion of financial reforms and development', FF [2012] 3.. After the CPC's 2017's 5th National Financial Work Conference, the Supreme People's Court issued Several Opinions on Further Strengthening Financial Trials requiring 'the People's Courts at all levels to thoroughly study and implement the spirit of the conference, and to effectively align their thoughts and actions with the Central Committee of the CPC with Comrade Xi Jinping as the core, in their analysis, of judgement and decision-making for financial work.' FF [2017] 22.

part in the management of financial markets. Essentially the judiciary ensures it is in lockstep with the CPC.[81] Of course, the judiciary's approach is not rigid, although in early days it was considered that the judiciary's approach was merely to interpret policies, and thus was limited.[82] In recent years, it is evident that the judiciary do not simply regurgitate the CPC policies, but interpret and incorporate them into the area of adjudication. For example, by way of the 2017 *Several Opinions on Further Strengthening Financial Trials,* the Supreme People's Court issued directives on substantive matters concerning usury practices, security interests in crypto assets, the legality of online intermediaries, and issues concerning zombie companies.[83]

The above discussions are focused on the judiciary's implementation of CPC policies via its judicial documents[84]; in turn, the CPC policies determine the contours of judicial policies concerning the financial sector. In addition, individual cases also indicate the power of the CPC in the judiciary.

It is most visible when the CPC rules and policies are explicitly referred to in individual rulings of the courts. These cases are rare but show a glimpse of the

[81] Hou Meng, *A Study on the Supreme People's Court of China: Starting with Judicial Influence* (Law Press, 1st ed, 2007) 62.

[82] See Zhou Daoluan, 'Review of Judicial Interpretation Work in New China and Thoughts on Improvement' in Wang Shengjun (ed), *Compilation of Judicial Interpretation of the Supreme People's Court of the People's Republic of China* (Renminfayuanchubanshe, 1994) 4.

[83] Detailed examples such as ch 2 art 2: 'Strictly, lawfully stipulating usury and effectively reducing the cost of financing in the real economy.' ch 2 art 3: 'Lawfully determining the legal effect of new types of securities and expanding the financing security modes of micro, small and medium-sized enterprises. ... if a contract conforms to the provisions on security interests in the Property Law, its effect with respect to real rights shall be determined in accordance with the law.' ch 2 art 4: 'Where a contract is a financing lease or factoring contract in name but a lending contract in fact, the rights and obligations of each party shall be determined according to the lending contractual relationship actually constituted.'ch 2 art 6: 'Accurately applying the Insurance Law ...'ch 2 art 7: 'The brokerage contractual relationship between online lending information intermediary agencies and parties to online lending contracts shall be accurately delimited. The form of brokerage fee by which an online lending information intermediary agency and the lender dodge the provisions on judicial protection of the upper limit of private lending interest rates shall be determined to be null. Illegal criminal acts relating to or in the name of internet finance shall be strictly cracked down upon, so as to regulate and ensure the sound development of internet finance.'ch 3 art 11: '"Zombie enterprises" without market competitiveness or operation value shall be subjected to liquidation and bankruptcy in a timely manner for them to leave the market in an orderly manner, in order to effectively reduce ineffective supply, resolve overcapacity, release factors of production, reduce corporate leverage ratios, and provide powerful judicial services and guarantees for deepening supply-side structural reform'.

[84] For the varying degrees of legal effects of the directives issued by the Supreme People's Court, see Huang Tao, 'The Judicial Document of Chinese Supreme People's Court: Status, Problems and Prospects' (2012) 4 *Legal Forum* 124, 124–9.

ubiquitous presence of the CPC. For example, in an appellate case[85] and the corresponding notice,[86] the Supreme People's Court stated that financial institutions, as creditors, are thus bound, and 'after ceasing to engage in business activities, and making arrangements for being a guarantor, the military and the armed police...will be relieved of all guarantor obligations under the guarantee.'[87] The uniqueness of the case is it predicates on the idea of 'The Party leads the Military'[88] which could be considered as something beyond the jurisdictions of the courts. The Supreme People's Court followed the CPC's rules that the military is prohibited from engaging in commercial activities, which set the example for other courts when it comes to similar cases.[89]

Alternatively, the judiciary would refer to CPC documents or policies in an attempt to support its reasoning. For example, in adjudicating a case, the Intermediate People's Court of Yichun rejected the application for a freezing order of bank

[85] *Dispute over Loan Guarantee Agreement concerning China Satellite Department of Measurement and Control System, China Yuan Wang (Group) Co., Ltd, and Guangzhou Zhong Yuan Real Estate Development Co., Ltd*, by making reference to the *Notice on Printing and Distributing the Implementation Plan for the Military and Armed Police to No Longer Engage in Business Activities* ZBF [1998] 24.

[86] *Notice on Printing and Distributing Four Supporting Documents for the Implementation Plan for the Military, Armed Police and Political and Legal Affairs Organs to No Longer Engage in Business Activities* ZBF [1998] 29.

[87] (2004) Supreme People's Court, Civil 2nd Instance Order No 159.

[88] The origin of the principle of 'the Party Leads the Military', the fundamental principle and system of the Party's absolute leadership over the military, originated from the Nanchang Uprising in 1927, and the specific document was the resolution of the Gutian Congress in 1929. In late December 1929, the 9th Meeting of the 4th Red Army was held in Gutian, Shanghang, Fujian. According to the instructions of the CPC Central Committee, a new Frontier Committee of the 4th Red Army of the CPC was elected at the meeting. Mao Zedong was elected Secretary of the Frontier Committee and adopted the *Resolution of the 9th Meeting of the 4th Red Army of the Communist Party of China*, which was drafted under the auspices of Mao Zedong, and that was the resolution of the Gutian Congress. The resolution of the Gutian Congress is a programmatic document for the construction of the CPC and the people's army. It solves the major problem of how to build an army with farmers as the main component into a new people's army under the absolute leadership of the Party. These principles are the fundamental principles underlying the CPC's cultivation of a people's army. They have a significant and far-reaching impact on the party's leadership of the army in all periods. As Xi Jinping said, 'Gutian is the place where our party has established the principle of 'build the party by ideology, build the army by politics', the foundation of our army's political work, and the place where the new people's army finally formed. It is Gutian where the people's army under the leadership of the party started, from small to large, from weak to strong, and from victory to victory.

[89] Similarly, in another appellate case, the People's Court of Shijiazhuang Hi-tech Industrial Development Zone explicitly made reference to the *Provisions of the CPC Central Committee and the State Council on Prohibiting Party and Government Organs and Officials from Doing Business and Running Enterprises* and *Provisions of the CPC Central Committee and the State Council on Further Preventing Party and Government Organs and Officials from Doing Business and Running Enterprises,* and determined that the breach of regulations resulted in the voiding of the underlying commercial loan agreement. On *Dispute over the Agreement concerning the Xinyingwan Office of Yangpu Economic Development Zone Administration Bureau and Hainan Danzhou Ganchong Rural Credit Cooperative*, (2003) Yangpu Intermediate People's Court, Final Appeal Order No 8.

accounts and a garnishee order, and the court used a CPC directive[90] as one of the grounds for such a decision.[91] It is important to acknowledge the rarity of such cases so far, and that they are considered as 'the exception to the rule'.[92] The courts and the judges by and large adjudicate in accordance with laws and regulations, and rarely explicitly refer to CPC directives. Nevertheless, the abovementioned cases illustrate the power or the extent of the power that the CPC could potentially exert over the judiciary.

In relation to a financial derivatives case in 2015,[93] in order to give emphasis to the fact that managing derivative markets falls under the scope of local governments, and thus that resolving the disputes concerning the rights of investors should be the task of local governments, the High Court in Guangdong Province referred to the

---

[90] *Opinions of the CPC Central Committee and the State Council on Creating a Sound Entrepreneur Growth Environment, Advocating Excellent Entrepreneurship and Better Using Entrepreneurs' Roles.*

[91] Dispute Over the Financial Loan Agreement concerning China Cinda Asset Management Co., Ltd. Jiangxi Branch and Industrial and Commercial Bank of China Limited Fengcheng Branch,(2019) GAN 09 Execution Review Order No 22. The court stated "in adjudicating cases involving private enterprises, court orders shall be carefully applied; and the court shall take into account ensuring current capital and accounts necessary for the operation of the enterprises, prohibiting excessive court-ordered seizure of property shall, and issuing the freezing orders of basic bank accounts with care, in order to minimise the adverse impact on the production and operation of enterprises.

[92] In the case of *Anshun Xixiu District Supply and Marketing Cooperative Member Stock Center Co., Ltd and Li Bangshun,* the Intermediate People's Court of Anshun decided that although the agreement in dispute was concluded contrary to the *Decision of the CPC Central Committee and the State Council on Deepening Comprehensive Reform of the Local Cooperatives* (ZF [2015] Order No 11) ZF [2015] 11, the *Opinions of the CPC Provincial Committee of Guizhou and People's Government of Guizhou Province on Implementing the Comprehensive Deepening Reform of Local Cooperatives* (QD [2016] Order No 5) QDF [2016] 5 as well as *Opinions of the CPC Municipal Committee of Anshun and People's Government of Anshun Municipality on Implementing the Comprehensive Deepening Reform of Local Cooperatives* (ASF [2016] Order No 24), under which local cooperatives were prohibited from taking deposits and lending, the court held that the abovementioned directives are not of law or regulation in nature, breach of which does not fall under the circumstances specified in Item (5) of Article 52 of the Contract Law of the People's Republic of China' (2017) QIAN 04 Civil Final Appeal Order No 586. In other words, the breach of the abovementioned directives should not be enforced by the courts. As a result, the validity of the agreement was upheld. In an insurance compensation case in 2019, a person of rural residency requested that the insurance company compensate under the principle of 'reforming the compensation system for personal injury, and unifying the compensation standards for urban and rural residents established under the *Opinions of the CPC Central Committee and the State Council on Establishing and Improving the Systems, Mechanisms, Policies and Schemes of Urban–Rural Integration.* This argument was rejected by the Yangyuan People's Court on the grounds that "the Opinions were not applicable in law", "judicial interpretation is superior to any directives" and "the relevant Judicial Interpretation of the People's Supreme Court on personal injury is still in force and should be complied with".See 'First Instance Civil Case of Liability Disputes of Motor Vehicle Traffic Accidents concerning Guo Shuzhi, Liu Mancheng and Ma Weibo' [(2019) JI 0727 Civil 1st Instance Order No 619].

[93] (2015) Guangdong Higher People's Court, Retrial Order No 67.

statement[94] in one of the CPC directives.[95] The court then concluded that such a dispute is of an administrative nature and does not fall under the purview of the court. The case arose when the Shenzhen Cultural Property Rights Exchange was cleared up by the local government. The case was concerned with investor losses as a result of investor accounts being frozen. From the court's viewpoint, it was not a civil dispute, since the local government was involved in the clearing-up of the markets which led to such a dispute. It would thus likely be the most efficient way for the local government to deal with these disputes. Although there was no clear legal basis, the court was able to refer to the CPC directives to justify the decision not to adjudicate such a case.[96] However, the appellate court, the Supreme People's Court, rejected such reasoning by the Guangdong High Court and stated that 'whether the clearing-up is of an administrative nature or not, the Exchange is a legal person, and thus it should not affect the court's power to adjudicate whether the Exchange bears any civil liabilities.'[97]

Thus, the CPC and the judiciary are not separate organs: on the one hand, the CPC influences the judiciary from all facets of judicial life; on the other hand, it is said that such influence is overarching and policy-driven.[98] The CPC and the judiciary are intertwined.[99] What is apparent is the leadership of the CPC in judicial activities. Instead of intervening in adjudicating individual cases, such leadership is primarily manifested via formulating and making judicial policies. The judicial directives concerning the financial markets resonate with and respond to the CPC and its policies to the extent that there is a fusion of the CPC financial policies and such policies of the judiciary. By and large, adjudication of individual cases is still based on laws and regulations with rare exceptions where the CPC policies were weaved into judicial reasoning.

---

[94] 'To improve the prevention and resolution mechanism of social conflicts and disputes, to improve and coordinate the workings of the dispute resolution mechanisms such as mediation, arbitration, administrative rulings and review, and litigation, … to improve administrative ruling mechanism, and to improve administrative departments resolving civil disputes related to the administration'

[95] *Decision on Major Issues Pertaining to Comprehensively Promoting the Rule of Law,* (23 October 2014) 4th Plenary Session, 18th CPC Central Committee.

[96] For analysis on the background reasons for 'screening' some financial dispute cases in the filing process of the courts, see Huang Tao, 'The Screening Mechanism of Financial Legal Disputes in Chinese Courts' (2011) 1 *Jurist* 114.

[97] See '*Retrial Decision on Case of financial derivatives transaction disputes concerning Chen Zhifen*' [(2016) Supreme People's Court, Retrial Order No. 411]; '*Retrial Decision on Case of financial derivatives transaction concerning Zou Zhonghai*' [(2016) Supreme People's Court, Retrial Order No 439].

[98] See Su Li, 'Political Parties in China's Justice System', in Su Li (ed), *Law and Social Science* (Law Press, 1st ed, 2006) vol 1, 266–7.

[99] According to some scholars, China's system of Party leadership over politics and law has reached beyond Mirjan Damaška's classification of the relationship between justice and state power. The CPC, as a political force independently leading the judiciary, takes the initiative to enter the judiciary, which shows a more complex relationship different from the path through which the Western world has developed the rule of law. See Hou Meng, 'Formation of Political-Legal System in Contemporary China' (2016) 3 *Chinese Journal of Law* 3.

3 Review and Assessment of the CPC's Roles in the Financial Markets

3.1 Guiding the Reforms Through Top-Down Design

The CPC initiates reforms in the financial sector and determines the directions of such reforms. Since the introduction of Deng's opening-up policies, the CPC has been present in all corners of the financial sector via making rules and enforcing rules. In other words, the history of the development of the financial markets in China is a history where the CPC's decisions and policies have been adopted, implemented and institutionalised. The interactions between the CPC and the financial markets were succinctly captured by President Xi when he stated in 2017 that 'Strengthening the Party's leadership in finance, adhering to the leadership of the Central Committee of the CPC, improving the mechanisms of the party's leadership in finance, and institutionalising (of the CPC rule).[100]

In the past four decades, the CPC's directions and measures have been critical to the success of economic transition. Since the beginning of Deng's opening-up reforms, the CPC's decisions and policies were the drivers behind reforms in the financial sector, which were manifested in multiple ways. In particular, key political figures push forward the reform agenda in the financial sector. The most illuminating example is Deng's views on stock markets. In the early days of the opening-up reforms, in responding to the questions such as whether stock markets are quintessentially capitalistic or could only be employed in a capitalistic economy, Deng stated in 1992: 'whether stock and stock markets are good, whether they are dangerous, whether they are exclusively capitalistic, or whether they could be utilized in a socialistic society? The proof of the pudding is in the eating.'[101] Deng's statements on the matter were determinative, and what ensued was the introduction of the stock markets in China and the establishment of infrastructure that was necessary for such markets. Similarly, Xi announced in November 2018 that 'setting up [of] a market in the Shanghai Stock Exchange catering for technology-based companies and piloting IPO registration reforms',[102] which re-started the process of IPO Registration Reforms. As discussed above, the *Securities Law* was amended in 2019 to effect such changes.[103]

[100] See 'During the 40th Collective Learning Session of the Central Political Bureau of the CPC, Xi Jinping Stressed the Importance of Financial Vitality for Economic Vitality, the Importance of Financial Stability for Economic Stability, and the Importance of Carrying out Good Financial Work and Maintaining Financial Security' *People's Daily* (27 April 2017).

[101] *Selected Works of Deng Xiaoping* (People's Publishing House, 1993) vol 3, 373.

[102] See 'Shanghai Stock Exchange will set up a Science and Technology Innovation Board and pilot a registration system' *Economic Daily* (6 November 2018).

[103] Among the ten important institutional reforms of the new *Securities Law* summarized by the CSRC, 'comprehensively implementing the securities issuance registration system' sits at the top. See 'Perfecting the Basic System of the Securities Market and Ensuring the Reform and Development of the Capital Market: CSRC Celebrates the Adoption of the Amendment to the *Securities*

While it is most visible to effect changes at the legislative level, it is important to acknowledge that the CPC's leadership is not only confined to such a level and is much more comprehensive. As discussed earlier, the CPC's leadership extends to the regulation of the markets as well as the judiciary. Overall, under the banner of 'the Party leads Finance', the legislature, regulatory bodies and the judiciary have been in lockstep with the CPC. What follows is a more coordinated approach among the legislature, regulatory bodies, and the judiciary when it comes to matters concerning the financial sector. For example, on 2 November 2020, the CPC's 16th meeting of the Comprehensive Deepening Reforms Committee passed the *Several Opinions on Cracking Down on Illegal Activities in the Securities Markets (the Opinions).* This is first directive that the CPC directly issued since the introduction of the opening-up policy with a view to sanctioning misconduct in the securities markets.[104] Against the backdrop of the amendments to the *Securities Law*, the *Opinions* could be considered as a signal—not only to the legislature, but also to regulatory bodies, the judiciary, and law enforcement authorities. More recently, more detailed directives were issued by the CPC Central Office and the Office of the State Council on the similar matters.[105]

3.2 Determining the Trajectory of the Reforms

Through the development of financial markets in China, the leadership of the CPC also has the effect of determining the trajectory of reforms. The CPC believed that 'Reforms are the second revolution for China,'[106] which indicates the magnitude of the impact of reforms on the Chinese society.[107] In the context of reforms in the financial sector, there are a variety of divergent interests among central and the local governments, among regulatory bodies, among financial institutions, among financial

---

Law of the People's Republic of China', *China Securities Regulatory Commission* (29 December 2019). http://www.csrc.gov.cn/pub/newsite/zjhxwfb/xwdd/201912/t20191228_368688.html.

[104] It stated that "we should accelerate the improvement of the judicial mechanisms for securities law enforcement, strengthen the investigation and punishment of major crimes, uphold the rule of law and maintain integrity in the capital markets, strengthen cross-border supervision and enforcement cooperation, and promote sound market orders.'.

See 'Xi Jinping Chaired the 16th meeting of Central Comprehensively Deepening Reforms Commission and Gave an Important Speech', *Chinese Government* (2 November 2020). http://www.gov.cn/xinwen/2020-11/02/content_5556789.htm.

[105] *Opinions on Cracking Down on Illegal Activities in Securities Markets* (General Office of the CPC Central Committee and General Office of the State Council, 6 July 2021). http://www.gov.cn/zhengce/2021-07/06/content_5622763.htm.

[106] *Selected Works of Deng Xiaoping* (People's Publishing House, 1993) vol 3, 113.

[107] The work report of the 2nd plenary session of the 13th CPC Central Committee held in 1988 recognised the existence of interest groups in Chinese society for the first time: 'under the socialist system, there are still conflicts between different interest groups among the people'.

institutions and investors, and among investors themselves,[108] which in turn would determine the directions or the successes or failure of reforms.[109] For example, the IPO Registration Reforms was referred to by the former CSRC Chairman Gao Xiqing was 'a revolution deep in the soul'.[110] The proposed reforms would adversely affect the interested parties who were the beneficiaries of the regulatory arrangement since the inception of the stock markets. The interested parties would be well entrenched in the system and wield significant powers. It is thus plausible that these interested parties would by all means pose obstacles or slow down the reform process.[111]

Among the struggles of different interest groups, the CPC would be required to play a role as an arbiter, not siding with any groups. In doing so, it seems that the issue of path dependence could be overcome.[112] The CPC could adopt policies that are conducive to long-term economic growth and allocate resources according to productivity considerations. Ideally, this would create a disinterested government under the CPC's leadership.[113] Such an approach would also resonate with the CPC's own narrative that the CPC has no special interest of its own.[114] In this sense, the CPC could be in a position to balance the interests of different groups in the system, and thus pave the way for reforms.

The evidence has shown that the CPC has a unique role to play which determines the directions of such reforms and removes obstacles to such reforms on the way. The aforementioned IPO Registration Reforms started off in 2013 but had been stalled. The CPC's leadership pushed ahead and then the corresponding reform measures were finalised in the form of legislative amendments. The IPO Registration Reforms

---

[108] For economic studies from this perspective, see, eg, Lu Lei, 'Information Structure, Interest Group and Public Policy: The Theoretical Problem in the Selection of Present Financial Supervision System' (2000) 12 *Economic Research Journal* 3; Xie Ping, Lu Lei, 'Coercion and Collusion of Interest Groups: On the General and Departmental Characteristics of Financial Supervision Corruption' (2003) 7 *Journal of Financial Research* 1; Luo Jinsheng, *Interest Groups and Institutional Transitions* (China Financial Publishing House, 2003); Jiang Chun, Xu Licheng, 'Political Economics of Financial Development' (2007) 8 *Research on Financial and Economic Issues*; Xu Jiagen, *Research on Action Mechanism of Interest Group in Financial Institution Reform* (Southwestern University of Finance and Economics Press, 2nd ed, 2015).

[109] Douglas North, *Institutions, Institutional Change and Economic Performance* (Cambridge University Press, 1990).

[110] Gao Xiqing Talking about the IPO Registration Reforms; the Biggest Achievement of the year for the Regulator, https://www.thepaper.cn/newsDetail_forward_1253142.

[111] See Mancur Olson, "The Logic of Collective Action" (Harvard University Press, 1965) 55–56.

[112] Path dependence in institutional economics refers to the phenomenon that, after the initial choice of a specific system by people, due to the reasons of economies of scale, coordination effect, learning effect, adaptive expectation and the vested interest constraints, the selected system will continue to strengthen itself along the existing direction, resulting in the difficulty of institutional change, and as a result an efficient system never emerges. See Douglas North, *Institutions, Institutional Change and Economic Performance* (Cambridge University Press, 1990) 100.

[113] Yang Yao, "The Disinterested Government: An Interpretation of China's Economic Success in the Reform Era" in Augustin Fosu (ed), *Achieving Development Success* (Oxford University Press, 2013).

[114] See 'People Always First, and the Communist Party of China Does not Have Its Own Special Interests', *People's Daily* (19 August 2020).

measures have now been officially introduced.[115] This is an illustration of a situation where the CPC has played the role of a mediator and an arbiter of various interest groups.

The reforms of the regulatory institutional structure concerning financial markets also serves as an example. The Office of the CPC's Public Sector Reform Committee had to intervene in the aforementioned struggle between the CSRC and the National Development and Reform Commission concerning regulating private securities funds. Another example is the reforms to establish the Shanghai Financial Court and Beijing Financial Court so that financial disputes which could involve parties across the nation are to be adjudicated in Shanghai and Beijing. Such reforms would step on the toes of local judiciaries.[116] The reforms were propelled by the Office of the CPC's Public Sector Reform Committee, which ensured the implementation of such reforms.[117]

To some extent, through the reforms, the CPC and the government under its leadership have forged a role of an 'all-encompassing organisation',[118] or the ultimate decision maker. This reflects some political theorists' view that, instead of following pressure from particular interest groups, an authoritarian government can neglect them and push through reforms.[119]

---

[115] A fact for reference is that one of the disciplinary violations reported by the Central Commission for Discipline Inspection in October 2019 of Liu Shiyu, former Chairman of the CSRC, is considered 'ineffective implementation of the major decisions and arrangements of the CPC Central Committee'. See 'Liu Shiyu, Former Deputy Secretary of the Party Group and Director of the Council of the All-China Federation of Supply and Marketing Cooperatives, Was Placed on a 2-year Probation in the Party and Expelled from His Governmental Office', *Central Commission for Discipline Inspection* (4 October 2019). http://www.ccdi.gov.cn/toutiao/201910/t20191004_201995.html. The new *Securities Law* authorizes the State Council to stipulate the specific scope and implementation steps of the securities issuance registration system.

[116] These two financial courts are 'local' in nature as they are accountable to the local Standing Committee of the People's Congress in terms of finance and personnel. See *Decision of the Standing Committee of the National People's Congress on Forming the Shanghai Financial Court* (27 April 2018) 2nd Session of the Standing Committee, 13th National People's Congress; *Decision of the Standing Committee of the National People's Congress to Form the Beijing Financial Court* (22 January 2021) 25th Session of the Standing Committee, 13th National People's Congress.

[117] For research on this point, see Huang Tao, '"Nationwide" Financial Market and "Local" Court: from the Perspective of Central-Local Relations in China's Financial Justice' (2016) 3 *Law Review*.

[118] The description of 'pan-profit' organisations comes from Olson. He believes that the existence of such organisations is crucial to the rise and fall of the country, and those interest groups keen on income redistribution policy are the biggest challenge to a democratic society. See Mancur Olson, *The Rise and Decline of Nations: Economic Growth, Stagflation, and Social Rigidities* (Yale University Press, 1982). The CPC has to compensate interest groups in return for support for the reforms See Yao Yang, *Global Implications of the Chinese Experience* (Peking University Press, 2011) 58–62.

[119] SP Huntington, *Political Order in Changing Societies* (Yale University Press, 1968) and A Kohli, 'Democracy and Development' in JP Lewis and V Kallab (eds), *Development Strategies Reconsidered* (Transaction Books, 1986).

3.3 Leveraging on the Authority of CPC to Legitimise Reforms

To some extent, the CPC or the endorsement of the CPC provides legitimacy to the activities undertook by the legislature, regulatory bodies, and the judiciary concerning the financial markets. One would argue otherwise that relevant laws such as the *Legislature Law*, the *Banking Supervision and Regulation Law*, the *Securities Law*, and the *Civil Procedure Law* provide a legal basis, and extend powers and authority to the legislature, the regulatory bodies, and the judiciary concerning their respective activities in the financial markets.

In practice, as demonstrated, the CPC is ubiquitous in the activities undertook by the legislature, regulatory bodies, and the judiciary. In some cases, in light of the decisions of the CPC, authorities are adopting relevant measures without the measures first being legislated, which is evident in the case of the IPO Registration Reforms.[120] One explanation is that the presence of the CPC is indicative of the fact that by resorting to the CPC, the legislature, regulatory bodies, and the judiciary aim to strength legality and legitimacy of their own activities.[121] In other words, the CPC is considered as the authoritative voice which renders authority to the aforementioned bodies and activities undertaken by them.

In contemporary China, to some extent, it is necessary for the legislature, regulatory bodies, and the judiciary to resort to the authority of the CPC.[122] After the introduction of the opening-up policy, the CPC has passed the period of 'Charismatic Authority'[123] and hinges its authority on the economic development and economic welfare of the Chinese people.[124] The CPC is perceived to drive such economic development and the economic welfare of the people. At the times when the development of financial markets is at a crossroad, what is seen as necessary is the authoritative voice which could push forward reforms in a resolute manner. Resorting to the CPC is not only politically symbolic as demonstrated by aforementioned examples, but also is of pragmatism.

As illustrated above, after 2016, the emphasis in the markets has shifted to combatting financial risks and cracking down on internet financing activities. In doing so, the

---

[120] After double-checking the reform direction of the stock issuance registration system at the highest political level, the Shanghai Stock Exchange officially launched the Science and Technology Innovation Board in June 2019 and began the trial of the registration system, which was earlier than the introduction of the new *Securities Law* in December 2019.

[121] See Max Weber, *Economy and Society: An Outline of Interpretive Sociology*, translated by E. Fischoff et al. (University of California Press, 1978) volume 1, 215 and David Dyzenhaus, *Legality and Legitimacy: Carl Schmitt, Hans Kelsen and Hermann Heller in Weimar* (1997).

[122] Habermas held the view that under the truth-dependency of belief in legitimacy, appeal to the state's monopoly on the creation of rules does not suffice: Jürgen Habermas, *Legitimation Crisis*, translated by Thomas McCarthy (Heinemann London, 1976) 98.

[123] Max Weber, *Economy and Society: An Outline of Interpretive Sociology*, translated by E. Fischoff et al. (University of California Press, 1978) volume 1, 241.

[124] For the concept of Performance Legitimacy, see Zhao Dingxin, *Politics of Legitimacy: The State-Society Relations in Contemporary China* (National Taiwan University Press, 2017) 117–50.

authorities would often refer to the CPC's policies and directives. From the perspective of socio-linguistics, it is not mere rhetoric but has practical implications. In 2014 and 2015, the State Council had adopted a supportive tone to internet financing activities in its *Report on the Work of the Government*.[125] Regulatory authorities at the central level have also taken a hands-off approach when it comes to regulation of internet financing.[126] However, triggered by the scandals which led to public outcry in 2015, the central regulatory authorities took a U-turn in their approach. By pointing to or resorting to the role of the CPC, and the CPC's policies, the regulatory authorities sought to legitimise their actions and unify various interests and forces under the banner of the CPC, which in a way allayed the concern on the central regulatory authorities' ability to mobilise local regulatory forces.[127]

Again, relying on CPC rules and policies lends legitimacy to the acts of other authorities in the markets. The judiciary is no exception. As discussed in Part 2.3, judges are willing to make references to CPC directives. This illustrates that, in reference to the CPC, a higher authority or a more authoritative voice, judges intended to render the decisions 'legitimate'. In some cases, the CPC directives probably serve as the only basis for a judgement. In the case mentioned earlier concerning that 'the military should not undertake commercial activities', the court would not have another ground, apart from the CPC's directives, to use as the basis for the decision.[128]

What also must be acknowledged is that while the CPC renders authority and legitimacy to the authorities such as the legislature, the judiciary and the regulatory authorities; in turn, these authorities give effect to the CPC's policies and other directives. Through these authorities, the CPC's policies and other directives are implemented. More technically speaking, the CPC's policies and other directives are legislated, regulated, and enforced via these authorities.[129] Such arrangements would echo Xi's views of 'modernizing the country's governance system under the rule by

---

[125] *2014 Government Work Report of the State Council* (14 March 2014). http://www.gov.cn/guowuyuan/2014-03/14/content_2638989.htm; *2015 Government Work Report of the State Council* (16 March 2015). http://www.gov.cn/guowuyuan/2015-03/16/content_2835101.htm.

For the policy and legal disputes over the early development of Internet Finance in China, see Huang Tao, 'Internet Finance in China: Market, Supervision and Law' (2017) 4 *Journal of Southeast University (Philosophy and Social Science)*.

[126] Weiping He, *The Regulation of Securities Markets in China* (Palgrave Macmillan, 2018) 245.

[127] The struggles between local and central authorities are well illustrated in Weiping He, 'The Regulation of the Financial Sector in China: A Tale of Two Governments' (2018) 18(2) *Journal of Corporate Law Studies* 339, 342.

[128] Under the Party leads the military, there are no laws and regulation applicable in this instance.

[129] For example, the Party's internal discipline needs to respond to the reality of the development of the rule of law in t financial markets, so as not to be considered "inappropriate". In April 2001, the General Office of the CPC Central Committee and the General Office of the State Council issued the *Provisions on Party Organ and Government Personnel's Personal Investment in Securities*, which announced that the provisions on 'prohibiting leading cadres at or above the county (division) level of the Party or government organs from buying and selling stocks', which had been implemented since 1993, would be replaced by the decree that 'the ban on the purchase and sale of stocks by the staff of the Party or government organs shall be relaxed with restrictions, and under certain conditions, the staff of the Party or government organs shall be allowed to invest in the securities market, buy

law' and 'only through a comprehensive rule by law framework can we effectively guarantee a systemic, standardised and coordinated national governance system and achieve public consensus'.[130]

3.4 The CPC Diversifies the Governance Mechanisms in the Financial Markets

Across the globe, due to the nature of financial markets, different means are employed to govern and regulate markets.[131] There are multiple parties involved in the governance of financial markets, such as the central bank, administrative supervisory and regulatory authorities, the judiciary, and self-regulatory bodies. As illustrated, the CPC has played a role in the governance of financial markets in China that is unseen in the other jurisdictions.

From the viewpoint of economics, any society is at risk of disorder and dictatorship. In theory, there are four means of public control: namely, private orderings, private litigation, regulation, and state ownership.[132] These means 'are associated with progressively diminishing social costs of disorder and progressively rising social costs of dictatorship'.[133] In the context of China, in addition to the means of private litigation, regulation, and state ownership, the CPC could be seen as a force of public control.[134]

As a way of illustration, in the context of cracking down on internet financing activities in 2016, regulatory authorities often referred to CPC directives in the course of their regulatory activities. The CPC departments such as the Political and Legal Affairs Commission, Office for Maintaining Stability, and Department of Propaganda would also be involved alongside the regulatory authorities.[135] Importantly, in addition to the aforementioned legitimising of their regulatory actions, under the

and sell stocks and securities investment funds according to law'. The reason for this change lies in that 'the development of China's securities market has walked onto the track of legalisation' and 'It is a support for the national construction for the staff of the Party and government organs to invest their legal property in the securities market in a legal way.'.

[130] Xi Jinping, 'Unswervingly Follow the Path of Socialist Rule of Law with Chinese Characteristics to Provide a Strong Legal Guarantee for the Comprehensive Construction of a Socialist Modern State' (2021) 5 *Qiushi.*

[131] Bank for International Settlements, *Central Bank Governance and Financial Stability* (Report, May 2011).

[132] Simeon Djankov, Edward Glaeser, Rafael La Porta, Florencio Lopez-de-Silanes, Andrei Shleifer, 'The New Comparative Economics' (2003) 31 *Journal of Comparative Economics* 595.

[133] Simeon Djankov, Edward Glaeser, Rafael La Porta, Florencio Lopez-de-Silanes, Andrei Shleifer, 'The New Comparative Economics' (2003) 31 *Journal of Comparative Economics* 595, 598.

[134] Most Anglo-Saxon countries have opted for a combination of regulation under the administrative arm of the state and private litigation under the judiciary.

[135] The special rectification of Internet financial risks is jointly carried out by 17 departments, including the Publicity Department of the Central Committee of the CPC, Office of the Central Cyberspace Affairs Commission, and the Central Office for Maintaining Stability. See 'The Leading

banner of the CPC, the regulatory authorities are also able to utilise the resources that are available to the CPC.

The CPC has the advantage over the other authorities which are usually plagued with bureaucracy: the CPC is able to respond in an efficient manner[136] due to its policy of 'One Case, One Matter, One Squad',[137] which could be considered a 'campaign-style governance' approach.[138] The participation of the CPC departments in cracking down on internet financing activities enables the state to respond quickly, and mobilize all resources expeditiously.[139] Such an approach goes beyond the two means of public control identified earlier, i.e. regulation and private litigation, and has the effects of stabilising the markets in particular and society at large in a timely manner.[140] The existence of the campaign-style governance mechanism is perhaps a result of deficiencies and failures in the state governance mechanisms.[141] In other words, the campaign-style governance mechanism is a characteristic of a Chinese state, which compliments the governance mechanisms of the state.[142] The state governance mechanisms sometimes were not equipped to resolve problems facing financial markets in an efficient manner.[143]

Group for the Special Rectification of Internet Financial Risks Meets the Press', *State Council Information Office* (13 October 2016). http://www.scio.gov.cn/xwfbh/qyxwfbh/Document/1494001/1494001.htm.

[136] Wang Puqu, Tang Bin, 'An Analysis of the Party-Government Structure and Functional Mechanism of Contemporary Chinese Governance' (2019) 9 *Social Sciences in China* 4.

[137] In the field of financial risk management, the working mode of 'one matter, one case and one squad in local jurisdictions' was favourably recognised by the Office of the Central Committee for the Comprehensive Rule of Law in March 2021, and was reported nationwide as a model experience and practice. See *Circular of the Office of the Central Committee for the Comprehensive Rule of Law on the Principal Leaders of the Party and Government Performing Duties as the First Responsible Person for Promoting the Construction of the Rule of Law and the Model Experience and Practices Discovered in Field Investigation of the Construction of Government Ruled by Law* (17 March 2021). http://www.moj.gov.cn/Department/content/2021-03/17/582_3268570.html.

[138] For further discussions on Campaign-style Governance, see Zhou Xueguang, 'The Mechanism of Campaign-Style Governance: Rethinking the Institutional Logic of China's State Governance' (2012) 9 *Open Times* 105; Zhou Xueguang, 'Authoritarianism and Effective Governance: The Institutional Logic of State Governance in Contemporary China' (2011) 10 *Open Times* 67.

[139] For previous cases dealing with the protection of investors in financial markets by mobilising political resources rather than conventional administrative supervision and judicial mechanisms, see Huang Tao, 'Why Isn't the Court So Important? An Observation of China's Securities Market' (2012) 9 *Law and Social Sciences*.

[140] The 2008 US Subprime Mortgage Crisis could serve as an interesting comparison. The Federal Reserve Bank in the US was not able to intervene to assist several investment banks in trouble due to legal constraints, which led to the worsening and the spreading of the crisis. The legal constraints were overcome by the Dodd-Frank Act, see Evan A Johnson, 'Revisions to the Federal Reserve's Emergency Lending Rules' (2016) 36 *Review of Banking & Financial Law* 530, 530–549.

[141] Zhou Xueguang, *The Institutional Logic of Governance in China—An Organisational Approach* (SDX Joint Publishing Company, 2017) 129.

[142] See Jing (n 14).

[143] Another example is the *Implementation Plan for Special Rectification of Risks in Internet Financial Advertising and Financial Activities in the Name of Investment and Wealth Management* (GSB [2016] 61). http://www.gov.cn/xinwen/2016-10/13/content_5118616.htm.

The rules and disciplinary mechanisms governing the CPC and its members also have effects beyond the CPC itself. In the early days of the reforms of financial markets, one key objective was 'making a bank bank' i.e. transitioning banks into commercial banks. At the legislative level, the 1995 *Law on the People's Bank of China* and the *Law on Commercial Banks* stipulated that 'the People's Bank of China shall, under the leadership of the State Council, independently implement monetary policies, perform its functions and carry out its operations according to law, free from any intervention by local governments, government departments at all levels, public organizations or individuals'[144] and that 'commercial banks [shall] conduct business in accordance with laws, free from any interference by organisations and individuals'.[145] However, in practice, banks were subject to the interference of the local CPC and the local governments, and ended up with a considerable amount of non-performing loans due to their extension of credit to local SOEs. This problem was not resolved until 1998 when the CPC acted to further reforms in the financial markets.[146] The key objectives of the reforms was to set up the CPC Central Financial Work Committee to lead the reforms, as well as making the personnel in PBoC, CSRC, and state-owned commercial banks subject to the hierarchical management of the CPC.[147] In particular, the appointment and removal of key personnel is subject to the approval of the CPC Central Financial Work Committee.[148] In other words, such powers once vested in the hands of the local CPC and local governments had been shifted either to within the organisation itself or CPC Central. As a result, the influence of the regions on these financial institutions was diminished to the extent that they no longer wielded the power they once had over decisions of the financial institutions to allocate credit. The aforementioned rules in the 1995 *Law on the People's Bank of China* and the *Law on Commercial Banks* were finally being complied with in 1998 or soon after when the financial institutions removed the

This document involves the regulation and governance of Internet financing advertising. The document is led by the State Administration for Industry and Commerce in the government system, but also involves the Publicity Department and the Central Office for Maintaining Stability. This is because the government's authority is limited. Once it involves matters such as the Internet and advertising, pulling in the Party's resources will improve efficiency.

144 Art 7.

145 Art 4.

146 Released the *Notice of the CPC Central Committee on Issues Related to Improving the Party's Leadership System in the Financial Sector and Strengthening and Improving the Party's Work in the Financial Sector.*

147 In addition to adjusting the subordination between the Party organs of the People's Bank of China and State-owned commercial banks, in terms of the administrative system, the State Council approved and transmitted the *Implementation Plan of the Provincial Institutional Reform of the People's Bank of China* (GF [1998] No. 33) in November 1998 to reform the management system of the People's Bank of China. This plan abolished all provincial branches and set up nine inter-provincial (autonomous regions and direct-administered municipalities) regional branches.

148 Ibid.

influence of localities.[149] It also paved the way for further reforms taking place in state-owned financial institutions.[150]

In addition, the CPC, via its internal disciplinary mechanisms, fulfils a supervisory role with respect to key personnel in financial markets. Due to the powers of the authorities and their officials in the financial markets, corruption is an acute problem.[151] Combatting corruption is not only a pressing task for the government but also for the CPC.[152] The CPC's disciplinary resources provide support to the government's sanctions on corruption. The CPC utilises its internal mechanisms to install checks and balances, and investigates the misconduct of its members, which in turn lends legitimacy to the CPC and the State.[153] Since the 18th National Congress of the CPC in 2012, the CPC's Central Leading Group for Inspection visited 22 financial institutions, which accounted for all the financial institutions under the management of the central government.[154]

---

[149] An ideal fiscal Federalism is where the local governments have no access to unlimited credit, see Barry R Weingast, 'Second Generation Fiscal Federalism: Implications for Decentralized Democratic Governance and Economic Development' (Working Paper, Hoover Institution and Department of Political Science, Stanford University, 2006) and Barry R Weingast, 'The Economic Role of Political Institutions: Market-Preserving Federalism and Economic Development' (1995) 11 *Journal of Law and Economic Organization.*

[150] In the late 1990s, China's institutional reform in the field of banking law actually reflects the needs for a mutual adaptability between the economic decentralisation route after the Reform and Opening Up and the highly organised Party system. See Guo Yue, 'From Party "Building" finance to Financial Party Building: Rethinking the Relationship between the Communist Party of China and Finance' (Doctoral Thesis, Central Party School of the CPC, 2017) 70.

[151] Li Xiaohong, Dong Hong, *Anti-Corruption Theory in Finance* (China Fangzheng Press, 1st ed, 2017) 228. The interventions of the government in markets provides opportunities for corruption or rent-seeking activities.

For studies on the influence of "financial repression" in China's financial system on the development of the rule of law, see Huang Tao, 'The Legal Mirror of "Financial Repression" and Its Reform: Reflection on the Chinese Financial Market' (2013) 8 *Finance and Economics* 1. he extent or the severity of corruption is correlated with the extent of government interventions in the markets. There is a high probability of corruption in the authorities which control finance or access to finance See Xie Ping, Lu Lei, 'Unwilling Bribery and Collusion within an Interest Group: The General and Sectoral Characteristics of Financial Regulation Corruption' (2003) 7 *Journal of Finance* 1.

[152] In a large number of previous financial corruption cases, the facts of 'violation of discipline' of leading cadres was often intertwined with the facts of 'violation of law'. However, it should be noted that the party's discipline will cover a wider field than national laws. For example, one of the discipline violations reported by the Central Discipline Inspection Commission of Sun Deshun, former Deputy Secretary of the Party Committee and President of the China CITIC Bank was that '(he) grossly violated the decision and deployment of the CPC Central Committee that "finance must serve the real economy' and restricted and curbed loans in the manufacturing industries'. See 'Sun Deshun, Former Deputy Secretary and President of China CITIC Bank Co Ltd., was Expelled from the Party for Gross Violation of Discipline and Law', *Central Commission for Discipline Inspection* (20 March 2020). http://www.ccdi.gov.cn/scdc/zggb/djcf/202003/t20200320_213972.html.

[153] See Huang Wenyi, 'Normative Doctrines of the Political-Legal System in China' (2020) 4 *Chinese Journal of Law* 3.

[154] See Li, Dong (n 138) 286–7. In September 2021, such visits from the CPC have been extended to regulatory authorities in the financial sector 'The 8th round of Discipline Inspection of the 19th CPC Central Committee will Target the Party Organs of 25 Financial Institutions', *Central*

In combating corruption, it is observed that there is an amalgamation of the State and the CPC machineries (departments and units) where the resources are shared, and mutual goals are achieved. The most evident is that the State Council's Supervisory Office and the Party's Disciplinary Office work in tandem.[155] In October 2018, the CPC Central Office pushed reforms of disciplinary mechanisms in central government-affiliated financial institutions, and strengthened and extended the reach of the disciplinary agencies.[156] After the IPO Registration Reforms mechanisms were introduced to the Shenzhen Stock Exchange's second board, the Shenzhen Stock Exchange incorporated the CPC's disciplinary rules into its regulations.[157] Similarly, in 2021, the CBIRC advocated a similar approach.[158] At the 5th Plenary Session of the 19th Central Commission for Discipline Inspection taking place in January 2021, Xi emphasised 'concentrating on the coordination between anti-corruption and mitigation of financial risks, and strengthening regulation as well as internal governance in the financial sector'.[159] Therefore, at the highest level, anti-corruption is also considered as a means to mitigate risks in financial markets.

Overall, the CPC's machineries are an integral part of the governance of financial markets in China. In particular, the CPC's disciplinary mechanisms have provided and added another dimension to the means of governance. The CPC's mechanisms

Commission for Discipline Inspection (26 September 2021). https://www.ccdi.gov.cn/toutiao/202109/t20210926_251271.html. In 2020 alone, the CPC Disciplinary and Supervision Committees sanctioned 9420 officials due to corruption.

See 'The Former Chairman of the Board and Deputy General Manager of China Everbright Industry (Group) Was Stripped of Party Membership and Expelled from Public Office, Releasing a Strong Signal of Anti-Corruption in the Financial Realm Again', *Central Commission for Discipline Inspection* (19 March 2021). http://www.ccdi.gov.cn/pl/202103/t20210319_238208.html.

[155] Jiang Bixin, Zhang Yu, 'Theory of Law-Based Power Supervision in Xi Jinping's Thought on the Rule of Law' (2021) 2 *Chinese Journal of Law* 3.

[156] *Opinions on Deepening the Reform of the Agencies of the Central Commission for Discipline Inspection and the National Supervisory Commission*, under the *Opinions*, the disciplinary agencies are empowered to investigate and sanction officials not only based on the CPC rules but also on laws and regulations See 'The General Office of the CPC Central Committee Printed and Distributed the *Opinions on Deepening the Reform of the Accredited Institutions of the Central Commission for Discipline Inspection and the National Supervisory Commission*', *Central Commission for Discipline Inspection* (30 October 2018). http://www.ccdi.gov.cn/toutiao/201810/t20181030_182414.html.

[157] The *Opinions on the Implementation of Strengthening the Reform of Second-Board Markets and Piloting Registration-Based Supervision against Corruption.*

[158] 'Promoting regulation by strengthened disciplinary supervision, scrutinising the exercise of power in relation to licensing, rating of regulatory activities, on-site inspection, off-site supervision and administrative sanctions, investigating, in the course of exercising power, instances of non-compliance of law, breach of law, acting for personal gains, and abusing power' See 'The Party Committee of China Banking and Insurance Regulatory Commission Held a System-Wide Work Conference on Comprehensively Administering the Party Strictly and Building a Clean and Honest Government in 2021', *China Banking and Insurance Regulatory Commission* (27 January 2021). http://www.cbirc.gov.cn/cn/view/pages/ItemDetail.html?docId=962900&itemId=915.

[159] See *Communiqué of the 5th Plenary Session of the 19th Central Commission for Discipline Inspection of the CPC* (24 January 2021) 5th Plenary Meeting, 19th Central Commission for Discipline Inspection of the Communist Party of China.

should be viewed as an indispensable aspect of the overall framework that exerts control of the financial markets in China.

4 Final Remarks

Let us now step back to see the big picture: the CPC founded the People's Republic of China in 1949. The construction of the financial markets in China from scratch since 1978 was led by the CPC. There is a contrast between deliberate design and planning and spontaneous forces of society.[160] The Chinese markets had come about as a result of human design, which was different that of the major financial markets in the West which largely resulted due to human action. Under the constitution, the CPC is the one and only governing party. Through the control of the stakes of state capital in banks, securities companies, insurance companies, and fund companies, the CPC is the dominant participant in the markets. The CPC makes and enforces rules in the markets.[161] The establishment of the Central Financial Commission and the Central Financial Work Commission in March 2023 signified the effort to formally centralize and strengthen the role of the CPC in the China's financial markets.

If we compare the operation of the CPC as a firm as put forward by R. H. Coase, the CPC plays the part as a firm in a larger organism, the markets. The operation of the markets costs and by forming an organisation, such as a firm and allowing some authority to direct resources, certain marketing costs are saved.[162] That to some extent would explain the fast development of the financial markets in China.

The CPC so far played a dominant role in the financial markets with distinct advantages.[163] It is a system that mobilized resources with the 'needed institutions' that enforces contracts, protects property rights, and facilitates markets that allocate resources.[164] However, it is also observed that that there are limitations and boundaries that such approach could provide.

Our analysis has shown that the role of the CPC is multi-faceted in the financial markets: it simultaneously acts as a law-maker, a regulator, and an adjudicator. This all highlights the CPC's manifesto in governance that 'the Party leads legislative activities, guarantees regulatory activities, supports the judiciary, and sets the

160 Hayek, Friedrich A. (1969). Studies in Philosophy, Politics and Economics. Touchstone. 96.

161 In July 2018, the CPC central and the State Council stressed that "Bringing the CPC's leadership and corporate governance together; Legalizing the role of the CPC in the corporate governance structure in state controlled financial institutions; Standardizing the process in which the CPC takes part in the decision making; see in *Guidelines on Improving the Management of State -controlled Finance Capital.*

162 Ronald Coase, The Nature of the Firm. Economica, 1937, 4 (16): 392.

163 Joseph E. Stiglitz, The Economic Role of the State, Oxford: Blackwell,1989, 66.

164 Mancur Olson, Power and Prosperity: Outgrowing Communist And Capitalist Dictatorships, New York: Basic Books, 2000, 185.

example in abiding by laws and regulations.'[165] Once not so visible hand of the CPC has been replaced by a hand that is dominant for the workings of the China's financial markets.

More importantly, at the practical level, the CPC is in a position to utilise its considerable resources and act as a control mechanism in the governance of financial markets. The role of the CPC in financial markets seems to be omnipotent; it exerts powers that determine the direction of reforms and manages the financial markets.[166] Control or governance mechanisms under the CPC and the one under the other authorities of the State are integrated: they complement and interact with each other. As illustrated, for example, the CPC was instrumental in forcing through the IPO Registration Reforms. Such reforms would also assist the CPC's anti-corruption stance.[167] These interactions assist in comprehending the intricacies of the party and the state: there is little distinction.[168]

Furthermore, what can be readily overlooked is that the CPC is able to fill the gap in the governance of financial markets under the legislature, regulatory authorities and the judiciary. While the rules have gradually been introduced to regulate the markets since the introduction of the Deng's opening-up policy, these rules sometimes fall short due to the nature of financial markets. The participation of the CPC in markets brings another means of control. In particular, while the legislature, regulatory authorities, and the judiciary might prove slow to act, the CPC seems to be able to tackle the issues in an efficient manner, which if not, could further trigger economic and social instability. The CPC has seemingly proven to be instrumental in the governance of the financial markets in achieving goals such as maintaining the stability of markets, combatting misconduct, and mitigating systemic financial risks.

Consistent with the Coasian theory, through various means, the CPC carries out its functions by saving transaction costs.[169] Acting as a de facto law maker, a de facto regulator, and a de facto adjudicator, the CPC ensures the functional financial markets at less cost. This approach is also considered as legal paternalism.[170] As a result, after four decades of development, it seems that the CPC has made substantial

[165] Xi Jinping, 'Strengthening the Party's Leadership in Comprehensively Promoting Law-Based Governance' (2019) 4 *Qiushi*. See Jing Yuejin et al., *Contemporary Chinese Government and Politics* (Renmin University Press, 2016) 5.

[166] Some scholars believe that China's current system is a separate yet integrated 'Party-State interaction system'. The ruling party can not only 'govern the country' with the help of both systems, the Party and the State, but also by getting total control of the state machine, jointly implementing its governance ideas in different ways attuned to the distinct nature of each institution, without the need to resort to administrative institutions as in Western countries. See Qiang Shigong, 'From Administrative Law to Political Party Law: Jurisprudential Thinking on the relationship between Party Law and State Law' (2016) 3 *China Law Review* 35.

[167] The IPO Registration Reforms is a step further from the approval IPOs by the authorities which limits the window of rent-seeking activities of officials.

[168] See Xu Xianming, 'The CPC is in, under and above the Law', *Sohu* (15 April 2017). https://www.sohu.com/a/134191503_662101.

[169] Ronald Coase, The Nature of the Firm. Economica, 1937, 4 (16): 392.

[170] Joel Feinberg, Legal Paternalism, In Rolf Sartorius (ed.), Paternalism, University of Minnesota Press, 1983,pp. 3, 7.

progress. Such an approach could be arguably desirable at an early stage of the system development. Similarly, as recognised by Coase, there are costs of organising transactions within the firm.[171] 'The costs of organising certain transactions within the firm' may become greater than 'the costs of carrying out the transactions' in the markets.[172] There are costs associated with the approach that has adopted by the CPC. 'The costs of organising certain transactions within the firm' could well become greater than 'the costs of carrying out the transactions' in the markets for the CPC. What if when narrow interests replace the encompassing interest?[173] The biggest concern for the Chinese could be the inefficiencies of property rights, which existed because rulers would not upset interested groups by enacting efficient rules that were opposed to the interests of such groups.[174]

The role of the CPC in the development of the financial markets over time, especially under Xi, is reflective of ever increasingly blurring demarcation between the Party and the State, and further, the ascendency of the Party over the State. Under Deng and prior to Xi, there was an official emphasis of distinction between the Party and the State.[175] There has been a shift to the separation of works undertaken by the Party and the State.[176] The most telling manifestation is the ordering of officials' designations. Prior to Xi's era, officials' designations in the government would be listed before their designations in the Party. Under Xi, the official's designations in the Party are listed first.[177] Thus as indicated by the title of the chapter, it is observable that the commonly understood 'the Party State' has been seemingly shifting towards 'the Party is the State'. The authors will continue to make observations of such trajectory in the years to come.

While acknowledging that control or governance mechanisms under the CPC and the ones under the other authorities of the state are integrated, we need to recognize that there are times that the CPC internal disciplinary mechanism failed. For example, in the Baoshang Bank Bankruptcy incident, the bank's internal governance

---

[171] Ronald Coase, The Nature of the Firm. Economica, 1937, 4 (16): 396.

[172] Ronald Coase, The Nature of the Firm. Economica, 1937, 4 (16): 396.

[173] Mancur Olson, Power and Prosperity: Outgrowing Communist And Capitalist Dictatorships, New York: Basic Books, 2000, 170.

[174] Douglas North DC, Institutions, institutional change, and economic performance, Cambridge, Cambridge University Press, 1990.52.

[175] Selected Works of Deng Xiaoping (People's Publishing House, 2001) vol 3, 176–177.

[176] The Essence of Separation Between the Party and the State, Bejing Daily, 25 March 2013, http://theory.people.com.cn/n/2013/0325/c49150-20899102.html

[177] Tianjing Officials' Changing Business Card: the Party Designations come First, China Discipline and Inspection Newspaper, 23 May 2015, http://politics.people.com.cn/n/2015/0523/c70731-27045416.html.

mechanisms failed when the senior party officials in the bank acted in the interest of the majority shareholder to the detriment of the bank, and contrary to the stability of the bank.[178] Dong Hong, the duty director of the aforementioned CPC's Central Leading Group for Inspection which was assembled to combat corruption turned out to be corrupt.[179]

Last but not least, it should be acknowledged that there is a significant drawback for such an institutional setting: without a formal legal or statutory recognition and support of the CPC as part of the governance structure in the financial markets, there is an issue of lack of clarity and certainty.[180] There is no means to ensure that the implementation and the enforcement of such CPC rules is consistent and thus brings clarity and certainty to both the markets and investors.[181] Of further concern is the checks and balances on power. Xi pointed out that individual CPC institutions and individual party officials must obey and comply with law.[182] There have been many

[178] Zhou Xuedong, 'Financial Risks of Medium & Small Banks Coming Mainly from Failure of Corporate Governance' (2020) 15 *China Finance* 19.

[179] CPC Discipline Commission, Former Director of the CPC Central Leading Group for Inspection Dong Hong Expelled from the Party, 12 April 2021, https://www.ccdi.gov.cn/yaowenn/202104/t20210412_86168.htm

[180] For instance, some scholars propose that the institutionalised role of Party groups in the Party's intervention in State power should be improved (see Fang Lei, Jiang Yongxi, 'On the Law-Based Governance of the CPC' (2015) 7 *People's Tribute* 22). Some scholars also suggest that for state affairs that involve the Party, the specific organisations or individuals of the party should become a legal subject in the judicial process against which action can be commenced (see Wang Ruolei, 'Relationship Between Rule-based Party Governance and Law-based State Governance in China' (2016) 6 *Chinese Journal of Law* 17).

[181] For instance, in terms of central-local relations, a non-institutionalised approach has long been characterised as 'negotiate and get things down', which not only is detrimental to the development of China's unified market economy, but also threatens the unity and stability of the political system. See Su Li, 'The Division of Power between the Central and Local Governments in Contemporary China: Reinterpretation of Chapter Five of "On the Ten Prominent Relations" by Mao Zedong' (2004) 2 *Social Sciences in China* 42; Deng Xiaoping, 'Emancipate the Mind, Seek Truth from Facts and Look Forward in Unity' (Speech, Closing Meeting of the Central Work Conference, 13 December 1978). Some scholars believe that for political party organisations, the institutionalised pressure brought by political modernisation is not only reflected in the internal rational management conducive to the improvement of their ability, but also reflected in the standardisation of the interaction process between political parties, the state and society. This institutionalised operation of political parties is an important symbol of the modernisation of political parties. It is the inevitable result of the secularisation of modern culture and economic rationalisation. See Luo Feng, *Embeddedness, Integration, and the Reconstruction of Party Authority: A Survey on the Relations of China's Ruling Party, State and the Society* (Shanghai People's Publishing House, 2009) 109–10.

[182] See Xi (n 118); Xi Jinping 'Speech at the Special Seminar for Major Leading Cadres at Provincial and Ministerial Levels to Study and Implement the Principles of the 4th Plenary Session of the 18th CPC Central Committee and Comprehensively Promote the Rule of Law' (Speech, 2 February

instances where individual institutions or party officials advance personal interests while breaching laws and regulations, as well as CPC disciplinary rules.[183]

2015) in Literature Research Office of the CPC Central Committee (ed), *Compilation of Xi Jiping's Commentaries on Comprehensive Law-Based Governance* (Zhongyang Wenxian Press, 2015) 37.

[183] Lai Xiaomin, the former chairman of Huarong Asset Management Company, acted contrary to laws and regulations and the CPC rules while abusing his powers as a senior Party official.

The comment on Lai Xiaomin's case by the Central Commission for Discipline Inspection and the National Supervisory Commission was 'a combination of political and economic issues, financial chaos and financial corruption'. See 'Lessons from Lai Xiaomin's Case to Promote Reform', *Central Commission for Discipline Inspection* (18 January 2021). http://www.ccdi.gov.cn/toutiao/202101/t20210118_234021.html. Special interest groups such as the one represented by La Xiaoming are one of the causes that lead to the decline of a nation: see Mancur Olson, *The Rise and Decline of Nations: Economic Growth, Stagflation, and Social Rigidities* (Yale University Press, 1982).

Chapter 3
Redistribution of Powers in the Case of Asset Management Product Regulation in China

Abstract China is aiming to reform its financial regulatory structure by adopting a function-based structure. This involves the merging of regulators and the introduction of new laws and regulation. At the heart of it, the reforms would require a redistribution of the regulatory powers of the regulators. Through the lens of asset management product regulation, this chapter outlines the financial regulatory structure resulting from the 2018 reforms. One key point that can be discerned is that China's regulatory structure did not adequately protect the interests of investors. This inadequacy not only provided fertile ground for investors to lose their savings through the unscrupulous and inappropriate practices of bad actors in relation to asset management products, it also heightened the possibilities for systemic financial risks and financial instability. The chapter concludes that without redistributing the powers of the regulators, the 2018 reforms will have a limited impact on the manner in which the financial system is regulated.

The original version of the chapter has been revised. A correction to this chapter can be found at https://doi.org/10.1007/978-981-97-9176-7_9

T. Huang and W. He, *Politics Meets Markets*, Contemporary Chinese Civil and Commercial Law, https://doi.org/10.1007/978-981-97-9176-7_3

1 Introduction

Politics affects financial regulation in various ways.[1] Understanding the extent and the scope of the powers of regulators in a financial regulatory structure is the key to understanding the nature of financial regulation in a given jurisdiction. In the contemporary setting of the financial sector in China, asset management products regulation provides a good means for understanding this seemingly changing financial regulatory structure.

There has been a noticeable growth of asset management products in China in recent times, reflecting the growth of the economy and wealth. As of the end of 2016, the total assets under management by Chinese institutions totalled RMB 84.82 trillion, of which: RMB 29.05 trillion was managed by banks; RMB 20.22 trillion by trust companies; RMB 1.77 trillion by insurance companies; and RMB 38 trillion by securities companies, fund management companies and private fund management companies.[2]

Products listed in Table A have common features. First, assets are managed by asset managers located within licensed institutions such as banks, securities companies, fund management companies and insurance companies or registered institutions

[1] See generally Stephen Haber, Douglass C North and Barry R Weingast (eds), Political Institutions and Financial Development (Stanford University Press, 2008) (affirming that financial development is an outcome of specific laws and regulations, which are the product of politics and political institution.'); Stavros Gadinis, 'From Independence to Politics in Financial Regulation' (2013) 101(2) California Law Review 327 (showing that elected politicians have increasing influence over banking); Efraim Benmelech and Tobias J Moskowitz, 'The Political Economy of Financial Regulation: Evidence from U.S. State Usury Laws in the 19th Century' (2010) 65(3) The Journal of Finance 1029 (suggesting that financial regulation is 'being used by incumbents with political power for their own private interests'); Stavros Gadinis, 'The Financial Stability Board: The New Politics of International Financial Regulation' (2013) 48(2) Texas International Law Journal 157 (arguing that 'elected politicians can shape international financial regulation' through the Financial Stability Board); Reinout Arthur van der Veer and Markus Haverland, 'The politics of (de-)politicization and venue choice: A scoping review and research agenda on EU financial regulation and economic governance' (2019) 26(9) Journal of European Public Policy 1395 (discussing the political inputs of public opinion and interest groups, which impact financial regulation and economic governance). Political actors can exploit the financial systems for their own interests at the expense of the general economy. For example, they can do this by changing the banks' required reserves according to when they need to borrow money, by allowing only their political allies to open banks, or by refusing to enforce the debts of politically unfavoured creditors. (Stephen Haber, Douglass North, and Barry Weingast, 'Political Institutions and Financial Development' in Stephen Haber, Douglass North, and Barry Weingast (eds), Political Institutions and Financial Development (Stanford university press, 2008) 1,4.) Appointment to the agencies leadership is highly politicised (Laurenz Ennser-Jedenastik, 'The Politicization of Regulatory Agencies: Between Partisan Influence and Formal Independence' (2016) 26(3) Journal of Public Administration Research And Theory 507.). The legislation behind creating the financial agencies and their management are also highly politicised (Gerald F. Davis, 'Politics And Financial Markets' in Karin Knorr Cetina and Alex Preda (eds) The Oxford Handbook of the Sociology of Finance (Oxford University Press, 2012) 34, 39).

[2] The PBoC Press release on Guidelines on Standardizing Financial Institutions' Asset Management Products (Public Consultation) http://www.pbc.gov.cn/goutongjiaoliu/113456/113469/3420458/index.html accessed on 25/06/2018.

such as private fund management companies. Secondly, investing in these products involves the transfer of ownership of assets from investors to asset managers. Ownership is held in trust for investors. As a result, asset managers manage assets under their own names. Thirdly, investors depend on the performance of asset managers for financial gains or losses.[3] The investors pay management fees in return for the services provided by the managers. These features tend to resemble the legal structure of trust operating in common law jurisdictions.

The chapter investigates the evolution of the China's financial regulatory structure in the light of asset management product regulation. Establishing a function—based regulatory structure would not only require the introduction of laws and regulations, but also a redistribution of regulatory powers among the regulators involved, the achievement of which would require political resolve.

Focusing predominantly on the three regulatory dimensions of systemic, prudential, and business conduct, the function-based approach involves three separate regulatory agencies charged with three well-defined obligations. This structure maintains one single agency across segregated functional lines of financial services, namely, banking, insurance, and securities. In Australia, for example, while the Reserve Bank oversees systemic regulation, two other regulatory agencies, the Australian Prudential Regulation Authority (APRA), and the Australian Securities and Investments Commission (ASIC), undertake prudential regulation and conduct of business regulation respectively. Under this regulatory structure, the ASIC is the body regulates asset management products across the entire financial system.[4] This regulatory structure has been accredited that Australian banks survived the global financial crisis in good shape.[5] In giving effect to their respective mandates, regulators can find themselves attempting to resort to the same regulatory means or regulating the same subject, in effect treading on each other's toes which could give rise to regulatory dissonance.[6] It was revealed that in the 2001's HIH Insurance Collapse and in the 2009's Trio Capital Collapse that the regulators failed to coordinate.[7] Thus this structure places a premium on coordination between regulators.[8]

Through the lens of asset management products regulation, this chapter provides a good example of the manner in which politics shakes up the landscape of financial regulation. The structure of the chapter is as follows. Part II outlines the problem

[3] Tao Huang, Financial Markets Regulation: From Institutional to Functional Regulatory Structure, Fa Xue, 7, 2011.

[4] The Australian Securities and Investments Commission, How to register a managed investment scheme, https://asic.gov.au/for-finance-professionals/fund-operators/establishing-and-registering-a-fund/how-to-register-a-managed-investment-scheme/ accessed on 19/03/2019.

[5] OECD, OECD Reviews of Regulatory Reform, AUSTRALIA, TOWARDS A SEAMLESS NATIONAL ECONOMY 41.

[6] See detailed discussion of regulatory dissonance in the context of China's banking regulation in Weiping He, Banking Regulation in China, 2014, Palgrave Macmillian.

[7] HIH Royal Commission Report, at vol. III, 466; Parliamentary Joint Committee on Corporations and Financial Services, Trio Capital Inquiry Report, 153.

[8] Australian Government, 2014, Financial System Inquiry, http://fsi.gov.au/publications/final-report/chapter-5/ accessed on 19/03/2019.

behind the various types of asset management products, and the practices of funds managers and product promoters that place investors at risk. Part III provides an outline of the financial regulatory system and explains the gaps that exist in the regulatory systems, which it is argued have led to the inadequate coverage of asset management products. After outlining the nature of the 2018 reforms, Part IV points out that in the context of asset management regulation, as a result of politicking among various authorities, the reforms do not solve the problems that plagued the industry, in part because the basic laws relating to asset management products remain inadequate.

There are a variety of asset management products in the market. They are variously described as funds, wealth management products or asset management products and are provided by different institutions (see Table 1). Table 1 outlines the products and their provider institutions as well as the regulators and the relevant laws and regulations.

2 The Inadeqacy of the Sector-Based Regualtory Structure: The Rise of Ponzi Schemes, Regulatory Arbitrage and a Regulatory Vacuum

The fast growth of asset management products in China has been aided by technology, more specifically the internet. For example, internet companies, such as the Alibaba Group, Tencent Holdings, JD.com Inc. and Baidu Inc, have built financial services platforms to distribute asset management products developed by third parties, as well as their own products.[9]

At the same time, technology has posed considerable challenges for the regulators. It often enables miscreants to engage in harmful conduct in circumstances where there is no clear regulatory authority to deal with the behaviour. Promoters of some asset management products use the internet as a conducive platform to reach out to investors.

Since the first internet-based asset management product, Yu'e Bao which was released in June 2013, the sector has been growing at a dramatic rate of around 100% per annum.[10] These products emerged in a regulatory vacuum in which there were no entry requirements for platform operators. The Chinese regulators initially adopted a hands-off approach as internet-based asset management products were considered as providing much needed funding to small and medium enterprises. As a result, some platforms allegedly engaged in dubious Ponzi schemes.[11] In 2014, 367 companies operating those platforms were forced to close down after the companies

[9] Such as Du Xiaoman Asset Management, https://8.baidu.com/ accessed on 25/10/2018.

[10] Yan Shen & Yiping Huang, Introduction to the special issue: Internet finance in China, China Economic Journal, Volume 9, 2016-Issue 3.

[11] Jingyi Wang, Yan Shen & Yiping Hua, Evaluating the regulatory scheme for internet finance in China: the case of peer-to-peer lending, China Economic Journal, 2016 9, 3.

Table 1 The rules applicable to asset management products with different names

Issuer	Products	Regulators	Features	Laws/regulation
Fund management companies	Public funds	The China Securities Regulatory Committee (CSRC)	For a public fund, fund shareholders are to gain and loss in proportion to their respective shares in the fund	Securities Investment Funds Law 2015
Subsidiaries of fund management companies	Private funds	The CSRC	Only available to qualified investors (investing no less than RMB 1,000,000 in a single fund and the total financial assets is no less than RMB 300, 000)	Provisions on the Administration of Subsidiaries of Securities Investment Fund Management Companies 2016
Private fund management companies[12]	Private funds	Asset Management Association of China under the CSRC	The distribution of gains and losses for non-public fund shareholders is determined by the fund contract[13]	Interim Measures for the Supervision and Administration of Privately Offered Investment Funds 2014

(continued)

[12] Private Fund management companies are licenced by the CSRC and the private fund management companies are required to register with the industrial association Securities Association of China.

[13] Securities Investment Funds Law (2015) s3.

Table 1 (continued)

Issuer	Products	Regulators	Features	Laws/regulation
Commercial banks	Wealth management products	CBIRC[14]	Commercial banks can only sell products with a risk rating equal to or lower than the client's risk tolerance[15]	Measures for the Administration of the Sale of Wealth Management Products of Commercial Banks 2011
Securities companies and their subsidiaries	Asset management products[16]	CSRC	Securities companies can only sell these products to qualified investors, and proceeds are vested in a custodial financial institution[17]	Measures for the Administration of the Customer Asset Management Business of Securities Companies 2013
Futures companies and their subsidiaries	Asset management products	CSRC	Only available to investors who invest more than RMB 100,000	Measures for the Pilot Program on the Asset Management Service of Futures Companies 2017

(continued)

[14] These products were regulated by the CBRC prior to the 2018 Reforms.

[15] Measures for the Administration of the Sale of Wealth Management Products of Commercial Banks(2011) s 9.

[16] The most common type is that securities companies bundle the money of multiple clients and invest in ventures.

[17] Measures for the Administration of the Customer Asset Management Business of Securities Companies (2013) s26.

Table 1 (continued)

Issuer	Products	Regulators	Features	Laws/regulation
Insurance assets management companies[18]	Asset management products	CBIRC[19]	Only available to investors who invest more than RMB 1,000,000 and the number of investors for one fund is capped at 200	Notice on Insurance Assets Management Companies Conducting Pilot Asset Management Business 2013
Trust investment companies	Trust products	CBIRC[20]	A typical Plan would involve a trustee holds the money from separate two or more trustors/settlors (the trustee company) under the single account which is set up for the purpose of the Plan. The trustee then manages the money under its own name and for the benefit of the beneficiaries[21]	Measures for the Administration of Trust Companies' Trust Plans of Assembled Funds 2009

[18] In addition, there are unlicensed/unregistered companies via internet conducting fund management business against the law.

[19] These products were regulated by the CIRC prior to the 2018 Reforms.

[20] These products were regulated by the CBRC prior to the 2018 Reforms.

[21] Measures for the Administration of Trust Companies' Trust Plans of Assembled Funds (2009 Revision) article 2, Trustee companies provide Collective Capital Trust Plan which is regulated under the CBRC's Trust Companies Collective Plan Regulation.

were either exposed to credit risk or involved in fraudulent activities.[22] Ezubao, once praised for its new and innovative approach to financial services, was found to have defrauded 900,000 investors of up to RMB 50 billion. This case was pursued by the State prosecutor.[23] The prevalence of internet financing frauds was attributed to the fact that there was a lack of any effective regulation of peer to peer (P2P) products.[24]

The regulatory responsibilities for internet financing remained unclear until the publication of the *Guidelines Concerning Promoting Healthy Development of Internet Financing* (the *Guidelines*) in July 2015 by the People's Bank of China (PBoC), the China Banking Regulatory Commission (the CBRC), the China Securities Regulatory Commission (the CSRC), the China Insurance Regulatory Commission (the CIRC) and the other six other ministries.[25] Under the *Guidelines*, the PBoC is responsible for the payment systems; the CBRC is responsible for internet-based peer to peer lending and other small loans, internet-based trust assets management, and internet-based consumer finance; the CSRC is responsible for equity-based crowd-funding, and sales of funds and the CIRC is responsible for internet-based insurance.

However, in the aftermath of Ezubao, it remained unclear as to where the regulatory power and responsibility rested for P2P products.[26] Confusion over regulatory responsibility was exacerbated by the involvement of local governments, which were active in exercising their regulatory powers. The Chongqing, Shenzhen and Shanghai governments, for example, suspended the P2P platforms. On 8 January 2016, the Beijing local government suspended all marketing and promoting of P2P products, and suspended the registration of all private fund investment companies.[27] On 11 January 2016, the Shenzhen government similarly suspended registering investment companies.[28] At the national level, on 15 January 2016, the PBoC announced that it had devised an auditing system for internet-based financing activities which monitors the activities of borrowers and lenders in relation to P2P products.[29] On 19 January 2016, the National Equities Exchange and Quotations Market which is under the supervision of the CSRC suspended all new listings by private fund investment companies.

Under the sector-based regulatory structure, financial institutions could "choose and pick" lax rules. This led to a "race to the bottom" situation. For example, under the CSRC's directions, securities companies have been always prohibited from using

---

[22] He Jianfeng, Legal issues of Internet Finance Regulation, Jinan Review, 2016, 1, 58.

[23] China Courts, Ezhubao Investigation 31/01/2016, http://www.chinacourt.org/article/detail/2016/01/id/1801878.shtml accessed on 15/02/2016.

[24] He Jianfeng, Legal issues of Internet Finance Regulation, Jinan Review, 2016, 1, 58.

[25] In April 2018, the CBRC was merged with the CIRC to form the China Banking and Insurance Regulatory Commission. It was abolished in March 2023 and was replaced by the National Administration of Financial Regulation.

[26] For further analysis regarding P2P and other internet financial products, please refer to Tao Huang, China Internet Finance: Markets, Regulation, and Law, Southeast University Newspaper, 4, 2017.

[27] Beijing Government, http://www.beijing.gov.cn/ accessed on 7/03/2017.

[28] Shenzhen Government, http://www.sz.gov.cn/cn/ accessed on 7/03/2017.

[29] PBoC, Media Conference on 15/01/2016.

the proceeds from issuing asset management products and investing them in certain products. By contrast, banks were able to make such investments, until 2013 when the CBRC issued the *Notice on Standardizing Commercial Banks' Wealth Management Products Investments*. In other words, until 2013, despite the prohibition by the CSRC, securities companies could still invest in trust loans by using bank channels to avoid the prohibition.

For further illustration, in 2007, the CSRC issued the *Trust Company Collective Trust Investment Schemes Rules* which imposes requirements on individual collective trust investment schemes under which the number of investors should not exceed 50.[30] This rule has been routinely circumvented by banks. A bank is able to raise funds from the investors (the number of whom may well exceed 50) and invest the funds in a scheme in which the bank appears to be the sole investor. The investors thus are not visible to the regulator or the public. Therefore, technically speaking, such a scheme would still seemingly comply with the 50 investors limit rule.

In addition to the arbitrage problems discussed above, technology exposed the inadequacy of the regulatory system in other ways. The regulation of internet-based financing activities is a case in point. Internet-based financing has undergone rapid growth in the past decade. It provides investors with higher returns. For example, the lending rates of mainstream P2P platforms ranged between 15 and 20% in 2014, and the average lending interest rate was 17.86%.[31] The internet-based financing was able to assist medium, small and micro companies whilst the banking system was largely supporting state-owned entities (SOEs).[32] It proved a challenge for traditional retail deposit business in the big four banks in China since would-be depositors would invest in P2P products, which brought better returns.[33]

The presence of local governments further compounded the situation given they were driven by different incentives to those of the centralized regulators.[34] Prior to 2015, the internet-based financing sector was largely regulated by local governments. For example, Beijing, Shenzhen, Nanjing and other similar governments provided favourable policies supportive of the development of the sector.[35] The Beijing government provided senior management personnel with Beijing HuKou.[36] Local governments largely resorted to industry self-regulation in substitution for government regulation. In 2014, for example, the Shenzhen Internet Finance Association, an

---

[30] Measures for the Administration of Trust Companies' Trust Plans of Assembled Funds (2009 Revision).

[31] Boao Review and Lufax, *P2P Lending Market in China*, (2015) 6.

[32] The State Council, *Government Report*, 05/03/2015.

[33] Editorial, Internet Finance Challenging Traditional Banking, Internet Finance and Law, 2014, 3,38.

[34] For detailed analysis of the regulatory powers of the local governments, please refer to Weiping He, (2018). The regulation of the financial sector in China: a tale of two governments. Journal of Corporate Law Studies. https://doi.org/10.1080/14735970.2018.1426982.

[35] Editorial, Local Governments Supporting Internet Finance, Internet Finance and Law, 2014, 9, 46.

[36] Handian government, Rules on Key Enterprises Services and Support, 2012.

industry association, issued the *Shenzhen P2P industry Self-regulation Convention*, and *Shenzhen Crowd-funding Self-regulation Convention*.

At a national level, in May 2014, the State Council issued the *Suggestions on Further Promoting Development of Capital Markets*, under which the State Council encouraged and supported internet-based financing innovation but encouraged set up industry regulations and rules. In December 2014, one of the industry self-regulatory bodies, the Securities Association of China, released the *Rules on the Management of Crowd-funding Private Funds* for public consultation. Overall, it is safe to conclude that there were multiple regulators at both local and national level without clear responsibility demarcations, ensued from which were issues of regulatory arbitrage and a regulatory vacuum. The institutional regulatory structure is reflective of politics that underlies the distribution of regulatory powers. In other words, any reforms concerning the regulatory institutional structure would require political resolve and willingness at the very top of the political hierarchy.

3 Moving Towards a Function-Based Regulatory Structure?

There appears to be some changes occurring more recently at the regulatory structure level to address the concerns about regulating asset management products. On 17 March 2018, the 1st meeting of the 13th National Congress announced reforms to the sector-based regulatory structure, which had been in existence since 2003 (the 2018 Reforms). As a consequence, the financial markets in China will undergo two major regulatory changes. First, the China Banking and Insurance Regulatory Commission (CBIRC) will replace the China Banking Regulatory Commission (CBRC), and the China Insurance Regulatory Commission (CIRC). Secondly, the People's Bank of China (PBoC) will make regulations and prudential regulatory rules about the banking and the insurance sectors. The new CBIRC was subsequently established in April 2018.[37] This was seen as a response to the shift at the policy level, which now aims to control systemic risks. In July 2017, the National Financial Works Meeting, convened by the China Communist Party proposed the establishment of a functional regulatory structure.[38] It is understood that the objective of the 2018 Reforms is to move towards a functional regulatory structure.[39]

In order to gain an informed understanding of the likely impact of the 2018 Reforms, it is necessary to gain a sense of the way in which the system operated

---

[37] The State Council, *Institutional Reform Program of the State Council*, http://www.gov.cn/xinwen/2018-03/17/content_5275116.htm accessed on 23 March 2018.

[38] The meeting is paramount in a sense that it sets the agenda for China's financial system and financial regulation in the next five years. For detailed analysis of different regulatory structures, please see Weiping He, *Banking Regulation in China* (2014) 43.

[39] The State Council, the National Financial Works Meeting Held in Beijing, http://www.gov.cn/xinwen/2017-07/15/content_5210774.htm accessed on 12/07/2018.

before the reforms. The financial institutions that issued investment products were under the purview of different regulators. Banks were licensed by the CBRC. Fund management companies and futures companies were licensed by the CSRC, and private fund management companies were registered with Securities Association of China, which was under the leadership of the CSRC. Likewise, insurance companies were regulated by the China Insurance Regulatory Committee.

Different regulators issued rules regulating products provided by their respective regulatees. The regulatory approach was known as the sector-based regulatory structure, which was established in 2003. There was no one single common approach to regulating the institutions. Rather the rules regarding approval conditions and procedures, eligibility of investors, information disclosure requirements, investment risk tolerance requirements, enforcement rules, and legal obligations on the part of issuers for these products varied depending on the nature of the products.

The introduction of the *Laws of Commercial Banks* in 1995 was the first step towards establishing the sector-based regulatory structure. Section 43 of the *Laws of Commercial Banks* reiterated the separation of businesses principle. This principle was established in 1997 by a PBoC directive prohibiting commercial banks from engaging in trust assets management and securities business.[40] The regulatory structure that led to the separation of sector policy emerged with the establishment of the CSRC in 1993, and the CIRC in 1998. In 2002, the 16th CPC National Meeting urged further reform in the financial sector.[41] Subsequently, the *Laws of People's Bank of China* (1995) and the *Laws of Commercial Banks* (1995) were amended to allow for the establishment of the CBRC for the banking sector in 2003. At the same time, revisions to the *Law on the People's Bank of China (1995)* strengthened the PBoC's responsibility for monetary policy. Under section 1 of the *Laws of People's Bank of China (2003)*, the PBoC became primarily concerned with making and implementing monetary policies to manage the macro-economy and maintain the stability of the entire financial system. The objective of monetary policy was to stabilize the currency, and promote economic growth.[42] The sector-based structure governed the financial markets until the 2018 reforms.

The sector-based structure had the capacity to enable a means for playing to the strengths of each regulator. Regulators were well placed to provide effective oversight as they each had specialised knowledge of their respective areas of regulatory responsibility. Individual regulators possessed all-encompassing powers in relation to the respective regulated institutions under their purview. Each regulator was responsible for licencing the entities under its purview. Regulatory responsibility applied to these entities regardless of the products and services they offered. The reforms distinguish

[40] PBoC, Notice on Forbidding Bank Capital Entering the Stock Markets 1997.

[41] Report on 16th the Communist Party of China National Meeting, 2002, and Weiping He, Banking Regulation in China, Palgrave Macmillan, New York, 163.

[42] *Laws of People's Bank of China 1995* s3.

between commercial banking and investment banking, which could help prevent risk contagion and reduce systemic risks.[43]

At the same time, under this sector-based regulatory structure, there was a clear demarcation between the regulatory responsibilities of the respective Chinese regulators. This institution-based regulatory framework was entrenched by the applicable legislation. The CBRC, the CSRC, and the CIRC respectively administer the *Law of Commercial Banks* and the *Trust Law*, the *Securities Law*, and the *Insurance Law*. For example, the CSRC was responsible for commercial banks, trust investment companies, financial investment management companies and financial leasing companies. The CSRC was responsible for securities companies, fund management companies and futures brokerage companies. The CISR was responsible for insurance companies, insurance brokerage companies and insurance asset management companies. Under the relevant laws, the regulators licensed respective regulated entities and regulated these entities in their own sphere. The regulator that licensed an entity was responsible for the ongoing regulation of that entity. In other words, the regulator who had the power to grant an entity the market access was vested with the role of regulating the business conduct of the entity after it entered the market. The regulator also regulate any products the entity provided. For example, for a bank, its products were subject to the supervision of the CBRC whether they were of deposit nature or securities nature. This was reflective of the nature of a sector-based institutional regulatory model. Therefore, similar products provided by different entities might be subject to the purview of different regulators.

The regulators also effectively controlled the regulated entities through a personnel system. That is, the senior management of a regulated entity was normally elected by, or their election was subject to, the approval of their respective regulator. The China Communist Party (CCP) committee in a regulated entity was accountable to the CCP committee at their respective regulators.

In the earlier days of the Chinese financial industry, owing to legislative and regulatory demarcations and the limited financial products on offer, the sector-based regulatory structure was seemingly effectively in regulating the different sectors across the financial markets.

With the emergence of technology and new financial products, this regulatory arrangement was sorely tested. Asset management products is a good example of the challenges the technology presented. As discussed above, some products provided by fund management companies are of a trust nature. However, clients of fund management companies were not protected by Chinese trust law since this law explicitly excluded the products offered by fund management companies as trust products. The law gave no recognition of a fund manager as being the legal owner of the asset on behalf of the investor. Clients purchasing securities products from a bank would similarly be unable to avail themselves of the protection of the *Securities Law*.

In 2014, the State Council's *Notice on Strengthening Shadow Banking Regulation* reinforced the existing regulatory structure for the regulation of asset management

---

[43] Guo Dexiang, Thoughts on Universal Banking in China's Financial Sector, HeBei Law, 2003, 5, 133.

products. The CBRC regulated asset management products offered by banks, the CSRC regulated asset management products by securities and futures companies and private fund management companies and the CIRC regulated asset management products by insurance companies. The central bank, the PBoC regulated and coordinated cross-sector asset management products by financial institutions. While the reforms has gained the support of the top of the political apparatus, a redistribution of political powers would be the pre-requisite for any meaningful reforms.

4 Systemic Risks and Investor Protection

What makes asset management products an inherently risky proposition is that they are pooled investments: money is pooled together with multiple investors (often hundreds or even thousands of investors) and used for investing in multiple projects undertaken by multiple enterprises. In essence, these investors are brought together to contribute money or money's worth to gain an interest in multiple enterprises. The specific legal or other interest an investor has in any project is not easily identifiable. Risks could also arise in circumstances where there is a mismatch between short-term investor input and long-term investment output. As a result, it is difficult to determine or ascertain risk levels for individual investors.[44] This is of concern for regulators such as the PBoC and the CBRC. Since 2011, the CBRC has attempted to manage risks by restricting commercial banks from pooling funds and requiring them to match clients to their investments on a one to one basis.[45]

Some bankers have acknowledged that they are unsure about how to quantify risks associated with asset management products.[46] First, the products sold by commercial banks are normally designed by trust companies or management companies. A banking license allows commercial banks to sell products to the public, whereas trust companies and management companies are unable to do so. In other words, trust companies and management companies use banks as avenues to sell products that they otherwise are not allowed to sell. Secondly, from the banks' perspective, these products are considered off-balance sheet products and consequently there is no compliance requirement with the prudential standards that are imposed on most banking products.

An undesirable aspect of this is that banks in China are largely owned by the governments (the central or local), investors often wrongly assume that the government guarantees apply to their investments. Investors often wrongly assume that

---

[44] Zhong Wei, Capital Pool Products Regulation, Bankers 2018 4.

[45] The CBRC's directives to this effect include *Commercial Banks Asset Management Products Meeting Notes* 2011, *Notice on Further Strengthening Commercial Banks Asset Management Products Risk Management* 2011, *Commercial Banks Asset Management Regulation Meeting Notes* 2013, and *Notice on Standardizing Commercial Banks Asset Management Business Investment Operations* 2013.

[46] First Finance, Guo Shuqing Charging Regulatory Storms, 18/04/2018.

the government will protect their investments from heavy losses. They assume the investment are risk free, when that is not the case.

Banks in part are to blame for investors forming this misimpression in that they sometimes implicitly or even explicitly state that their asset management products are risk-free. It was reported that one bank in Wuhan offered assets management products under the condition of "principal and interest guaranteed" when in fact the product was not guaranteed against investment losses.[47]

Similarly, internet-based financing products pose considerable risks to investors thus become a concern for the regulators.[48] The public nature of those products exacerbates the risk of contagion if something should go wrong.[49]

The number of disputes regarding asset management products has also increased. One of the key issues is the suitability of products for investors. Banks typically promote high risk products to low risk tolerance investors.[50] Other issues that arise are the eligibility of investors to invest in those products, the compliance of products with regulatory requirements and the compliance of disclosure obligations on the part of the issuer.[51] In light of these inappropriate practices, which expose investors to heavy losses, consumer protection has become a vital issue.The authorities, perhaps belatedly, are starting to take the issue seriously. For example, in 2006, for the first time, the concept of there being "financial consumers" was introduced by the CBRC.[52]Without providing clear definition of who qualifies as a financial consumer, the CBRC required commercial banks to protect their interests.[53]

The authorities including the State Council, the CBRC and the PBoC have issued various directives to protect consumers.[54]Furthermore, since 2011, the CBRC, the CSRC and the CIRC established specialized departments to deal with consumer protection issues.[55]Whether this has any systemic meaningful impact still remains to be seen.

---

[47] Hubei Daily, Some Bank in Hubei Guaranteeing Principal and Interest, http://news.cnhubei.com/xw/sh/201406/t2960989.shtml accessed on 22/03/2018.

[48] Meng Jianzhu, Mitigate Risks, http://legal.people.com.cn/n1/2016/0123/c42510-28078279.html accessed on 28/02/2017.

[49] Mao Lingling, Supervision of Internet Finance Law, East China University of Political Science and Law Review, 2014, 5.

[50] Yao Zhijian, Regulating Commercial Banks Selling Asset Management Products, Renmin Sifa, 2016, 32, 17.

[51] Shanghai Hongkou People's Court, Sheng Weizheng Suing Some Bank Shanghai Hongkou Branch Financial Services Contract Dispute 2016; Liu Nan and ABN AMRO Group Beijing Dongfang Square Branch Wealth Management Contract Dispute 2009.

[52] The concept of financial consumers was first introduced by the CBRC in its *Guidelines on Commercial Banks Financial Innovation* (2006).

[53] Guidelines on Commercial Banks Financial Innovation (2006)S 18.

[54] For example, the CBRC issued The CBRC's Banking Consumer Protection Blueprint (2012–2015) in 2012 and issued Banking Consumer Protection Guidelines in 2013; The State Council issued Guidelines on Strengthening Financial Consumer Protection in 2015; The PBoC issued Measures on Financial Consumer Protection in 2016.

[55] The CIRC established Insurance Consumer Protection Bureau, the CSRC Securities Investor Protection Bureau, the CBRC Banking Consumer Protection Bureau.

However, investor protection remains unsatisfactory, especially at the *ex ante* level. So far, asset management products related disputes have been adjudicated under the *Contract Law*. For example, in a case involving a bank managing an appellant's assets, the Supreme People's Court expressly pointed to the *Contract Law* as the governing law for the dispute.[56]

At the legislation level, there are technical barriers to extending protection to investors under other laws. China's *Securities Law* (the *Law*) defines "securities" narrowly. The issuance and trading of stocks, corporate bonds as well as other securities are recognized by the State Council as being subject to the *Law*.[57] In contrast, the *US Securities Act* of 1933 adopts a broader approach, referring to the term "security" as including any note, stock, bond, debentures as well as investment contract.[58] An investment contract, for purposes of the *US Securities Act*, means a contract, transaction or scheme whereby a person invests his money in a common enterprise and is led to expect profits solely from the efforts of the promoter or a third party.[59] In Australia, securities is defined to mean (a) debentures, stocks or bonds issued or proposed to be issued by a government; or (b) shares in, or debentures of, a body; or (c) interests in a managed investment scheme; or (d) units of such shares.[60]

In contrast to China's *Securities Law*, many jurisdictions have adopted a comprehensive approach in that these products are deemed to be financial investment products or financial products. South Korea introduced the concept of financial investment products under its *Capital Market Consolidation Act* in 2007 to solve a similar problem that China is now facing: namely, different (and sometimes conflicting) types of regulation are applied to the same financial investment products. Under South Korea's *Capital Market Consolidation Act*, financial investment products are comprehensively defined and classified.[61] Financial institutions are licensed to conduct different categories of financial investment products. Similarly, in Australia,

[56] Supreme Court of the PRC, China Construction Bank ShanXi Branch and Xian Changan Agricultural Credit Cooperatives Asset Management Contract Dispute 2015.

[57] S 2, Securities Law.

[58] SEC. 2. (a) DEFINITIONS.—When used in this title, unless the context otherwise requires— (1) The term "security" means any note, stock, treasury stock, security future, security-based swap, bond, debenture, evidence of indebtedness, certificate of interest or participation in any profit-sharing agreement, collateral-trust certificate, preorganization certificate or subscription, transferable share, investment contract, voting-trust certificate, certificate of deposit for a security, fractional undivided interest in oil, gas, or other mineral rights, any put, call, straddle, option, or privilege on any security, certificate of deposit, or group or index of securities (including any interest therein or based on the value thereof), or any put, call, straddle, option, or privilege entered into on a national securities exchange relating to foreign currency, or, in general, any interest or instrument commonly known as a "security", or any certificate of interest or participation in, temporary or interim certificate for, receipt for, guarantee of, or warrant or right to subscribe to or purchase, any of the foregoing.

[59] SEC v. Howey Co., 328 U.S. 293 (1946).

[60] Corporations Act 2001, S 92.

[61] Kim Dong-hwan, The Capital Market Consolidation Act and the.

Korean Financial Market, in Korea's Economy 2008, the Korea Economic Institute and the Korea Institute for International Economic Policy, Volume 24.

http://www.keia.org/sites/default/files/publications/Dong-hwan1.pdf

a financial product is defined as a facility through which, or through the acquisition of which, a person either makes a financial investment, or manages financial risk or makes non-cash payment.[62]

China's *Securities Investment Funds Law* (2015) only applies to securities investment funds (that is public funds).[63] Public funds can only be issued and managed by a fund management company licensed by the CSRC and the issuance of non-public funds must be registered with Asset Management Association of China, an industrial body accountable to the regulator, the CSRC. There are therefore investor protection provisions in place for securities investment funds, but the protections under the Law are not available for investors in non-public funds. There is, for example, stringent qualification requirements placed on the manager of a public fund and disclosure requirements are mandated during the life of a fund.[64] Non-public funds must only be offered to qualified investors, and the number [of what] must not exceed 200 for a fund.[65]

As a result, asset management products that are not issued by the above-mentioned entities do not fall within the scope of the *Law* and the *Securities Investment Funds Law*.

Asset management products investors are not protected by the investor protection schemes that are available under the *Law*. Chinese investors are equally left unprotected by trust law. Chinese trust law defines a trust in this context as a circumstance in which the trustor on the basis of confidence in the trustee, entrusts certain property rights they own in the trustee and the trustee manages or disposes of the property rights in their own name in accordance with the intentions of the trustor and for the benefit of the beneficiary or for specific purposes.[66] The trust law was subsequently clarified by a State Council directive that ruled that only trust investment companies and fund management companies are allowed to deal with trust products.[67] In other words, some products, although of trust products in nature, are not considered as trust products in a legal sense. Therefore, the protection of trust law does not extend to investors who invest in these products. For example, legal principles that provide that a trustee must not obtain profits for his or her own benefit do not apply in the context of managers managing asset management products.[68]

The 2018 reforms were introduced because of the inadequate protection provided to investors. This inadequacy was seen as creating systemic risks to the financial system, hence the need for reform.[69]

---

[62] Corporations Act s 763A.

[63] Securities Investment Funds Law (2015) Article 2.

[64] Securities Investment Funds Law (2015) Chapter 2 and chapter 7.

[65] Securities Investment Funds Law (2015) Article 87.

[66] Trust Law of the People's Republic of China, 2001 Article 2.

[67] The State Council, Notice on Implementation of the *Trust Law* 2001.

[68] Trust Law of the People's Republic of China, Article 26.

[69] Wang Yong, Details on the State Council's Institutional Reform, speech at the 13th National People's Representatives first meeting (13/03/2018), http://cpc.people.com.cn/n1/2018/0314/c64094-29866184.html accessed on 12/07/2018.

5 Regulatory Coodination Among the Regulators

A prime concern about the sector-based regulatory structure was the lack of coordination among regulators. Under the sector-based regulatory system, China lacked effective monitoring, coordination and response mechanisms. The three main regulators, the CBRC, the CSRC, the CIRC and the PBoC were on par with each other in terms of their administrative hierarchy and they were not obliged to be accountable or co-operative with each other. There was no one overarching or leading regulatory agency.

Section 9 of the *Law of People's Bank of China* requires the State Council to establish a financial regulatory coordination system and to devise and implement the rules for its operation. Section 6 of the *Laws of People's Republic of China on Banking Regulation and Supervision* and section 35 of the *Law of People's Bank of China (2003)* further required the PBoC and the CSRC, the CBRC and other financial regulators to establish a system for sharing regulatory information. These laws emphasised the element of transfer of material resources, such as information.[70] However, the statutory provisions went no further than requiring a system of information sharing and, in particular, did not impose any conciliation process or a mutual or unilateral adjustment mechanism in the event of disagreement.

The relevant law requires early coordination, but then fails to provide a means for how it will be enforced and for the consequences of non-compliance. The extent to which these systems have been implemented has not been made publicly available. The 2008 initiative of the State Council noted below suggest that there had been no real progress in enhancing the sharing of information among regulators.

There was pressure from both the public and the central government for the CBRC and the CSRC to coordinate the way they undertook the regulation of the conduct of relevant entities. For example, the public had called for improved coordination among regulators in relation to P2P products.[71] The coordination among the regulators was considered integral when it comes to the regulation of financial conglomerates.[72] A direct political effort from the central government was also made in 2008 to address and improve regulatory enforcement. The State Council urged the PBoC to establish coordination mechanisms with financial regulators with particular respect to regulatory rules.[73] The State Council also raised the establishment of a joint committee as a means of enhanced coordination.

---

[70] Aspects of coordination can be distinguished between volitive communications and resource transfers. See Fritz W. Scharpf, 'Interorganizational Policy Studies: Issues, Concepts and Perspectives' in Kenneth Hanf and Friz W. Scharpf (eds), *Interorganizational Policy Making: Limits to Coordination and Central Control* (SAGE Publications, 1978) 351,352.

[71] The American Chamber of Commerce People's Republic of China, 'American Business in China' (White Paper (2011) 178.

[72] Ba Shusong, Coordinating Mechanisms of Regulator, West Review, 2006(11).

[73] *Zhong Guo Ren Min Yin Hang Zhu Yao Zhi Ze Nei She Ji Gou He Ren Yuan Bian Zhi Gui Ding [Rules on the PBoC's Main Objective, Institutional Structrue, and Staffing] 2008.*

To some extent, coordination did occur among the Chinese financial regulators notably through collective regulatory action. This can be seen, for example, with respect to the enforced abolition of certain bank fees. Some banks charged service fees for various over-the-counter transactions, including withdrawals or deposits.[74] In 2013, the CSRC, the PBoC and other financial regulators issued the *Notice on Risk Management of P2P Products*. Additionally, in 2014, the CSRC, the CBRC, the PBoC and the CIRC jointly promulgated the *Notice Concerning Inter- Financial Institutions Business (2011)* to standardise business dealings among financial institutions. In May 2014, the PBoC with the CBRC, and CSRC issued the *Notice on Regulating Business Between Financial Institutions* which stipulated that financial institutions under repurchase agreements or mutual investments should not accept or provide any direct or indirect, explicit or implicit third-party credit guarantee.

Any shift to collective regulatory action will be a departure from the original regulatory design, which involved individual regulators operating as specialised regulators with distinct areas of regulatory oversight. It also became unclear whether such a move would sacrifice the regulatory utility of the individual authorities because the degree of authority projected by each of them alone might be diluted by collective regulatory action.[75]

Another criticism of coordination among the regulatiors is that a lack of leadership (or lead agency) will lead to stasis, which would mean that it will be less likely for any outcome to result. The PBoC advocated that it should have a leadership role in coordination.[76] It is significant that the former Governor of the PBoC, Zhou Xiaochuan, is politically ranked higher than the Chairmen of the other regulators.[77] In its various institutional documents, the PBoC referred to itself as acting as "Hui Tong" (together with) other regulators.[78] This Chinese term carries the connotation of a leadership role for the PBoC. Indeed a joint committee was set up in 2003 with the PBoC "Hui

[74] Xinhua, *Yin Hang Zan Ting Shou Qu Ling Chao Qing Dian Fei [Banks Stopped From Charging Some Fees For Over-the-counter Transactions]*, http://www.jx.xinhuanet.com/news/2010-06/05/content_19989691.htm at 7 Oct 2011.

[75] Tatsuya Kameda et al., 'Democracy Under Uncertainty: The Wisdom of Crowds and the Free-Rider Problem in Group Decisio Making' (2011) 118(1) *Psychological Review* 76.

[76] PBoC, *Ren Min Yin Hang Ru He Kan Dai Jin Rong Jian Guan Xie Tiao Ji Zhi de Jian Li? [PBoC's View on Financial Regulatory Coordination Mechanism]*, http://rmyh.gzlps.gov.cn/art/2009/2/27/art_5787_105349.html at 19 Oct 2011.

[77] State Council, the Institutional Structure of the State Council, http://www.gov.cn/guowuyuan/zuzhi.htm accessed on 3/04/2017.

[78] PBoC, '2007 Nian Zhong Guo Fan Xi Qian Bao Gao [2007 Report On China's Anti-money Laundering]' (PRC http://www.pbc.gov.cn/publish/fanxiqianju/1282807157712/_fileupload/426CBD8C.pdf (2008) 6.

Tong" other financial regulators in this matter.[79] The PBoC thus assumed responsibility to coordinate the regulatory actions of the other authorities.[80] The PBoC has also advocated a leadership role for itself when the opportunity arises.[81] This regulatory approach represented some elements of the primary/secondary regulator model where the primary regulator coordinates other authorities in the handling of issues.[82]

In February 2016, a key PBoC official, Li Bo, who was in charge of the PBoC monetary policy, proposed regulatory structure alternatives. His proposal largely followed the UK model and built on the central role of the PBoC. In essence, his proposal involved having a prudential regulator under the PBoC together with a separate business conduct regulator.[83] In 2017, the PBoC has furthered its leadership role in the existing regulatory structure. According to s 24 of the *Guidelines on Financial Institution Asset Management Business* (2017) advanced by the PBoC, together with the CSRC, the CBRC, the CIRC and the State Administration of Foreign Exchange, the PBoC is responsible for the macro-prudential regulation of asset management business and the PBoC, the CBRC, the CIRC and the State Administration of Foreign Exchange regulate market entry and day-to-day regulation in relation to asset management products. The balance of power is consequently directed towards one particular authority. This would be a departure from the initial institutional regulatory design which maintained specialist regulators of equal footing.

It is safe to state that any meaningful institutional regulatory structure changes would require a redistribution of political power. The latter would be an onerous undertaking and would take time. A co-ordination mechanism established within the CCP, outside the formal regulatory structure, would probably work the best in the short term, and would lead to a change in the formal institutional regulatory structure in the long term.

[79] PBoC, *Fan Xi Qian Gong Zuo Bu Ji Lian Xi Hui Yi Zhao Kai Di Yi Ci Gong Zuo Hui Yi First [Meeting of the Anti-money Laundering Joint Committee]*, http://www.pbc.gov.cn/publish/fanxiqianju/3291/2010/20100825152559202913905/20100825152559202913905_.html at 14 Nov 2011.

[80] In addition to the CBRC, the PBoC also coordinates with other two regulators: China Insurance Regulatory Commission, and China Securities Regulatory Commission see in PBoC, '2007 Nian Zhong Guo Fan Xi Qian Bao Gao [2007 Report On China's Anti-money Laundering]', http://www.pbc.gov.cn/publish/fanxiqianju/1282807157712/_fileupload/426CBD8C.pdf (2008) 6, 7.

[81] Zhou Xiao Chuan, 'Jin Rong Zheng Ce Dui Jin Rong Wei Ji de Xiang Ying [Financial Policy in Dealing with Financial Crisis]' Beijing University, 15 Dec 2010) http://www.pbc.gov.cn/publish/hanglingdao/2950/2011/20110104191901596935544/20110104191901596935544.html accessed on 2/10/2017.

[82] Jeremy Cooper, 'The Intergration of Financial Regulatory Authorities-the Australian Experience' Australian Securities & Investments Commission, (2006) 3.

[83] PBoC, Li Bo, Centring on Marco-prudential Regulation, Pushing Financial Regulation Reform, http://www.cf40.org.cn/plus/view.php?aid=10619 accessed on 06/04/2016.

6 Final Remarks

Through the lens of asset management products regulation, the chapter examines the evolving nature of the regulatory institutional structure of the China's financial system. The sector-based regulatory structure in place prior to the 2018 reforms supported and promoted the development of the Chinese financial system over the past three decades. It was well entrenched, and to some degree, represented different interests and compromises of those who wield the power.

The ultimate control of the regulators rested with the State Council. Issues among the regulators tended, somewhat unsurprisingly, to be referred up to this next level of the political hierarchy, for resolution. For example, at the end of 2013, the State Council issued the *Notice on Strengthening the Supervision over Shadow* Banking which prohibited trust assets management companies from undertaking business with shadow banking features. Another example is in relation to regulation of internet financing, where the final demarcation of responsibilities among various regulators in 2015 was agreed to by the State Council.[84] The power struggle between the authorities provided opportunities for mediation by the State Council. The adjudicatory role of the central government increases the possibility that regulatory authority will be transferred back to the central government, either to be effectively retained there or to be redistributed again between the four regulatory authorities. It was reported that the State Council Financial Stability and Development Committee at its inaugural meeting in July 2017 noted its purposes to "monitor and control financial risks and strengthen regulatory coordination".[85] The Committee is chaired by Ma Kai, one of China Vice-Premiers. This denotes its elevated political status.

At the National Financial Works Meeting held in July 2017, the notion of functional regulation or conduct regulation was proposed under which, for example, a bank which sells a asset management product would need to obtain a licence from the CSRC.[86] This proposal, if realised, would clearly redistribute regulatory powers already vested in the regulators. This would require amendments to present laws to allow, for example, the CSRC to extend its regulatory power over commercial banks if they offer fund management products. In 2015, there was an attempt to do this. The definition of securities was expanded to include publicly traded securities investment funds therefore extending protection to certain fund investors.[87] However, this extension was not formally adopted by the national legislature.

In the light of the 2018 reforms, there will also be adjustments or reconciliation under these proposed changes to specify which particular regulator has responsibility for a particular entity since they would be subject to regulation of a particular regulator under the prior-to-2018 regulatory structure. Under the 2018 reforms, the function

---

[84] The State Council, Guidelines on Promoting Internet Finance Development 2015.

[85] The State Council, Inaugural Meeting of the Financial Stability and Development Committee, http://www.gov.cn/guowuyuan/2017-11/08/content_5238161.htm accessed on 12/12/2017.

[86] Editorial, the National Financial Works Meeting's New Concepts: Functional Regulation and Conduct Regulation, China Economy Weekly 2017 (29).

[87] Securities Law Amendment (Draft) 2015, Section 3

of making regulations and prudential regulatory rules concerning the banking and the insurance sectors has been transferred to the PBoC. This could be considered as an improvement in a sense that the PBoC is now the sole body to make prudential rules.

The 2018 reforms appears to be driven with a view to a function-based regulatory structure. However, as it stands, it is important to note that this is a mere organizational change. In other words, it remains an institutional regulatory structure, not a functional one: individual regulators are empowered to licence and regulate entities and regulate the products and services these entities provide. It is also noticeable that under this structure, Yi Gang, the Governor of the PBoC, is the deputy—secretary of the PBoC CCP committee. While Guo Shuqing, the Chairman of CBIRC, holds the position of the secretary of the PBoC CCP committee. This cross personnel system, as a rare political arrangement, potentially would improve coordination between the PBOC and other regulators. Any movement towards a genuine function-based regulatory structure would require further redistribution of regulatory powers among regulators. This would require considerable political will and commitment. Overall, the 2018 reforms, as a change of form rather than substance will not mitigate or address the challenges and the concerns the sector-based regulatory structure had confronted in recent years.

Overall, the sector-based regulatory structure established in 2003 facilitated the development of China's financial sector in the past 15 years. In the light of technological development and emergence of new financial products, it is evident as illustrated in the case of asset management products regulation, such a structure was failing the regulatory needs of the financial sector. Under the structure, systemic risk and investor protection issues have become increasingly concerns for the policy-makers and the regulators. In particular, with multiple regulators on the scene and without clear legal definition of those products, protection is only available to investors via contract law.

While Chinese policy-makers are willing to bring ahead changes, the 2018 reforms should be seen as a mere change of form and not of substance. The 2018 reforms stopped short of redistributing the powers that vested in individual regulators and will thus have only a limited impact on the manner in which the financial system is regulated including the manner in which asset management products are regulated. In other words, the underlying regulatory structure will still prove inadequate to effectively meet regulatory challenges. In the case of asset management products, laws reform aimed to comprehensively defining asset management products and clarifying the nature of those products is a prerequisite to resolve the regulatory issues discussed above. The 2018 reforms are unlikely to bring about noticeable changes.

Institutional regulatory structure reforms is a matter of redistribution of underlying political power. This is not a simple technical undertaking, instead, it would involve a redistribution of vested interests. The reforms which has seemingly taken place would not bring meaning changes to tackle the problems plagued the financial sector. Only a redistribution of political powers can.

Chapter 4
Why China's Judiciary is not that Important? Through the Lens of Regulating China's Securities Markets

Abstract China's securities markets have experienced rapid growth in the past two decades. The Shanghai Stock Exchange, for example, was ranked the fourth-largest stock exchange in the world as of end of June 2018. China's judiciary has been absent in protecting the interest of investors in its securities markets. This therefore raises the obvious question of who plays the role in protecting Chinese investors in this fast-growing and potentially volatile market. This chapter finds the Chinese state, by deploying various political resources, plays a direct role that is often more significant than that played by the judiciary in protecting the interest of investors. China's capital markets are reflective of its unique historical and contemporary conditions. The establishment and development of China's securities markets are made possible under the direction of the state.

1 Introduction

It is undeniable that the development of China's securities markets over the past two decades has been rapid. As of end-June 2018, despite the turmoil that engulfed the market in June and July 2015, Shanghai Stock Exchange (SSE) was ranked the fourth-largest stock exchange globally, with a total market capitalisation of around US$4.526 trillion, and over 136 million shareholders and 2,558 listed companies.[1] At the same time, China's securities markets are "renowned" for their speculative

[1] Securities and Futures Commission, Hong Kong, Market Capitalisation of the World's Top Stock Exchanges (as at End June 2018)", at https://www.sfc.hk/web/EN/files/SOM/MarketStatistics/a01.pdf [(August 2016)].

T. Huang and W. He, *Politics Meets Markets*, Contemporary Chinese Civil and Commercial Law, https://doi.org/10.1007/978-981-97-9176-7_4

nature,[2] and have also been likened to a casino.[3] China's status as the world's fourth-largest securities market is not solely attributed to the tens of millions of investors that speculate in unregulated markets. Foreign investors are also investing in the markets with access through QFII (the Qualified Foreign Institutional Investor scheme), and Shanghai and Hong Kong Connect.

The chapter examines the nature and dynamics of China's investor protection mechanisms. It explains why the judiciary is marginalised in protecting investors, after reviewing the political and legal circumstances. The chapter is organised as follows. The second section examines the roles played by the judiciary and the regulator in protecting investors in China. The third section details the manners in which the state musters its political resources to protect investors. The fourth section looks into the causes and effects of this institutional framework in protecting investors and addresses the question as to how the state exerts its social control in the securities markets.

2 The Struggle Between the Judiciary and the Regulatory Authority

In China, various executive bodies at different levels are regulating market activities. The central government, central government departments, local governments, local government departments and sometimes even unauthorised government bodies from diverse sources exercise regulatory force on the market. Law promulgated by the National People's Congress (NPC) is implemented nationwide but has very limited application. For example, the *Securities Law* enacted in 1998 was a response to the 1997 Southeast Asian financial crisis and was merely concerned with risk control of financial markets. The *Securities Law* was silent on civil liability measures in relation to false statements, insider trading and market manipulation in the marketplace. Admittedly, the silence was actually an oversight on the part of policymakers.[4] One contributing factor to the limited applicability of laws is the dynamic and fast-paced economic and social development across China. Thus, laws at the national level are unable to meet the rapidly changing needs of localities. Another factor is the limited legislative powers of the NPC which is only empowered to legislate certain matters. The executive bodies are expected to make regulations related to matters over which the NPC has no jurisdiction.

---

[2] Mei Jianping, Jose A. Scheinkman and We Xiong, "Speculative Trading and Stock Prices: Evidence from Chinese A-B Share Premia", *Als of Economics and Finance* 10 no. 2 (2009): 225–255; Sheldon Gao, "China Stock Market in a Global Perspective", *Dow Jones Indexes*, September 2002.

[3] CCTV, Interview with Wu Jinglian in the correspondent of Half-Hour Economy 12 January 2001. See also Hongo Jing, "China's Securities Markets Are Still a Gaming House", at http://www.forbeschina.com/review/201304/0025298.shtml [21 November (2004)].

[4] Research Office of the National People's Congress Standing Committee, *Guidelines on the implementation of China's Securities Law*, (Beijing: Reform Press, 1999), p. 348.

Regulations have always been the prominent source of rules that regulate China's securities markets. Historically, the establishment of SSE preceded the enactment of the Securities Law by almost a decade. Directives from the Securities Committee under the State Council and China Securities Regulatory Commission (CSRC) at the time filled the vacuum before the enactment of the Securities Law.[5] The Securities Commission of the State Council issued the Interim Measures for Prohibiting Securities Frauds (1993)[6] and the CSRC released a Circular concerning Prohibiting Manipulation of the Securities Market (1996) to deal with activities that otherwise would be deemed illicit in the markets.[7] The revised Securities Law (2005), enacted about seven years later, had to some extent established formal rules in the areas of fraud and market manipulation.[8] However, given the rapidly changing nature of the securities markets, the Securities Law (2005) was unable to address all issues and relevant sanctions. The CSRC then issued a large number of regulations, guides and notices to provide comprehensive regulation of the markets.

The Securities Law authorised the CSRC to supervise and regulate securities markets in a centralised manner.[9] The legislation also recognised the CSRC's power to prescribe rules and regulations relating to supervisory and regulatory activities in the markets.[10] The CSRC exercised regulatory power over the issuance, listing, trading, registration, depository and clearance of securities.[11] The CSRC promulgated regulations related to market operators and market intermediaries. The CSRC also formulated rules for companies intending to be listed on the markets,[12] and duly drafted rules in relation to information security and risk management.[13] Thus, the CSRC's regulatory reach has encapsulated all aspects of the market activities.

Under the newly revised Securities Law (2014), the CSRC is given extensive powers in enforcement as well.[14] The Supreme People's Court (SPC) also holds

---

[5] Both the Securities Committee under the State Council and China Securities Regulatory Commission (CSRC) were established in 1992 to manage the securities markets. In 1998, the Securities Committee under the State Council was merged with the CSRC.

[6] Interim Measures for Prohibiting Securities Frauds, issued by the Securities Commission of the State Council, 2 September 1993.

[7] "Circular concerning Prohibiting Manipulation of the Securities Market", issued by China Securities Regulatory Commission (CSRC), 31 October 1996.

[8] *Securities Law of the People's Republic of China*, issued by the Standing Committee of the National People's Congress on 29 December 1998 and amended in 2004, 2013 and 2014.

[9] Ibid., Art. 7.

[10] Ibid., Art. 179.

[11] Ibid.

[12] *Measures for the Administration of Initial Public Offering and Listing of Stocks*, issued on 17 May 2006 and amended on 30 December 2015.

[13] *Measures for the Risk Control Indexed of Securities Companies (2008 Revision)*, issued on 20 July 2006 and amended 24 June 2008 at http://www.csrc.gov.cn/pub/newsite/flb/flfg/bmgz/zjgs/201012/t20101231_189810.html [7 September 2014]

[14] Th CSRC is empowered to conduct on-site inspection / investigation and to collect evidence, request persons of interest to explain their conduct, inspect make copies of property registration and correspondence records, to ding records, registration of transfer, ad accounting or other relevant materials of interest parties;, seize documents and materials which are likely to be hidden or

some residual legislative power due to its ability to promulgate judicial interpretation. The judicial interpretation of the SPC has the effect of law,[15] but it is confined to the application of law in specific cases.[16] It should also be noted that the SPC only exercises such power in special cases.[17]

The SPC has made judicial interpretations on the application of law for both substantive and procedural matters, such as rules on civil disputes caused by false statements related to the securities markets, and civil compensation for false statements and disputes on the futures market. In its 2003 judicial interpretation regarding rules on civil disputes caused by false statements related to the securities markets, the SPC not only defined "false statements," "investors" and "securities markets," but also prescribed that only intermediate courts are allowed to adjudicate such cases.[18] The promulgation of judicial interpretation is a response to new issues arising in rapidly evolving securities markets. Judicial interpretation statements can be treated as low-cost legislation that is flexible and timely, in contrast to the process of legislation via the NPC.

In sum, it is apparent that the CSRS and the SPC share residual legislative power as a result of the nature of securities law.

In terms of law enforcement, the Chinese courts are unwilling to adjudicate cases related to securities markets. For instance, in the case of *Lu Jiahao (an independent director of the listed company Zhenzhou Baiwen) v. CSRC* where the CSRC allegedly unfairly penalised the plaintiff, the court used procedural reasons to dismiss the case. In 2001, some investors attempted to instigate litigation for civil compensation as a result of false statement by a listed company in relation to its securities. The SPC responded by publishing the Notice of Temporary Dismissal of Securities Related Civil Compensation Cases[19] (hereinafter "the Notice"), which the following.

The capital market in China is in a constant state of development. Many problems such as insider trading, fraud and market manipulation harm the integrity of the market, infringe the legal rights of investors, and negatively impact on the development of the capital market. These issues should be regulated gradually. These new problems have attracted close attention by the judiciary. However, due to legislative

---

damaged;, inspect capital accounts, securities accounts and bank accounts of interest parties;, seize capital or securities which have been or could be shifted or hidden, and important evidence which have been or could be hidden, forged, or damaged, and to restrict the trading of parties of interest. See also fn. [18], Art. 180.

[15] The Standing Committee of the National People's Congress, "Resolution of the Standing Committee of the National People's Congress Providing an Improved Interpretation of the Law", 10 June 1981.

[16] Ibid.

[17] What qualifies "special" is at the discretion of the court. Wu Aiping, "The Legal Effect of Judicial Interpretation", the People's Court, at http://www.dyzxw.org/html/article/201306/27/135428.shtml [(5 January 2015)].

[18] "Some Provisions of the Supreme People's Court on Trying Cases of Civil Compensation Arising from False Statement in Securities Market", 1 February 2003, issued by the Supreme People's Court.

[19] "Notice of the Supreme People's Court on the Relevant Issues concerning the Acceptance of Cases of Disputes over Civil Tort Arising from False Statement in the Securities Market", (*Fa Min China* ([2001)] no. 406, 15 January 2002, issued by the Supreme People's Court.

limitations and judiciary constraints, the courts are not able to adjudicate cases of such nature. Through our careful contemplation, the courts will not adjudicate cases caused by the above-stated misconduct in securities markets.

The Notice literally deprived investors of their rights stipulated under the Civil Procedural Law,[20] and had invited wide criticism from investors and the public. This position was later abandoned by the SPC. On 15 January 2002 and 9 January 2003, the SPC published two sets of judicial interpretations to allow the court system to adjudicate civil compensation cases as a result of false statements, provided that an enforcement action had already been undertaken by the CSRC.[21] Hence, the judiciary's deference to the regulatory authority is obvious when dealing with these matters. The CSRC's enforcement action became a prerequisite for instigating litigation in the judicial system. This rule has restricted investors seeking to initiate legal action. The SPC also stated that jurisdiction of cases depends on the domicile of origin of listed companies whether the intermediate people's court have jurisdiction over them.[22] Such rule has again restricted investors' access to judicial redress.

The legal barriers to civil litigation with respect to insider trading and market manipulation remain. In 2007, one of the vice presidents of the Supreme People's Court, Xi Xiaoming, stated that the revised *Securities Law* (2005) confirms civil liability for insider trading and market manipulation. If investors commence such litigation, courts should refer to the preconditions and jurisdictional rules set for false statement related to securities trading in the Supreme People's Court interpretation.[23] This alluded to the courts' more active role in protecting investors against insider trading and market manipulation. Acceptance of such cases by courts has been reported in Nanjing and Beijing.[24] In 2015, the "case registered is case accepted" principle was introduced under which the court is only required to review the procedural matters instead of substantive matters before the case is accepted.[25] Courts accept and adjudicate insider trading and market manipulation cases. In practice, a

---

[20] *The Civil Procedural Law of the People's Republic of China*, issued by the National People's Congress on 9 April 1991, amended in 2007, 2012 and 2017, Art. 2. The Law purports to protect the rights of civilians.

[21] "See Provisions of the Supreme People's Court on Trying Cases of Civil Compensation Arising from False Statement in Securities Markets", 1 February 2003, issued by the Supreme People's Court; and "Reply of the Supreme People's Court on Issues concerning the Trial of Tort Cases Involving Misrepresentation"", 3 July 2003, issued by the Supreme People's Court.

[22] Domicile of origin refers to where the company is registered, e.g. registered in a municipality, a provincial capital or a municipality with independent planning status and a special economic zones. Therefore, for example, an intermediate people's court has jurisdiction over companies registered in a municipality where the court itself resides.

[23] Address by Xi Xiaoming, Vic-President the Supreme People's Court, on "National Conference of Work on Civil and Commercial Trials—Bringing into Full Play the Trial Function on Civil and Commercial Cases to Provide Judicial Protection for Building a Socialist Harmonious Society", 30 May 2007.

[24] SoNG Yixin, *Rights Protection on the Securities Market* (1st edition), Shanghai: Shanghai Academy of Social Science Press (2009), p.10.

[25] The CPC Reform Committee, "Suggestions Concerning People's Courts Implementing Registration Reform", (11 April 2015).

limited number of cases undergo adjudication, due to the fact that the CSRC's penalty determination is a prerequisite for courts to accept cases. In fact, as of end-2017, only one insider trading civil litigation case had been adjudicated.[26]

The courts are still very reluctant to adjudicate cases of such nature. According to a survey conducted by Song Yixin, a lawyer practising in this area, although there were 15,000 cases filed by investors between 1990 and 2013 against listed companies for civil compensation as a result of alleged false statements on the part of public companies, only 101 were accepted by the courts.[27]

Courts may suspend cases at any stage after commencement, e.g. at hearing, judgment or enforcement stage. The suspension could be a result of political intervention from the government.[28] The uncertainty does not serve to enhance investors' confidence or encourage them to file the cases. As of 1 April 2009, 46 listed companies were sued for making false statements but only 12 were charged.

There are some characteristics of the Chinese judicial system that lead to the phenomenon of judicial failure. These include the lack of judicial independence,[29] indefinite delay to trial period,[30] and alteration and revocation of punishment by the CSRC,[31] and thereby engendered a public perception of insignificant or non-existent gains from litigation. Therefore, some investors have discounted litigation as a means of seeking resolution or redress.

Insider trading and market manipulation cases generally involve a considerable number of investors. For example, the number of eligible plaintiffs in the Zhongguancun case had reached 130,000.[32] Given their scale, these cases could potentially

---

[26] See *Yang Jianbo v. the CSRC 2013*.

[27] Song Yixin, *Reflection on Civil Cases Relating to China's Securities Markets, 1990–2013*), Beijing: Peking University Press (2003), p. 19.

[28] Huang Tao and Zhao Yuan, "The Closed Doors of Courts: China's Judicial Filtration of Financial Litigations",, *2urnal of Contemporary China* 24, no. 93 (2015): 493–510 (20).

[29] The Supreme People's Court (SPC) has published a judicial interpretation, which regulates the cases of civil compensation arising from false statements in securities market. The shermediate people's courts have the jurisdiction over and issuer's or listed company's locality. Tis raises the likelihood of local protectionism in the judicial system.

[30] For example, the civil compensation case related to an alleged false statement by a listed company, Dongfang Electronics, lasted by more than six years. See "Civil litigation of Dongfang Electronics Is Finally Over", *China Securities Journal*, 26 May 26, 2009. Long duration of litigation pe not uncommon in large civil cases. For example, the Duke Group Litigation in South Australia countinued for more than a decade.

[31] Article 11 of "The Supreme People's Court's Regulation on Hearing Civil Compensation Cases Caused by False Statements in the Securities Market" implemented in 2003, (200me Provisions of the Supreme People's Court on Trying Cases of Civil Compensation Arising from False Statement in Securities Market", 1 February 2003, issued by the Supreme People's Court, which indicates after the acceptance of civil compensation cases with respect to false statement, the court can order a suspension of the case when the party refuses to obey the regulator's verdict and order the party to apply for administrative reconsideration or administrative litigation.

[32] *Civil Proceeding initiated on Huang Guangyu Insider Trading Case*, ava, http://news.hexun.com/2010-09-13/124873486.html [(22 July, 2014)].

be politically sensitive.[33] Courts dealing with these cases may succumb to concerns about the political consequences of their judgements. It is further observed that the courts, acting on their self-interest, are unwilling to adjudicate cases involving large number of participants. In China, judges' performance is measured, *inter alia*, by the number of cases they have presided.[34] For instance, between a litigation filed by multiple persons and a case initiated by one person, both are considered as one case in terms of case load but the former involves more time and effort to adjudicate.

In contrast to the courts' reluctance to be involved in settling disputes, CSRC plays a more active role or has more political resources at its disposal (to be discussed later). More specifically, the CSRC had set up a hotline to handle complaints from investors about products and services in securities markets.[35] If the CSRC declines to adjudicate a dispute or its resolution outcomes are adverse to the litigant, the litigant has a legal claim against the CSRC. In fact, there are cases where litigation has been launched against the CSRC for its inaction when a complaint was made.[36] In order to avoid reputational loss for its inaction, the CSRC thus intervenes in civil disputes. In this way, regulatory power is used as a substitute for judicial power. This also partly explains the unwillingness of the SPC to accept tort litigation related to the securities markets, instead referring it to the regulator.[37]

In China, the courts are not the preferred avenue for resolution of disputes in terms of efficiency. Simply, the courts are largely absent from the field out of choice, and not because they have been outperformed. The courts' passive role contrasts sharply with the role played by the regulator. The courts' deference to the regulatory authority and their reluctance to adjudicate cases related to the securities markets is a distinctive feature in China's institutional investor protection system.

Indeed, over the past two decades, many have questioned the effectiveness of the securities markets regulatory authority.[38] Although the CSRC possesses extensive enforcement powers, it has often been criticised for failing to or being unable to protect the interests of investors. The stock price rigging case of Yi'an Tech is a

---

[33] The average number of investors involved in a class case in the Uited States was 45,055. See Thomas E. Willging, *Empirical Study of Class Actions in Four Federal District Courts: Final Report to the Advisory Committee on Civil Rules*, University of Michigan Library, (1996).

[34] Wu Yuanzhong, *Judges' Appraisal, A Difficult Question*, People's Courts, published on 25 January 2013.

[35] CSRC, 123troduction of CSRC's Hotline 12386"", va http://www.csrc.gov.cn/pub/newsite/tzzbh1/tb12386rx/tbrxjs/201311/t20131114_238301.html [(2 March 2014)].

[36] For example, Ai sued the CSRC for its inaction. See Gao Xiqing and & Cen Dagang, (*Cae Study of Securities Law*) (st edition), (eijing: Intellectual Property Publishing House, 2005), p.19.

[37] *The Supreme People's Court's Notice on Issues Concerning the Acceptance of Civil Infringement Cases Caused by False Statement in the Securities Market* (*Fa Min Chuan*) [2001] 43. (S also "Some Provisions of the Supreme People's Court on Trying Cases of Civil Compensation Arising from False Statement in Securities Market", 1 February 2003, issued by the Supreme People's Court.

[38] Hao Xuguang, Li Fang and& Zang Shiyu, "(China's Securities Markets Regulator's Actions and Their Consequence"), 0 *na Industrial Economics*), (2013): 96–107 (Xao Xuguang, Fan Honggang and& ZOU Zhili, ("Ientifying the Efficiency of Regulation on Chinese Securities Market—nEx post Criteria Based on the Excess Return and Market Volatility""), (*ance and& Economics*), (2010): 33–38.

good example.[39] The CSRC had also taken an approach considered radical: e.g. the punishment of Lu Jiahao, an independent director of the listed company Zhengzhou Baiwen.[40] The CSRC's ineffectiveness could be attributed to the multiple regulatory goals it has to achieve. The CSRC is mandated to protect investors; to ensure the fairness, effectiveness and transparency of the markets; and to reduce systematic risks.[41] Protecting investors is by no means the primary goal of the CSRC. These goals are internally consistent and centred on the primary objective of protecting investors, since maintaining a fair, effective and transparent market, and reducing systematic risks serve in the interest of investors.

In addition to protecting the interests of investors, promoting the development of the securities markets is also clearly on the regulatory authority's agenda. One aim of the Securities Law (1998) was to facilitate the development of the socialist market economy.[42] The securities markets were tasked to finance the reform of state-owned enterprises (SOEs).[43] If the regulatory authority shouldered these political responsibilities, it would be seen to serve not only investors but also the government. Promoting the development of the securities markets and the CSRC's primary mandate of protecting investors do involve pursuit of conflicting goals. In this scenario, it is challenging for regulators to maintain its independence and adhere to both mandates. For example, if the CSRC initiates an investigation into a particular listed company, the stock price of the company will drop. If a state-owned listed company happens to be the target of probe, it is not in the interest of the government for such an investigation to occur. Research has shown that the CSRC pursues cases against private corporations more promptly than against SOEs.[44] The CSRC's deliberate delay in taking actions against SOEs would be counterproductive to its role to deter possible illicit activities in the markets and to protect the investors.[45] This also explains the CSRC's concern about the possible impact of its own behaviour on the market (e.g. causing investors' confidence to waver), and on regulatory behaviours such as controlling the pacing of securities issuance.[46] When stock prices are high,

---

[39] Alhough te CSRC imposed heavy penalties on the parties involved in Yi'an case, there wase no actionable assets available to remedies for investors;, se "Yi'an Tech profited RMB 46 million, and fined RMB 47 million", ava http://finance.qq.com/a/20101102/003726.htm [(11 March, 2014)].

[40] Huang Tao and& Cen Rudan, *Study on the Legal Liability of an Independent Director: A Deliberation Based on Chinese Reality, 9n Ling Law Review*, 9(2005): 144–160.

[41] International Organization of Securities Commissions, *Objectives and Principles of Securities Regulation*, May 2003, at, http://www.iosco.org/library/pubdocs/pdf/IOSCOPD154.pdf [(11 November, 2014)].

[42] See *Securities Law of the People's Republic of China (1998)*, Art. 1.

[43] In the early 20th century, securities markets were established to address the issue of lack of capital in SOEs. See Shao Chang, "Development of Securities Markets and SOEs' Reform", *Sdy of Finance and Trade*, 2(1998): 46–-491

[44] Si Ru, "Political Connections and Effectiveness of CRSC's Regulation and Supervision", *Journal of Central University of Finance & Economics*, no. 6 (2013): 91–6.

[45] Xu Nianxing, "Do Political Connections Affect the Efficiency of Legal Enforcement?", *Economic Quarterly*, 1, no. 2 (2013): 373–406.

[46] If the CSRC initiates an investigation of a particular listed company, itock price of the company will certainly goop. Therefore, in order to sustain stable stock prices, the CSRC exercises extreme

the CSRC allows issuance of new listings to cool the market; and when stock prices are low, the CSRC slows down the issuance of new listings.

The CSRC also acts as market administrator as well as a regulator. From securities issuance, regulation of corporate governance, market access of intermediaries to risk management, approval of new products and investor education, the CSRC is an all-purpose caretaker of the securities markets. The CSRC is also tasked to maintain stability in the markets. During market downturns, the CSRC implements measures for the bailout of troubled companies. When the market turns bullish, the CSRC implements measures to prevent formation of bubbles.[47] For example, in 1994, the CSRC implemented three measures to stimulate the markets after years of stagnation: i.e. suspend the issuance of new stock; control the rights of issuance; and encourage injection of new capital into the markets. Such responsibilities and behaviours are once again contradictory to the objective of protecting investors.

Overall, the role that the judiciary could play in investor protection is very limited. This suggests that the CSRC might be expected to step forward to protect investors, on top of its other objectives to attain. The CSRC sometimes has to prioritise other objectives at the expense of investor protection. Given China's political circumstances, in order to fully understand the issue of where the responsibility of investor protection should fall on in China, it is necessary to analyse beyond the interactions between the judiciary and the regulator, and examine the role of the central and local governments, as well as the role of political resources under their command.

3 Mobilising Political Resources as an Alternative to the Judiciary

As discussed earlier, the judiciary in China has failed in exercising its effectiveness in securities markets' investor protection, and the regulator has also been ineffective in practice. The Chinese securities markets have grown rapidly to attract a growing number of investors, but whether a mechanism is in place to protect the rights and interests of investors remains questionable.

Regulatory power is the power extended to a regulator by its authorising legislation or by other law. "Political resources", on the other hand, is defined as resources utilised by not only the regulator, but also other government authorities, such as the central committee of the China Communist Party of (CCP), local governments, the central bank, the State-owned Assets Supervision and Administration Commission (SASAC), Public Security Bureau and other government bodies. These authorities are normally mobilised beyond or without explicit mandates.

The most recent example was the 2015 stock market crisis. In response to the drastic fall of index by 30 per cent in the stock markets in June and July 2015,

caution is determining whether to initiate an investigation. It is clearly not in the interest of the government if any of the investigations ise launched against listed SOEs.

[47] Based on a research report by Shenzhen Stock Exchange in 2007.

China Securities Finance Corporation Limited, a state-owned company, reportedly extended RMB2.6 trillion credit to 21 securities companies on 8 June 2015 so that those companies could increase their shareholding in their proprietary dealings.[48] On the same day, SASAC ordered that stated-own companies were not allowed to decrease their shareholding.[49] On 9 July, the Central Huijin Investment Ltd., a state-owned investment company, not only committed not to sell any of its shareholding it held in the big four banks, but also promised to increase its shareholding of those banks.[50]

The "compensation first" policy is another example. In response to fraud related to initial public offerings of securities (hereinafter "IPO fraud"), the CSRC has considered a "compensation first" policy where relevant intermediaries such as underwriters will be required to step in to compensate investors promptly for the losses due to IPO fraud. The Wanfu Shengke case was one of the first cases identified by the CSRC for falsifying its financial status in its prospectus. The underwriter, Ping An Securities Company, stepped in, seemingly voluntarily, and compensated the investors.[51]

There are various reasons why intermediaries are willing to step in, while relevant regulations are being considered. First, prior to granting approval for IPO applications, the CSRC requires all intermediaries to commit to the "compensation first" policy. In absence of such a commitment, the CSRC would delay future IPO applications put forward by the securities company in question.

Local governments' proactive role is also recogniseable especially in recapitalising local listed companies, and this created a phenomenon known as "XX local concept securities". Issuance of securities directed or supported by the local government offers opportunities for speculation in the markets since the price of these securities would be over-priced. Although the local governments do not currently have the *de jure* or de facto power to regulate the securities market, they still play an influential role in providing and mobilising political and financial resources for the securities market. Their vested interest could be attributed to the fact that a majority of the listed companies are owned directly or indirectly by central or local governments. For instance, Shanghai municipal government is an active player in the securities markets. As early as in 1999, the Suggestion of Policy on Promoting the Development of Local Listed Companies was issued to provide political protection for the recapitalisation of local listed companies.[52] Leading up to the World Expo and the industrial restructuring climate, State-owned Assets Supervision and

---

[48] He Xun, "China Securities Finance Corporation Limit Provides 21 Securities Companies with RMB 260 Brillion Credits", ava http://hk.stock.hexun.com/2015-07-08/177380642.html [(14 March, 2016)].

[49] "SASAC Demands SOEs Not to Decrease Shareholdings", ava http://hk.stock.hexun.com/2015-07-08/177377195.html [14 March 2016].

[50] "Central Huijin Promises Not to Decrease Its Shareholding", at http://sc.stock.cnfol.com/gppdgdzx/20150709/21065846.shtml [14 March 2016].

[51] "Wanfu Shengke Case: Compensation First, Investors Protecting Their Rights", at http://www.csrc.gov.cn/pub/newsite/tzzbh1/tbtzzjy/tbfxff/201508/t20150803_282336.html [14 March 2016]

[52] "Suggestion of Policy on Promoting the Development of Local Listed Companies", issued by Shanghai Municipal People's Government, 8 November 1999.

Administration Commission of Shanghai Municipal Government carried out a large-scale recapitalisation of 20 listed state-owned companies. In the first 11 months in 2009, about RMB18.58 billion worth of state assets were securitised, boosting the asset-backed securitisation rate to 25.4 per cent of gross domestic product.[53] There are many cases where the authority, political power and assets of local governments have been utilised to improve the quality of listed companies and hence protect the investors' funds. The Guangdong provincial government published the "Suggestion on Enhancing Performance and Promoting Scale Development of Listed Companies in Guangdong Province" in 2000.[54] That same year, the Hubei provincial government published the "Notice of Suggestions on Promoting Asset Recapitalization and Healthy Development of Listed Companies in Hubei Province".[55] In April 2003, the Chongqing municipal government set up a working group for the recapitalisation of listed companies. Among its tasks were to "provide advice on policies and measures for recapitalisation of listed companies", and to "coordinate with listed companies resolving major problems in their recapitalisation, and to promote recapitalisation of listed companies and structural optimisation of these companies".[56]

Local governments have always been an important stakeholder in regulatory activities. The role is institutionalised by the State Council's "Regulations concerning Supervision and Management of Listed Companies (Exposure Draft)"[57] on 7 September 2007. Pursuant to Article 7(2), local governments at all levels are responsible for managing risks, and establishing and improving risk mitigation mechanisms associated with listed companies in their administrative territory. Article 92 empowers provincial governments to take over management of listed companies in following circumstances: when serious crises afflict the listed companies; and breakout of "social instability" due to shareholders' dissatisfaction with the board of directors' performance. As Zheng Yongnian posits in his book De Facto Federalism, local governments are more likely to exact favourable policies from the top by cooperating with the central government.[58]

The case of Qiongminyuan is a case in point. Hainan Minyuan Modern Agriculture Co Ltd. (hereinafter "Qiongminyuan") was listed on the Shenzhen Stock Exchange on 30 April 1993. Rumours later pervaded that its profit statements were false. The CSRC

---

[53] WU Fanglan, "A New Upsurge of Recapitalization of Local listed Companies in Shanghai", at http://stock.hexun.com/2009-12-28/122182044.html [18 July 2014]

[54] "Suggestion on Enhancing Performance and Promoting Scale Development of Listed Companies in Guangdong Province" issued by the People's Government of Guangdong Province, 2 March 2000.

[55] Notice of Suggestions on Promoting Asset Recapitaliszation and Healthy Development of Listed Companies in Hubei Province", issued by People's Government of Guangdong Province, 30 April 2000.

[56] Chongqing Municipal Government Sets Up Leading Group for Recapitaliszation of Listed Companies", st http://www.cq.xinhuanet.com/political/2003-04/02/content_359328.htm [14 May 2014]

[57] "Regulations concerning Supervision and Management of Listed Companies (Exposure Draft)", issued by the State Council, 7 September 7007.

[58] Zheng Yongnian "*e Facto Federalism in China: Reforms and Dynamics of Central--local Relations*" (Singapore: World Scientific Publishing, 2008).

passed a decision that the company falsified its 1996 financial statements to mislead investors.[59] On 28 February 1997 evening, Qiongminyuan applied to the exchange for suspension of trading. On 29 April 1998, the CSRC published an investigation report which stated that the company had committed various illegal acts including falsifying declarations of profits and capital reserves and market manipulation. Managerial personnel involved (including the chairman of the board) were subjected to criminal prosecution. However, the CSRC did not delist the company in accordance with Article 21 of the Interim Measures of Prohibiting Securities Fraud.[60] Instead, it called for recapitalisation through "additional issuance and share exchange" by stripping the non-performing assets of the company. By doing so, delisting Qiongminyuan was avoided and the interests of investors were thus protected. On 20 November 1998, the Beijing municipal government approved the parent company of Qiongminyuan to transfer 38.92 per cent of state-owned shares in the parent company to another company called Beijing Housing Development and Construction Group in exchange for its role in cleaning up Qiongminyuan. On 8 June 1999, Zhongguancun Science and Technology Company was established by Beijing Housing Development and Construction Group. Zhongguancun Science and Technology Company later issued around 187 million shares to Beijing Housing Development and Construction Group. With the consent of the CSRC, Beijing Housing Development and Construction Group exchanged these newly issued shares for those shares in Qiongminyuan which were held by the public. On 12 July 1999, Zhongguancun Science and Technology Company went public on Shenzhen Stock Exchange. Qiongminyuan was delisted on the same day.

Since 2006, various political authorities, such as the CSRC, the CPC Central, SASAC, Public Security Bureau and local governments, have been mobilised to solve the problem of major shareholders diverting capital of listed companies for other uses (known as "tunnelling").[61] For example, before 1 May 2001, majority shareholders in Sanjiu Yiyao stripped 96 per cent of the public company's assets.[62] In October 2005, the State Council endorsed the CRSC's Opinion on Enhancing Quality of

---

[59] The CSRC's Decision on Penalties Imposed on Hainan Qiongminyuan (1998), 27 April 1998)

[60] If any issuer issues a false statement as listed in Article 12 of the Interim Measures, the CSRC should consider such punishment ss issuance of warning, issuances of order for return of any capital illegally collected, confiscation of illegal proceeds, penalty imposition or evocation of qualification to issue new stocks or to be listed. These punishments could be imposed separately or collectively. See Interim Measures for Prohibiting Securities Frauds, issued by Securities Commission of the State Council, 2 September 1993.

[61] Tunnelling in China's securities markets is conducted through various related transactions. The most common form consists of transactions between the listed companies and shareholders or other related parties that create accounts receivable registered on the books of the company while the item to which the entry is related, in fact of greater market value, is transferred to the other party. Another form of tunnelling is accomplished through selling of shareholders' assets or products it a high price or purchasing corporate assets at a low price which squeezes the listed company.

[62] CSRC, "Notice on Sanjiu Yiyao and its Associates (2001)". Controlling shareholders were motivated by the secondary market's stock prices to improve the performance of the company. See Huang Tao, "Issues on the Legal and Institutional Environment of Governing the Tunneling of Listed Companies", *Lanzhou Academic Journal*, no. 4 (2009): 140–4.

Listed Companies, which states that controlling shareholders and controllers should not divert any funds of listed companies in the form of loans, guarantees and other arrangements.[63] Those that had already done so were required to make restitution by the end of 2006. In order to attain this goal, the CRSC endorsed a number of different restitutionary measures to expedite the repayment process. When the deadline was set as the end of 2006, the CSRC, securities markets operators and relevant listed companies made a concerted effort to achieve the goal. On 26 May 2006, the CSRC issued the Notice of Further Accelerating the Work of Debt Repayment to ensure that listed companies fully understand the importance and urgency of solving the problem and take measures to accelerate debt repayment.[64] This notice also encouraged listed companies to employ "innovative means" to solve problem. On 7 November 2006, the CSRC, the Ministry of Public Security, the People's Bank of China, SASAC, the General Administration of Customs, State Administration of Taxation, State Administration for Industry and Commerce and the China Banking Regulatory Commission (CBRC) jointly enacted the Notice of Advancing Work of Debt Repayment of Majority Shareholders that Divert Funds of Listed Companies,[65] reiterating the importance and urgency of the repayment work, and that it must be completed by the end of 2006. The repayment initiative yielded positive results. According to statistics published by the CSRC in early January 2007, by the end of 2006, 380 listed companies completed their repayment work that totalled RMB36.6 billion. Another 19 listed companies also approved the proposals for repayment by board resolutions or shareholders' meetings. The major shareholders of the aforementioned 399 companies had diverted RMB39 billion in total sum for other purposes. Senior officials were satisfied with the result of the repayment campaign.[66] It is noteworthy that the problem of majority shareholder's exploitation of minority shareholders was resolved only by mobilising the collective resources of the aforementioned authorities and local governments in a concerted effort.

Diverting funds from investors' settlement accounts has also long been a common practice among financial intermediaries in China.[67] When intermediaries are shut down or brought into bankruptcy liquidation proceedings, ordinary investors would

[63] "Notice of the State Council on Approving and Forwarding the Opinions of China Securities Regulatory Commission on Improving the Quality of Listed Companies", at http://www.gov.cn/zwgk/2005-11/01/content_88761.htm [15 December 2014].

[64] "Notice of Further Accelerating the Work of Debt Repayment", issued by CSRC, 26 May 2006.

[65] Notice of Advancing Work of Debt Repayment of Majority Shareholders That Divert Funds of Listed Companies, issued by CSRC, Ministry of Public Security, People's Bank of China, State-owned Assets Supervision and Administration Commission, General Administration of Customs, State Administration of Taxation, State Administration for Industry and Commerce and CBRC, 17 November 2006.

[66] Fan Fuchun, "The Problem of using Controlling Power to Tunnel Listed Companies has been Solved", *Shanghai Securities News,* Mar. 8, 2008.

[67] In 2001, the CSRC conducted a survey to investigate the extent to which funds were diverted from investors' settlement accounts. It found that 27 per cent of surveyed companies experienced this problem; See Shi Dong, "The Survey Shows that 27% of Securities Companies Diverted Funds from Customer Settlement Accounts", at http://stock.stockstar.com/SS2001061200156550.shtml [(5 January 2015)].

suffer financial loss. In order to address the problem, the People's Bank of China, the Ministry of Finance, the CBRC and the CSRC jointly issued the Opinions of Implementing the Purchase of Individual Credits and the Securities Trading Settlement Capital of Clients (the Opinions) on 15 October 2004.[68] As a result, all principal and interest in securities transaction settlement accounts of clients had to be purchased in full either by the central government or by local governments. The Opinions also detailed the division of responsibility for various aspects of the scheme among the regulatory bodies, the central bank, local governments and public security forces.[69] In the event of disputes arising from implementation of the scheme, the SPC held the view that "the Opinions is a special measure implemented by the state in tackling events with financial risks, and is aimed at maintaining market stability and protecting minority groups; it is of high political purpose and policy intention. If disputes arise during the process of screening, confirmation and purchase of personal credit and settlement account funds where litigation is initiated against work groups or related regulatory bodies, the court will inform the plaintiff to seek redress from the relevant government (local or central)".[70] The statement was later incorporated into the Notice of the Supreme People's Court on the Trial and Enforcement of Cases Related to the Securities Companies under Risk Disposal[71] promulgated by the SPC on 26 May 2009. This demonstrates that the SPC plays a passive role as it defers the authority to the local government.

Evidently, state action is an alternative to the judiciary and the regulatory authority in protecting investors in China. By mustering various political resources, the state plays a role in protecting the interest of investors.[72]As a specialist regulator, the CSRC is responsible for the regulation of securities markets. However, these regulatory actions normally involve various government bodies and are initiated by the CSRC. This is evident in notices or guidances that were released and issued in accordance to the CSRC's document sequence. According to Chinese conventions in politics, the CSRC is clearly the organ that initiates and coordinates the drafting

---

[68] "Opinions of Implementing the Purchase of Individual Credits and the Securities Trading Settlement Capital of Clients", issued by the People's Bank of China, the Ministry of Finance, the China Banking Regulatory Commission and China Securities Regulatory Commission, 5 October 2004.

[69] Accordingly, financial regulatory bodies may determine and announce the revocation, suspension or consolidation of business of financial institutions, as well as organise liquidation panels. Local governments shall facilitate liquidation panels by registering creditors' rights and formulating risk management plans in order to maintain social stability. The People's Bank of China and the Ministry of Finance shall supervise and be responsible for the approval of relending and loans for specific purposes. The public security organisations are responsible for investigating and meting out punishments for illegal and criminal behaviour of financial institutions and related persons.

[70] A speech by associate chief Judge Song Xiaoming on Symposium of Bankruptcy Cases of Financial Institutions and Other Entities Heard by Courts Around the Country, 10 November 2004.

[71] "Notice of the Supreme People's Court on the Trial and Enforcement of Cases Related to the Securities Companies under Risk Disposal", issued by the Supreme People's Court, 26 May 2009.

[72] During the early stage of development, the regulator used various methods, such as reducing stamp duty or placing encouraging editorials in *People's Daily* to support the market's steady and rapid growth. See Stephen Green, *The Development of China's Stock Market, 1984–2002: Equity Politics and Market Institutions* (Oxford: Routledge Curzon, 2004), pp. 225–332.

and implementation of the notice or guidance in question. For example, in 2005, the People's Bank of China, Ministry of Finance and CSRC jointly issued the personal creditor's rights and the clients' securities transaction settlement funds purchase opinions in document CSRC 2005 no. 59.[73]

4 Causes and Effects of Mobilising Political Resources

What has compelled the state to utilise political bodies to protect the interests of investors in the securities markets? The state, as the ultimate owner of financial resources, needs to actively promote the financial industry's development for economic growth.[74] The utilisation of state political resources is not aimed directly at protecting small and medium investors. The pursuit of macroeconomic goals, such as steady economic growth, financial stability and political stability, are more immediate concerns for the state. Collaterally, however, the protection of investors is consistent with the long-term aims of market regulators. In providing this support, the aim to maintain investor confidence in the markets is also achieved. Ultimately, through implicit guarantees, the state is standing by to extend protection to the investors.

Historically, the Chinese government has always adopted an interventionist approach since the inception of securities markets in China. For example, the planning department of the central government used to determine the total annual volume of stock issuance. The determined quotas were assigned to local governments and departments which selected the companies to go public. That is to say, only companies with quotas were qualified to go public. A parallel system that requires issuance of shares to be granted approval from both the provincial government and the CSRC was therefore in place. Theoretically, this mechanism was designed to benefit investors since it allowed local governments as well as state ministries and departments to select companies with good performance and promising prospects to be listed in the securities markets. Usually, local governments have an information advantage over the CSRC.[75] However, in reality, local governments and state ministries and departments did not select companies based on strong performance, believing that

[73] "Notice of Relevant Issues concerning the Purchase of Individual Credit's Rights of Securities Companies and the Securities Trading Settlement Capital of Clients", issued by the People's Bank of China, Ministry of Finance and CSRC, 30 June 2005.

[74] Zhang Jie, *Structure and Reform of Chinese Financial Institution* (1st edition) (Taiyuan: Shanxi Economy Press, 1998), p. 174.

[75] The quotas of stock issuance on Chinese securities market before March of 1 yielded positive effects in protecting investors according to some scholars. On the one hand, the quota system provided local officials with incentives to select for IPO companies with good performance, as a higher quota would be given subsequently to that area as part of award for local officials selecting quality companies. Se Katharina Pistor and XU Cenggang, "Governing Stock Markets in Transition Economies: Lessons from China", 7 (*American Law and Economics Review* 7, no. 1 (2005): 184–210; Lang Jinhuan and& XU Yngying, "A Lack of Law and Alternative Mechanism of Investor Protection: Based on the Research of Quota System", *Rearch of Institutional Economics 4* (2009): 152–165(2).

these companies had no capital pressure and could raise what they required by other means. Instead, they selected companies which have difficulties in raising capital. Local governments considered listing not simply a means of raising money but also a means of relieving cash flow difficulty.[76] Such enterprises tended to perform poorly after listing.[77]

The political guarantee also grew out of the intricate links between the government and listed companies. It should be highlighted that that a majority of listed companies in China's securities markets are effectively controlled by state entities, and thus stock prices are heavily dependent on government policy, and the market capital is mostly derived from SOEs and other state-owned financial institutions. There are cases where publicly listed SOEs purchase stock to support the securities markets.[78] As a result of the historical burden inherited from the planned economy, SOEs and government-controlled entities continue to shoulder many social responsibilities, such as providing life-time employment, the so-called "iron rice bowl".[79]

The protection provided by the government is relatively limited and not systemic. The governments only respond to serious issues that substantially affect investors to such degree that triggers "*quntixing shijian*", which is considered politically sensitive. *Quntixing shijian* refers to "matters that affect the mass", which could cause socio-political problems for the government. For example, the aforementioned 2004 Opinions of Implementing the Purchase of Individual Credits and the Securities Trading Settlement Capital of Clients[80] was only applicable to individual personal investors, and not applicable to corporations or other institutional investors who were also victims of the wrongdoings of financial institutions. In other words, damage to investors' interests at a confined level would not warrant government intervention. This in turn creates uncertainty in the markets over when a government rescue would be triggered.

The measures employed as a result of implicit government guarantees would be ineffective in the long term. Although the "*yanda*", i.e. "cracking down on crime",

---

[76] LI Jwen, *Study on Government Regulation of Chinese Securities Market (*1st edition), (Beijing: Economic Science Press (2007), P. 174.

[77] Such arrangements are amenable to corruption. Fr example, the scandal known to the Chinese public as the Kangsai Phenomenon uncovered the illegal behaviour of three ministerial officials, LiI Dqiang (vice governor of Hubei pProvince), XuU Pnghang (vice director of the State Commission of Science and Technology for National Defense) and WuU Wnying (President of the China Textile Association). See Liu peng, "Kangsai Phenomenon and the Institution of Stock Issuance and Listing in China", 1 Economic Herald, (2001): 53–5.

[78] For example, "Central Huijin Bought Stocks to Support the Securities Markets", av http://hkstock.cnfol.com/111011/132,1709,10868536,00.shtml [(11 April 2014)].

[79] Australian Government, "China's Unfinished State-Owned Enterprise Reforms", available at http://www.treasury.gov.au/PublicationsAndMedia/Publications/2013/Economic-Roundup-Issue-2/Economic-Roundup/Chinas-unfinished-SOE-reforms [11 April 2014].

[80] "Opinions of Implementing the Purchase of Individual Credits and the Securities Trading Settlement Capital of Clients", Article 4, issued by the People's Bank of China, the ministry of Finance, the China Banking Regulatory Commission and China Securities Regulatory Commission, 15 October 2004.

approach in law enforcement was implemented for a period of time by various political bodies to crack down on illicit activities,[81] the effects are quite limited. For example, the *Yyanda* approach was not able to did not deter the tunneling practice carried out by majority shareholders in listed companies over the longer term, and these illicit behaviours resurfaced when the *yanda* campaign was over.

The *ex post facto* nature of government intervention as a result of the government guarantees also aggravates the problem of moral hazard. When the issue affects a sizeable number of investors, the government cannot possibly choose not to intervene, and the expectation of government intervention has created the moral hazard problem for investors. Investors are more likely to make reckless decisions, knowing that the government will ultimately bear the risks.

In conclusion, the state bears the responsibility of institutional protection of investors in China's securities markets, whereas the CSRC and other political institutions orchestrate intervention to deter unsanctioned activities in the markets. The Chinese judiciary has little role in this process. However, the utilisation of political resources, which may protect investors in the short run, is however not a sustainable strategy. In economic terms, this is a form of "soft budget constraint" available in countries where the state's power is not restrained by legal institutions.[82] China has adopted a combination of strategies where regulations and the state enforce good behaviour and deter bad behaviour in the markets to attain the investor protection objective. The situation in China is one where the state is dominant and the principal mechanism of investor protection is centrally controlled, but the regulator participates to a certain degree.

5 Conclusion and Looking Ahead

In conclusion, understanding the role of the state is key to understanding the regulation of securities markets in China: political resources replace the judiciary in investor protection. The authors' research shows that investor protection in China's securities markets remains inadequate, and the judiciary has been marginalised in protecting investors. The regulator, meanwhile, is not able to fill the vacuum, and in effect, political resources need to be utilised in order to fulfil the investor protection role. It is still questionable whether this mechanism offers long-lasting effects in providing investor protection.

China's capital markets reflect its unique historical and contemporary conditions, a marked contrast to those of mature economies in the West. Indeed, the establishment and development of China's securities markets are made possible under the direction

[81] Ibid.

[82] The term "soft budget constraint" was first coined by János Kornai with respect to communist governments that were unable to promise not to use fiscal means to save SOEs. See János Kornai, *Economics of Shortage*, (Amsterdam: North Holland Press, 1980) (Amsterdam), p. 27).

of the state. This naturally leads to the situation whereby the state, instead of the judiciary, protects the investors in capital markets.

Chapter 5
Oracle of Delphi: How China's Judiciary Divines the Notion of 'Financial Security'?

Abstract In the past few years, the term financial security has been increasingly referred to by politicians in China's public discourse. This term was meant to broadly denote national security considerations in relation to financial markets. This chapter draws on and analyses a recent study of 242 Chinese court decisions undertaken by the authors and explores the nature and the extent of the term 'financial security' as used in judicial decisions in China. Our research demonstrates that the judiciary makes frequent use of this term even though it is a term which remains to be defined in legislation and regulation. This chapter offers a means of categorising the manner in which the term financial security is deployed, which may assist in a better understanding of the Chinese courts' judgments in the contemporary context as well as in the future. It also offers an account of the thinking and motivation behind legal reasoning that assists in gaining an insight into the use and implications of financial security that appear to underpin these decisions. The adoption of the term financial security, similar to the Greek myth of the Delphic Oracles, is indicative of the role played by the courts in the light of the Chinese political system.

1 Introduction

Financial security is a unique term when it is coined in the Chinese context.[1] There is no such single term in the West that conveys a similar meaning. However, to reflect the spirit of the term, the literature in the West supports the interdependency between the financial system and national security. The financial system is of central importance in the national economy and has considerable influence over both public and private activity. National security threats often exploit the financial system to achieve their goals or even target the financial system itself.[2] Consequently, the financial system must be addressed in tackling national security issues.

---

[1] The term financial security was first introduced by President Xi Jinping in 2014 at the first meeting of the Chinese Communist Party National Security Committee. Financial security in the West generally refers to the security of personal finance. See Xinhua Net (2014).

[2] Rodriguez (2010, p. 129); Borghard (2018).

T. Huang and W. He, *Politics Meets Markets*, Contemporary Chinese Civil and Commercial Law, https://doi.org/10.1007/978-981-97-9176-7_5

The integrity of and activities occurring within the financial system impact on national security. As one study notes: 'A secure financial market system is critical to [the US] national economy'.[3] The Security and Exchange Commission's (SEC)'s communalisation of the rights to market data reduces the incentives to invest in cyber security and exposes the US financial trading systems to a greater risk of cyber terrorism.[4] Terrorist groups (or other non-State entities) may exploit weaknesses in the financial system to obtain funding to finance their operations and conduct terrorism (or other criminal activities).[5]

'Critical infrastructure entities'[6] are vulnerable to offensive operations carried out by foreign adversaries in cyberspace, and cyber threats could fundamentally affect the stability of the financial sector as a whole.[7] Foreign threat actors have 'demonstrated a willingness and capability to target global financial services infrastructure'.[8] There is a direct link between the proper functioning of financial systems and the sound operation of a Western economy.[9] A major disruption to the financial system, such as the global financial crisis, also affects military and security expenditure.[10]

Moreover, the literature raises the idea that threats to national security and national security policies, in turn, impact on the financial system. Terrorism, one of the major threats to national security, is increasingly a serious issue in a largely connected financial market.[11] There is the potential for terrorists, or other malicious State actors, to use financial instruments to manipulate the financial system and threaten the national economy.[12] Corporate transactions in the form of the foreign acquisition of companies can pose national security concerns.However, these 'increased security concerns can unnecessarily add to investor uncertainty, reduce FDI [foreign direct investment] flow, undermine efforts to achieve investment liberalisation and invite retaliatory measures'.[13]

---

[3] Sarnikar and Johnsen (2009, p. 1).

[4] Sarnikar and Johnsen (2009, pp. 6–7, 14-21).

[5] Rodriguez (2010, p. 132).

[6] 'Support to Critical Infrastructure at Greatest Risk ("Section 9 Report") Summary', US Department of Homeland Security (Presidential Executive Order, 8 May 2018), https://www.dhs.gov/sites/default/files/publications/EO-13800-Section-9-Report-Summary-20180508-508.pdf. Section 9 of Executive Order 13636 defines critical infrastructure entities as organizations that control critical infrastructure in which 'a cybersecurity incident could reasonably result in catastrophic regional or national effects on public health or safety, economic security, or national security'.

[7] Borghard (2018, p. 1).

[8] Borghard (2018, p. 2).

[9] Rehman (2011, pp. 123–124).

[10] Rehman (2011, pp. 124–126). Accordingly, when a financial crisis occurs, an economic crisis ensues and governments are forced to review all expenditures, including defence plans and priorities.

[11] Rodriguez (2010, pp. 135–136).

[12] Rodriguez (2010, pp. 132–133).

[13] Malkawi (2011, p. 191). Malkawi points out how national security events, such as the September 11 terrorist attacks, result in governments adopting security measures that are antithetical to trade and investment.

It has been recognized that national security agencies and authorities are important to combat transnational financial crimes. The notion of threat finance was put forward by Kuester and it may be defined as 'any financial activity associated with actors, operations, or systems that threaten the security or stability of the U.S.'[14]

This chapter examines the nature and the extent of the term 'financial security' as used in judicial decision-making in China. After reviewing 242 court decisions, our research assists in gaining an insight into the use and implications of financial security that appear to underpin these decisions and assists in an enhanced understanding of the Chinese courts' judgments in the contemporary context as well as in the future.

This chapter proceeds in five parts. Section 2 provides the background to the term financial security as adopted in public discourse. Section 3 considers the use of such a term by the Supreme People's Court through its documents, decisions and reasons as well as by all levels of the court in their judicial reasoning. Section 4 analyses the reasons as to why such a term is used by the judiciary. Section 5 makes some observations as to the way in which the term is used. Section 6 sets out the conclusions.

2 The Adoption and Use of Financial Security in Public Discourse

In the past few years, it has been noticeable that financial security has entered public discourse in China and is frequently referred to by politicians. In 2014, President Xi Jinping proposed at the first meeting of the Chinese Communist Party National Security Committee the idea of Overall National Security. This expansive idea encompasses political security, sovereign security, military security, economic security, culture security, social security, technology security, information security, environmental security, resources security and nuclear security.[15] In November 2014, at the G20 Brisbane Summit, Present Xi Jinping included in his speech the aim of strengthening the global financial security network.[16]

In January 2016, at the CCP's Politics and Law Working Meeting, Meng Jianzhu, a member of the Chinese Communist Party (CCP) Politburo, elaborated on the subject of financial security.[17] Meng said that: 'Finance is the core of the modern economy.

---

[14] Kuester (2013, p. 75). Given the intersection between transnational financial crimes and threats to national security, foreign policy or the economy of the US, he argues, 'the tools of the national security community are important to worldwide efforts to combat these crimes'. Kuester explains how an exchange of influence between law enforcement authorities and national security agencies can be mutually beneficial for both parties.

[15] *Jianchi Zongti Guojia Anquanguan, Zou Zhongguo Tese Guojia Anquan Daolu* (坚持总体国家安全观 走中国特色国家安全道路) [Adhering to National Security and Following National Security with Chinese Characteristics], http://www.xinhuanet.com//politics/2014-04/15/c_1110253910.htm (accessed 20 February 2020).

[16] Sina News (2014).

[17] Meng Jianzhu was one of the most powerful politicians in China. See People.com.cn (2013).

Financial security is the key to economic security and social stability [...] FanYa, E-Zubao, DaDa Group's illicit fund-raising activities pose a threat to financial security and social stability [...]'. The introduction of the term has coincided with a period when the Chinese financial markets were plagued with various large-scale scandals.[18]

On 25 April 2017, members of the Politburo of the CCP gathered to discuss the theme of 'Maintaining National Financial Security'. President Xi expressed the view that:

Financial security is a key part of national security and an important foundation for stable economic development. Maintaining financial security is strategically essential for our national economic and social development [...]. The bottom line is to prevent systemic financial risks.

Financial security issues have thus become a recent theme of the Chinese national governance agenda. In July 2017, at the fifth National Financial Works Meeting, it was reiterated:

Finance is a key part of national competitiveness. *Financial security* is a key part of national security [...] deepen governance by rule of law in finance, safeguard national *financial security*, promote the development of the economy and finance [...] construct and complete a financial security line and risk management mechanisms.

It would appear from the way in which the term has been used by Chinese politicians and policy makers that financial security in the Chinese context should be referred to as national security in the context of the financial system.[19]

It is also important to ask how the Chinese legislative bodies incorporate this notion of financial security into their law-making agenda. The term financial security has not yet been embodied or defined in any laws enacted by the National People's Congress and its Standing Committee. In other words, this term has simply never appeared in any Chinese legislation.

However, at the same time, administrative regulations made by the State Council have indeed made reference to the term. Article 12 of the Regulation on Important State-owned Financial Institutions' Supervisory Committee (2000)[20] provides, for example:

If the board of supervisors finds, during the course of supervision and inspection, any business activities of the state-owned financial institution that may endanger *finance security*, result in asset losses or infringe upon the rights and interests of the

[18] See for detailed discussions on those scandals He (2018, p. 230).

[19] Similarly, successive US Administrations have identified the deterrence of threats to the international financial system as a national security goal: For over a decade, government administrations have emphasised the importance of deterring and combating threats to the international financial system by identifying it as a national security goal. As new financial threats emerge, government policies build upon and refine prior efforts. However, the policies remain roughly consistent with the goals of prior administrations. The common security concerns evidenced by National Security Strategy documents throughout the Clinton, Bush, and Obama Administrations have been to combat crimes within the international financial system.

[20] *Guoyou Zhongdian Jinrong Jigou Jianshihui Zhanxing Tiaolie* (国有重点金融机构监事会暂行条例) [Regulation on Important State-owned Financial Institutions' Supervisory Committee promulgated by the China Banking Regulatory Commission in 2000].

state, it should promptly submit a special report to the managing body of the board of supervisors, or may directly report to the State Council.

Article 2 of the Regulation on the Administration of Production Licences for Industrial Products (2005)[21] also makes an explicit reference to 'financial security':

The state shall implement the system of a production licence for the enterprises undertaking the production of the following important industrial products: tax cash registers, fake currency detectors, satellite television radio signal receiving facilities, wireless radio and television transmission equipment and other products concerning *financial security* and the safety of the quality of communications.

It is also significant that regulations made by agencies and ministries directly under the State Council have also made explicit reference to this term.

The China Banking Regulatory Commission (the CBRC) urges, in three regulatory instruments, those regulated to establish an information technology framework to meet the requirements of national financial security.[22]

The People's Bank of China (the PBoC) has similarly established rules requiring parties to take national financial security concerns into account. For example, in 2003, the PBoC listed maintaining financial security as one of the goals of anti-money laundering regulations.[23] In 2006, this regulation was revised and the reference to financial security was removed and replaced by financial order.

Another earlier example is the Provisional Rules on Financial Institutions' Security Works (1994) put forward by the Ministry of Public Security and the PBoC which provide that entities and individuals shall be rewarded if they are exemplary in safeguarding 'financial security'.[24]

---

[21] *Gongye Chanpin Shengchan Xukezheng Guanli Tiaolie* (工业产品生产许可证管理条例) [Regulation on the Administration of Production Licences for Industrial Products issued by the State Council in 2005].

[22] For example, *Zhongguo Jinchukou Yinhang Jiandu Guanli Banfa* (中国进出口银行监督管理办法) [Measures for the Supervision and Administration of the Export-Import Bank of China], promulgated by the China Banking Regulatory Commission (dissolved) on 15 November 2017.

According to Art. 33, the Export-Import Bank shall establish an information technology framework, an infrastructure and a network information system that meet the requirements of national financial security. See also Art. 32: the Agricultural Development Bank of China shall establish an information technology framework, an infrastructure and a network information system that meet the requirements of national financial security.

See also Art. 27: the China Development Bank shall establish an information technology framework, an infrastructure and a network information system that meet the requirements of national financial security.

[23] *Jinrong Jigou Fanxiqian Guiding* (金融机构反洗钱规定) [Provisions on Anti-money Laundering through Financial Institutions], promulgated by the People's Bank of China on 3 January 2003. According to Art. 1, the provisions were promulgated in accordance with the Law on the People's Bank of China and other laws and administrative regulations.

[24] *Jiceng Jinrong Danwei Zhian Baowei Gongzuo Zanxing Guiding* (基层金融单位治安保卫工作暂行规定) [Provisional Regulations on Local Financial Institutions' Security and Safeguarding Work], promulgated by the Ministry of Public Security and the People's Bank of China on 22 February 1994. According to Art. 34, the superior financial institution, the financial institution or the Public Security shall reward entities or individuals who have been exemplary in [...] 5) safeguarding financial security.

However, such references are limited, and the use of the term by law-making and regulatory authorities remains rare and non-systemic. The law governing financial activities, such as the law on Commercial Banks, Insurance law, and Securities law, has not incorporated the term, let alone defined it.

3 The Use of the Term by the Judiciary

While Chinese legislation and regulation are largely silent on the term, in stark contrast our study has shown that the Chinese courts have adopted this term in their reasoning. This section examines the use of the term financial security in Chinese judicial decisions.[25]

Since 2008, the Chinese courts have made reference to this term in several high profile cases. In 2008, in the highly publicised case of *Xu Ting—Case of Theft*, financial security was invoked as one of the key grounds under which the accused, Xu Ting, was convicted.[26] The High Court in Guangdong province held that due to a mechanical fault Xu Ting was able to use an ATM on 170 consecutive occasions to improperly withdraw a total of RMB 174,000, stealing the bank's property to the amount of RMB 173,826. This money was never recovered. Xu's conduct was held

---

[25] In recent years, the US courts have acknowledged the impact that the financial system has on national security. Judicial discussion in this area primarily revolves around the occurrence of illicit activities and transnational crimes, such as money laundering and terrorist financing. Given that these activities pose just as significant a threat to the US national economy and security, courts place weight on such considerations in their legal reasoning, particularly where legislation expressly requires this. In *United States v. Zarrab* 2016 WL 6820737, a defendant was accused of conducting international financial transactions and concealing from US banks the fact that the services were being provided to the Government of Iran. In this case, the Court expressly affirmed that the International Emergency Economic Powers Act (IEEPA) and the Iranian Transactions and Sanctions Regulations (ITSR) 'reflect the United States' interest in protecting and defending itself against […] Iran's sponsorship of international terrorism […] which implicate the national security, foreign policy, and the economy of the United States'. It was also accepted that the Iranian embargo was intended to deal with 'the unusual and extraordinary threat to the national security, foreign policy, and economy of the United States posed by the actions and policies of the Government of Iran'. Similarly, in *FBME Bank Ltd v. Lew* 125 F.Supp. 3d 109, the US Treasury Department's Financial Crimes Enforcement Network ('FinCEN') promulgated a Final Rule, which prevented a financial institution from continuing to do business in the US on the basis that it was of 'primary money laundering concern', and thus a threat to national security and the US financial system. In this case, the Court recognized the 'grave threat to national security that financing of terrorist activity and transnational crime poses'. The Court further emphasized that 'eliminating that financing, and extricating it from the U.S. financial system, are of paramount importance to the Government and the public'. Even so, the Court granted a preliminary injunction to the financial institution because it did not pose a current threat to the US financial system. The Court found that the financial institution was unable to access the US banking system, thus minimising the harm to the Government and the public from granting a temporary injunction.

[26] *Guangdongsheng Gaoji Renmin Fayuan* (广东省高级人民法院) [High Court of Guangdong Province], *Xingshi Caiding Shu* (刑事裁定书) [Criminal Order] (2008) *Yuegaofa Xingyi Zhongzi 170* (粤高法刑一终字第170号) [Criminal Case, Final Instance, No. 170].

to be tortious, not only infringing property rights and causing a loss to state property, 'but also threatening the stability of financial institutions, damaging financial security, and having a severe deleterious effect on society'.

In a 2017 case involving a listed company's dormant shareholder, *Yang Jingguo v. Ling Jinsheng Investment Dormant Shareholder Contract Dispute*, the Supreme People's Court relied on the ground of financial security to invalidate the contract in question.[27] The court reasoned:

The China Securities Regulatory Commission (the CSRC) regulates the securities markets pursuant to the Securities Law of the People's Republic of China. One of its functions is to protect the legal interests of retail investors. The CSRC requires listed companies to have a clear shareholding structure and to restrict the practice of dormant shareholdings. These are the prerequisite regulatory requirements for other requirements such as disclosure, related party transactions, and senior management's recusal. A failure to meet those requirements would harm the legal interest of retail investors, harm the stability of the capital markets and the security of transactions, harm *financial security* and social stability, and harm the public interest.

Both *Xu* and *Yang Jingguo* resulted in considerable public attention. However, the wider picture remains unclear. It is not known what approach is taken by the Chinese courts or the circumstances in which the courts have used financial security in their reasoning. From this section onwards, this chapter examines the documents of the Supreme Peoples' Court, including judicial interpretations, judicial directives or notices or minutes of meetings, speeches by officials, relevant reports, and other sources such as a judicial response and a typical case. The second stage of this study involves a scrutiny of all the cases that have been decided across all levels of courts where a reference has been made to the term 'financial security'.

3.1 Supreme People's Court's Judicial Documents

Our research has reviewed Supreme People's Court's judicial documents including judicial interpretations, judicial directives and notices, speeches by officials, meeting minutes and reports, and other judicial documents including judicial responses and typical cases.[28] In examining these judicial documents, it was evident that the relevant documents were released and concentrated in two periods, 2008–2012, and 2015-the present. During the 2008–2012 period, the Global Financial Crisis (GFC) persuaded the Supreme People's Court to prioritise financial security concerns, which has led to an increase in the use of the term. In the period from 2015 to the present, there have been stringent regulations imposed on the financial markets. The perceived

[27] *Zuigao Renmin Fayuan* (最高人民法院) [Supreme People's Court of China], *Minshi Caiding Shu* (民事裁定书) [Civil Order] (2014) *Minyi Zhongzi 30* (民一终字第30号) [Civil Case, Final Instance, No. 30].

[28] They all have varying degree of legal effects. See Guo (2018, pp. 170–192). See also, Huang (2012, pp. 124–129).

disorder and risks in the financial markets have highlighted the need for monitoring and managing the risks in finance.

Another finding, after reviewing the judicial documents, is that, while referring to the term of financial security, 27 out of those 31 judicial documents made reference to specific disputes. Those disputes cover financial crime (six documents), credit claims (five documents), non-performing credit claims (four documents), troubled financial institution resolution (four documents), private lending (three documents), and foreign exchange control (three documents). See Table 1 and Fig. 1. The Figure was compiled by the authors.

3.2 All Levels of the Courts' Decisions

A relevant qualification concerning the use of the data is that there has been limited access to all relevant court judgments. Since the introduction of the Supreme People's Court's Provisions on the Publication of Judgments on the Internet by the People's Courts in 2014,[29] the Peoples' Courts have made their judgments publicly available in a comprehensive and timely manner. This study has accessed judgments made available through http://wenshu.court.gov.cn. However, access to court judgments remains limited. For example, research shows that only 37.02% of all judgments were made available in 2014.[30] Decisions as to whether or not to publish a judgment are made arbitrarily.[31] Due to concerns as to the incompleteness of this platform, this study also accessed official publications by various courts including the Supreme Peoples' Court's Gazette[32] and the Guide on the Adjudication of Commercial Matters,[33] China Law Information by Peking University, and the official web pages of high courts and intermediate courts. The study cross-referenced judgments and ended up with a sample of Chinese judicial decisions consisting of 678 recent cases decided by four levels of the Chinese judiciary that contained the term 'financial security'.

The 678 judgments were reviewed individually and manually. Among these 678 judgments, our study excluded some judgments that do not use 'financial security' as part of the court's reasoning. In some cases, judges made reference to 'financial security' that was proposed by the parties but did not actually use the term in their own reasoning. For example, a commercial bank used the term to the effect that an adverse finding against the bank would affect national financial security. The court

---

[29] *Zhigao Renming Fayuan guanyu Renming Fayuan Zai Hulianwang Gongbu Caipan Wenshu de Guiding* (最高人民法院关于人民法院在互联网公布裁判文书的规定) [the Supreme People's Court's Provisions on the Publication of Judgments on the Internet issued by the People's Courts in 2014].

[30] OpenLaw (2016).

[31] Zhou Qiang, the then President of the Supreme People's Court, said that it was somewhat selective in deciding which judgments were to be made public. See Court.gov.cn (2016).

[32] *Zuigao Renming Fayuan Gongbao* (最高人民法院公报).

[33] *Shangshi Shengpan Zhidao* (商事审判指导).

Table 1 Supreme People's Court documents using the term financial security

The Supreme People's Court documents	Quantity	
Judicial interpretations	5	Rules on Adjudicating Cases in relation to Bills (2000) Circular of the Supreme People's Court on Relevant Issues concerning the Freeze and Deduction of Securities Trading Settlement Funds (2004) Rules on Adjudicating Cases in relation to Bills (2008) Reply of the Supreme People's Court to the Request for Instructions on the Unjust Enrichment Case of Guangzhou Zhonggu Investment Co., Ltd. v. Maoming Branch of Bank of China Co., Ltd., Guangzhou Office of China Orient Asset Management Corporation, and Shunwei United Asset Management Co., Ltd. (2010) Interpretations of the Supreme People's Court on Several Issues Concerning the Application of the Law of the People's Republic of China on Choice of Law for Foreign-Related Civil Relationships (I) (2012)

(continued)

Table 1 (continued)

The Supreme People's Court documents	Quantity	
Judicial directives and notices	12	Notice of the Supreme People's Court on Issuing Some Opinions of the Supreme People's Court on Providing Judicial Protection for the Construction of a Socialist Harmonious Society (2007) Notice of the Supreme People's Court on Issuing Several Opinions on Providing Judicial Guarantees and Legal Services for the Maintenance of National Financial Security and Comprehensive, Coordinated and Sustainable Economic Development (2008) Notice on the Judiciary Safeguarding a Steady Growth of the Economy (2008) Notice of the Supreme People's Court on Correctly Applying Interpretation II of Several Issues concerning the Contract Law of the People's Republic of China so as to Serve the Primary Objectives of the Party and the State (2009) Notice of the Supreme People's Court on Issuing Several Opinions on Providing Judicial Guarantees and Services for Accelerating the Transformation of the Means of Economic Development (2010) Guidelines on the Judiciary Safeguarding Works Preventing Financial Risks and Promoting Financial Reforms (2012) Notice of the Supreme People's Court on Several Issues Concerning Strengthening Civil Trials and Effectively Guaranteeing the People's Livelihood under the Current Situation (2012) Guiding Opinions of the Supreme People's Court on People's Courts' Provision of Judicial Protection for Acquisitions, Mergers and the Reorganization of Enterprises (2014) Opinions of the Supreme People's Court on Maximizing the Role of Trials to Promote the Development of New Urbanization Nationwide (2014) Opinions of the Supreme People's Court on Providing Judicial Services and Guarantees for the Coordinated Development of Beijing-Tianjin-Hebei (2016) Opinions of the Supreme People's Court on Providing Judicial Services and Safeguards for the Yangtze River Economic Belt Development(2016) Notice of the Supreme People's Court on Issuing Several Opinions on Further Strengthening Trial Finance-related Cases (2017)

(continued)

Table 1 (continued)

The Supreme People's Court documents	Quantity	
Speeches by officials	8	Tang Dehua's Speech on the Adjudication of Civil Cases (2000) Li Guoguang's Speech on the Adjudication of Civil Cases (2000) Xiao Yang's Speech on the national high courts' presidents' conference (2000) Xi Xiaoming's Speech on the adjudication of securities companies' liquidation cases (2005) Xiao Yang's Speech on the Adjudication of Civil Cases (2007) Xi Xiaoming's Speech on the Adjudication of Civil and Commercial Cases (2007) Xi Xiaoming's Speech on the Adjudication of Financial Crisis Commercial Cases (2009) Several Specific Issues by the Supreme People's Court on the Current Hearing of Commercial Cases (2015)
Meeting minutes and reports	2	National conference on the adjudication of financial crime (2001) Report of the Supreme People's Court on the Work of Civil Cases (2010)
Others (judicial responses and typical cases)	4	Key points of the Adjudication of Civil and Commercial Cases (2006) Key points of the Work of the People's Courts in 2009 (2009) Key points of the Work of the People's Courts in 2016 (2016) Ten Model Cases regarding the Hearing of Bankruptcy Cases according to the Law and the Promotion of Supply-Side Structural Reform (2016)

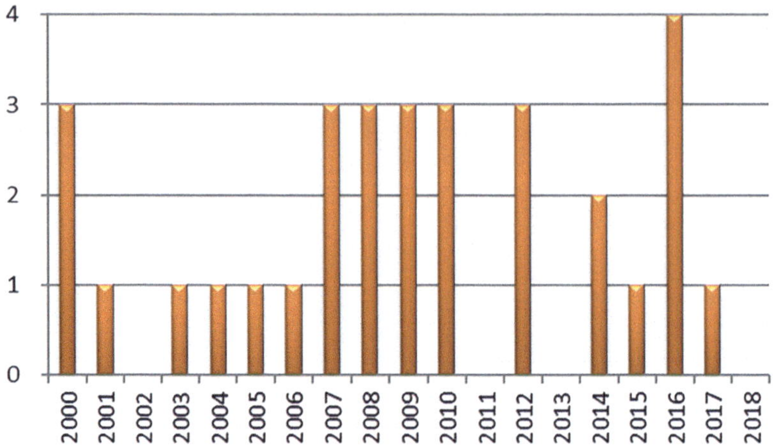

Fig. 1 Number of the Supreme People's Court documents using the term 'financial security' from 2000 to 2018

did not accept that argument.[34] In other cases, 'financial security' was just a name or a title and was not relevant to the substance of the case in dispute. For example, a party to one case was named as Qingdao Kangqiao Financial Security Print Ltd,[35] or, as part of the evidence, a document was put to the court which was entitled 'Financial Security Safeguard Documents', or a certificate was called a 'Financial Security Qualification Certificate'.[36] Excluding those cases, this study ended up with a total of 242 relevant judgments.

The first finding is that all four judicial levels have referred to the term financial security in their reasoning (Table 2). With regard to the distribution of decisions since 2006, most of the available decisions are from 2014 and thereafter (Table 3). This is largely attributable to the fact that the introduction of the Supreme People's Court's Provisions on the Publication of Judgments on the Internet by the People's Courts in 2014 has made it possible for the Peoples' Courts to make their judgments publicly available. The earliest relevant case found was a 2006 case where a bank had failed to recognize a forged bank card and incurred a loss as a result and the

---

[34] *Gansusheng Gaoji Renmin Fayuan* (甘肃省高级人民法院) [High People's Court of Gansu Province], *Minshi Panjue Shu* (民事判决书) [Civil Judgment] (2015) *Ganmin Zhongzi 207* (甘民二终字第207号) [Civil Case, Final Instance, No. 207].

[35] *Qingdaoshi Zhongji Renmin Fayuan* (青岛市中级人民法院) [Intermediate People's Court of Qingdao Municipality], *Minshi Panjue Shu* (民事判决书) [Civil Judgment] (2014) *Qingmin Yizhongzi 157* (青民一终字第157号) [Labour Case, Final Instance, No. 157].

[36] *Langfangshi Zhongji Renmin Fayuan* (廊坊市中级人民法院) [Intermediate People's Court of Langfang Municipality], *Minshi Panjue Shu* (民事判决书) [Civil Judgment] (2016) Ji 10 Minzhong 1719 (冀10民终1719号) [Civil Case, Appeal Instance, No. 1719]. See also, *Kaifengshi Zhongji Renmin Fayuan* (开封市中级人民法院) [Intermediate People's Court of Kaifeng Municipality], *Minshi Panjue Shu* (民事判决书) [Civil Judgment] (2016) *Yu 02 Minzhong 2899* (豫02民终2899号) [Civil Case, Appeal Instance, No. 2899].

Table 2 Distribution of judgments across four levels of the Chinese judicial hierarchy as of the end of Nov. 2018

	Sample judgments	Valid judgments
Supreme People's Court	15	10
High People's Court	67	22
Intermediate People's Court	208	73
Basic People's Court	388	137

Table 3 Distribution of judgments across four levels of the judicial hierarchy from 2006 to 2018

	Supreme People's Court	High People's Court	Intermediate People's Court	Basic People's Court
2018	1	6	8	7
2017	6	5	9	15
2016	2	2	19	27
2015		3	8	22
2014			19	23
2013		1		35
2012		2	4	4
2011		1	4	1
2010		1		
2009	1		2	
2008		1		2
2007				
2006				1
Total	10	22	73	137

court acknowledged financial security concerns as a result of technological developments.[37] It was also found that judges use 'financial security' most frequently in two types of cases: illegal futures transactions (41 examples) and defrauding loan transactions (77 examples).

[37] *Taizhoushi Luqiaoqu Renmin Fayuan* (台州市路桥区人民法院) [People's Court of Luqiao District, Taizhou Municipality], *Minshi Panjue Shu* (民事判决书) [Civil Judgment] (2006) *Luminer Chuzi 750* (路民二初字第750号) [Civil Case, First Instance, No. 750].

4 Why Do Courts and Judges Use the Term Financial Security?

Based on the sample decisions, there was, perhaps surprisingly, no attempt by the judiciary in any of the identified 242 cases to define the term 'financial security'. In individual judgments, the notion of financial security has not been clarified. At the same time, the Supreme People's Court made no attempt to define the term. For example, in the 2017 Notice of the Supreme People's Court on Issuing the Several Opinions on Further Strengthening the Adjudication of Finance-related Cases (Notice 2017),[38] financial security was mentioned on seven occasions. More specifically, Notice 2017 states that 'financial security is an important part of national security', and 'adjudication is to maintain national financial security'. The term appeared for the third time as part of a sub-title to 'mitigate financial risks and maintain financial security'. Notice 2017 also referred to financial security in cases that are typical in the context of the financial markets. Notice 2017 highlighted the risks in the real estate markets affecting financial stability and financial security, as well as financial security issues in relation to cross-border investment activities. There was no further clarification of financial security in those contexts. As a result, the term is left undefined, whether intentionally or unintentionally.

4.1 The Role of the Judiciary Within the State Apparatus

China's legal institutions are part of the state apparatus. Their roles are consistent with the ideology of the State and are subordinate to the leadership of the CCP.[39]

The role of the judiciary in any jurisdiction evolves over time. In the United States, in federalist times, the judiciary was initially seen as the least dangerous institution as it had 'no influence over either the sword or the purse'.[40] The courts then acquired the crucial authority of judicial review to check and balance the actions of the government (or the executive) and the legislature.[41]

In China, the judiciary is unambiguously a political institution that is subordinate to the Chinese Communist Party and the government.[42] While the notion of judicial independence has previously interested some Chinese judges and the courts, it is now widely regarded as a 'Western trap'.[43] This does not prevent Chinese judges from highlighting the importance of judiciary authority. In China, the assertion of judiciary power is not according to the American (or Australian) model of gaining

[38] *Guanyu Jingyibu Jiaqiang Jinrong Shengpan Gongzuo de Ruogan Yijian* (关于进一步加强金融审判工作的若干意见).

[39] China Court (2019).

[40] A. Hamilton, Federalist No. 78, 1788.

[41] *Marbury v. Madison*, 5 US 137 (1803).

[42] People.com.cn (2019).

[43] China News (2014).

the power of judicial review to act as a check and balance but rather according to using or sharing the common language with the state.[44]

Financial security in the Chinese context is not a legal term. From a socio-linguistic viewpoint, judges use language to express their identity or 'class aspiration', and seek to protect or increase their power.[45] The courts and the judges have adopted the term as part of their regular language.

The term 'financial security' itself in plain Chinese denotes some level of importance at the social and national level. It has become a part of legal reasoning. The use of the term by the Chinese judiciary could be considered as a means to strengthen the authority of the law.[46] It has the effect of elevating a relatively minor day-to-day dispute to a national level of importance. For example, in the case of *Xu Ying and Qing Dao Bank Asset Management Contract*, the High Court in Shandong Orovince held that '[...] in order to maintain national financial security and stability [...]'. This case involved a civil dispute concerning an asset management contract between an individual and a bank. The amount in dispute was RMB 212,000 which was negligible.[47] Therefore it was unclear as to why the term 'financial security' had any relevance to the facts of the case. It was seemingly intended to provide gravitas to the court's decision by linking it to concerns of financial security. The link between the facts of the case and financial security is difficult to discern.

It is suggested that there is an element of self-interest in that the courts and the judges are keen to adopt the term and sharing this language with the government.

4.2 Exercise of Judicial Discretion

Legal rules can be ambiguous and incomplete. The judiciary and the judges in any legal system have to resort to the exercise of discretion in their decision-making process. Boundaries need to be set to avoid a potential abuse or misuse of discretion. This especially arises in an environment where emphasis is placed on the legal reasoning in written decisions, and the courts have to demonstrate the appropriateness of the exercise of their discretion. In general, the courts and judges have to justify their decisions to these parties: the parties involved and the immediate senior (appellant) court. The courts and the judges have to persuade the parties involved that the legal decision is 'right' even if it is not the outcome that they were seeking. Furthermore, the judges are anxious to avoid the alarming prospect of an appellate court overturning a decision that may adversely affect the performance or standing of individual judges.[48]

---

[44] Ji (2006, pp. 4–20).

[45] Deckert and Vikers (2011, p. 44).

[46] Mattila (2006, p. 39).

[47] *Zaozhuangshi Shizhongqu Renmin Fayuan* (枣庄市市中区人民法院) [People's Court of Shizhong District, Zaozhuang Municipality], *Minshi Panjue Shu* (民事判决书) [Civil Judgment] (2016) *Lu 0402 Minchu 2823* (鲁0402民初2823号) [Commercial Case, First Instance, No. 2823].

[48] Ai (2008, pp. 98–151).

This study found that financial security forms some part of the legal reasoning of some judges to help justify the outcome. For example, in the civil case of *Plaintiff Ya Xiucheng and Defendant Liu Mingying and the Jiangsu Mei Zhi Lin Equity Investment Fund Management Ltd Property Dispute*,[49] the contention in question was the application of 'fault and loss cancel out' principle (similar to joint liability) under section 26 of the Tort Liability Law. The court ruled that this principle did not apply in the particular circumstances of this case. It explained:

Under Article 26 of the Tort Liability Law, where the victim of a tort is also at fault, the liability of the tortfeasor may be reduced. The courts shall determine the applicability of this section. If the tortfeasor deliberately causes harm or is at material fault, and the victim is at immaterial fault, then the tortfeasor's liability might not be reduced. In this case, the plaintiff was a financial consumer who lacked financial knowledge and did not understand the suitability of the fund product. However, the defendant Mei Zhi Lin Ltd failed to comply with the disclosure of obligations given the risks of the fund product and the circumstances of the plaintiff, and failed to make sure that the plaintiff was fully aware of the risks when entering into the transaction. Thus the court found that the defendant was at substantial fault. Therefore, to ensure that financial institutions comply with disclosure obligations, to maintain the confidence of financial consumers, to protect national *financial security* and stability, the 'fault and loss cancel out' principle does not apply, thus the defendant is liable to compensate the losses suffered by the plaintiff.

It is unclear in this judgment whether national financial security considerations would actually have any legal bearing in a civil dispute regarding a fund management product.

Another pertinent civil case, *Ningbo Libaidai Investment Advisory Ltd, Liu Zhongwei, Wang Wenze, Zheng Xiangzhong—the Case of Illegally Conducting Business*,[50] which was published in the Supreme People's Court Gazette, is also illustrative. This case concerned whether the accused had committed an offence by selling equity in a non-listed company to the general public. Under the Criminal Code, the accused only commits a crime if his conduct is severe. In deciding that the conduct was 'severe', the judges in this case considered that the conduct was detrimental to social stability and financial security as well as the amount of money involved. The judges used the reasoning of financial security in determining the severity of the conduct. In contrast, it is worth noting that Chinese securities law and regulation have so far not recognized the financial security aspect in cases involving the selling of equity in a non-listed company to the public. The judges in this case took a different approach.

---

[49] *Nanjingshi Xuanwuqu Renmin Fayuan* (南京市玄武区人民法院) [People's Court of Nanjing City, Xuanwu Municipality] *Minshi Panjue Shu* (民事判决书) [Civil Judgment] (2016) *Su 0102 Minch 3076* (2016) 苏0102民初3076号 [Commercial Case, First Instance, No. 3076].

[50] *Zhonghua Renmin Gongheguo Zuigao Renmin Fayuan Gongbao* (中华人民共和国最高人民法院公报) [the Supreme Peoples' Court's Gazette] *183 qi* (183期) [Issue 183].

4.3 Making Rules for Activities in the Financial Markets

In theory, there are two sources of rules for the financial markets: Parliament-made law and judge-made law. Given the dynamic and fast changing nature of financial markets and products, it is unlikely that Parliament would be able to promulgate rules in a timely and complete manner. As opposed to the judiciary in a civil law jurisdiction, judges in common law jurisdictions tend to be more active in making rules which affect the development of national and regional financial markets.[51] Judgments in a common law jurisdiction could be a source of law, and this fact accommodates or adapts to the needs of a changing economy, and this prompts the development of a financial market.[52] Research has shown that common law jurisdictions have more developed financial markets that tend to provide better protection to investors.[53] Through lawsuits, judges in a common law jurisdiction have been able to restrict insiders from harming investors and this ability is considered to be a 'smell test' in recognizing insiders' behaviour that is detrimental to the interests of investors.[54]

By law, legislative authority in China is vested in the National Peoples' Congress (the NPC) and the Standing Committee of the NPC, and Chinese judges have no formal authority to make rules. However, Chinese judges are in fact active in making rules. In a time of rapid social and economic changes, Chinese courts play an active role in interpreting and making law.[55] Judges have to make up the rules in order to fill in the legislative and regulatory gaps and omissions by the NPC and its Standing Committee, as well as other authorities. The example of financial security illustrates this point. The judicial documents and judgments examined as part of this study resorted to financial security as a means to make new rules.

In a 2015 example, a number of securities companies encountered financial problems. This was against the backdrop that China did not have laws of insolvency for financial institutions. Under the direction of the Supreme People's Court, the courts implemented a 'three termination' policy under which such cases are not accepted for adjudication, or are adjourned for adjudication, and the enforcement of judgments in such cases is suspended. The then Vice-President, Xi Xiaoming, stated that the introduction of the 'three termination' policy is for the purposes of 'the courts assisting the government to maintain financial order, maintain financial security, [and] maintain social stability'.[56]

Another case in point is that of *Jing Zuoyi and Shenzheng Qianhai Huifeng Jiayu Art Investment Management Ltd, Guangxi Huifeng Culture Corporate Group*

---

[51] The first tier financial centres including New York, London, Hongkong and Singapore are all common law jurisdictions, in which judge-made laws make up a considerable part of the rules governing the financial markets. See The Global Financial Centres Index 24 (2018), https://www.longfinance.net/media/documents/GFCI_24_final_Report.pdf.

[52] Posner (1973), Merryman (1985).

[53] La Porta et al. (1998).

[54] Coffee (2001).

[55] Chenguang (2006, pp. 524–549).

[56] China Insolvency Law (2014).

Contract Dispute.[57] In this case, the court extended the definition of securities and the laws relating to securities became applicable in this case:

The product in question is dividing a piece of artwork into intangible equal portions and selling those portions to the investors; in turn, the investors in those portions are able to trade the portions in an open market. The underlying transaction is conducted via means of securitization, and is of a financial nature and risky. This is of concern for national economic and *financial security* and social security. Therefore the transaction should be pre-approved by the relevant authority, and be conducted in designated markets.

The term 'securities' under the Chinese Securities Law includes stock, corporate debenture, and other securities determined by the State Council, as well as government debentures and public funds invested in securities.[58] As a result, the product in dispute in this case would not ordinarily have been considered as securities. This case involved the judges exercising their discretion and consequently broadening the scope of securities and relying on the concept of financial security in order to do so. This is a way for judges to make rules governing the financial markets and to try to ensure that the rules keep up with the rapidly developing nature of the financial markets. It is interesting to draw a comparison with the way in which 'securities' are defined in the US. The Securities Act 1933 does not prescribe what are securities. Instead, case law, through cases such as *SEC v. Howey Co.,* set out exactly what securities are.[59]

4.4 Significance in Evidence

In the case of *Wang Yaping and Pingan Bank Ltd, Beijing Branch-Bank Card Dispute*, the court gave particular weight to a piece of evidence as a result of national financial security considerations.[60] The court explained:

Banking transactional records concern national *financial security* and are subject to multiple layers of regulation. Therefore these records are very reliable. Since there

[57] *Shenzhen Qianhai Hezuoqu Renmin Fayuan* (深圳前海合作区人民法院) [People's Court of Shenzhen City, Qianhai Municipality] *Minshi Panjue Shu* (民事判决书) [Civil Judgment] (2016) *Ao 0102 Minch 380* (2016) 粤0391民初380号) [Commercial Case, First Instance, No. 380].

[58] *Zhonghua Renmin Gongheguo Zhenquan Fa* (中华人民共和国证券法) [Securities Law of the People's Republic of China], first promulgated by the Standing Committee of the National People's Conference on 29 December 1998. The law underwent major amendments in 2005 and 2019, and relatively minor changes in 2004, 2013 and 2014. The 2019 amendment will take effect from 1 March 2020. Hence it is customarily abbreviated as the 2005 Securities Law. See Art. 2: The present Law shall apply to the issuance and trading of stocks, corporate bonds as well as any other securities as lawfully recognized by the State Council within the territory of the People's Republic of China.

[59] *SEC v. Howey Co.*, 328 US 293 (1946).

[60] *Beijingshi Xichengqu Renmin Fayuan* (北京市西城区人民法院) [People's Court of Xicheng District, Beijing Municipality], *Minshi Panjue Shu* (民事判决书) [Civil Judgment] (2016) *Jing 0102 Minchu 32738* (京0102民初32738号) [Civil case, First Instance, No. 32738].

is no evidence that PingAn Bank forged Wang Yaping's credit card numbers and card information, the veracity of the evidence (in the form of transactional records) presented by the bank is confirmed.

This judgment again raises the issue as to the relevance of banking records for the concept of financial security. However, by somewhat creatively resorting to the argument of financial security, the court was able to place probative weight on banking records. While banking records are ordinarily of a private nature, in this case they were given considerable legal effect.

4.5 Judicial Recommendations

In the case of *Industrial and Commercial Bank of China Limited, Guiyang Zhongxi Sub-branch and Zhang Li Financial Loan Contract Dispute*, the court ruled that the claims made by the bank had not been substantiated by the evidence. The court urged the bank to conduct its business in a diligent manner:

Banks are financial institutions that affect the social and economic development of society. They have an obligation, in conducting their business, to verify accounts and manage financial risks, and to maintain economic and *financial security*.[61]

In the case of *Industrial and Commercial Bank of China Limited, Jining Sub-branch and Jiang Tao, Ma Yun Unjust Enrichment Dispute*, the court ruled that there were financial risks when the bank extended its credit to the extent that it affected the operation of the business.[62] As a state-owned financial institution, the bank should enhance internal control mechanisms, standardize operational procedures, avoid losses of state-owned assets and ensure national financial security.

The role of Chinese judges is not confined to adjudicating and resolving disputes. It is evident that, based on our study, they perceive and extend their role to that of a public-policy maker. This approach is consistent with the Supreme People's Court's view that 'people's courts should be proactive, and should extend beyond the role of a mere adjudicator'.[63] One of the goals of the Chinese judiciary is to resolve disputes and participate in social management.[64]

---

[61] *Guiyangshi Zhongji Renmin Fayuan* (贵阳市中级人民法院) [Intermediate People's Court of Guiyang Municipality], *Minshi Panjue Shu* (民事判决书) [Civil Judgment] (2018) *Qian 01 Minchu 367* (黔01民初367号) [Civil case, First Instance, No. 367].

[62] *Wulanchabushi Zhongji Renmin Fayuan* (乌兰察布市中级人民法院) [Intermediate People's Court of Wulanchabu Municipality], *Minshi Panjue Shu* (民事判决书) [Civil Judgment] (2009) *Wumin Chuzi 25* (乌民初字第25号) [Civil case, First Instance, No. 25].

[63] *Zuigao Renmin Fayuan Guanyu Jiaqiang Sifa Jianyi Gongzuo de Yijian de Tongzhi* (最高人民法院关于加强司法建议工作的意见的通知) [Notice of the Supreme People's Court of China on the Opinion of Enhancing Judicial Construction] issued by the Supreme People's Court on 15 March 2012.

[64] One noteworthy example is that in a competition called 'National Judicial Suggestions' organised by the Supreme People's Court in 2012. The Intermediate People's Court of Yancheng in Jiangsu Province was rewarded for being one of the top ten suggestions with its article 'Judicial Suggestions

It is common practice that Chinese courts make judicial recommendations. The courts have also developed a uniform approach in making judicial recommendations. There is generally a separate document entitled Judicial Recommendations which is appended to the individual judgment. The layout of such a document is also formalized.[65]

4.6 That's What Other Judges Do

The use of the uniform production of judgments is not uncommon in other jurisdictions. This is often referred to as increasing efficiency in the operation of the courts and the judicial system.[66] The use of templates in the judgments examined as part of this study appears to be an uncommon practice. In the context of the use of financial security, it is likely that judges have to rely on a prescriptive or at least standard document. They have achieved a degree of uniformity in their judgments and reasoning.

There were 242 relevant judgments as part of this study. As mentioned earlier the study shows that judges use 'financial security' most frequently in two types of cases: illegal futures transactions (41 examples) and defrauding loan transactions (77 examples). This raises the question as to why this term is most frequently used in these two types of cases. There are other likely illicit activities such as soliciting public money that would produce a more adverse impact on financial security than illicit future transactions. Similarly, activities such as currency forgery would have a more severe impact than defrauding loans.

It is therefore significant to ask what prompted the judges in cases of illegal futures transactions and defrauding loan transactions to use the term 'financial security'.

In the study, it is revealing that judges used very similar (if not identical) wording and references to financial security in cases involving illegal futures transactions. As one typical judgment set out:

---

on Resolving Financial Operation Risks and Optimising City-wide Financial Environment'. The reason for its award was that 'it is imperative to enhance city-wide financial security activities; it is significantly important to maintain financial order and security; the Intermediate People's Court of Yancheng targets resolving financial risks and proposes judicial suggestions to the municipal party committee and the municipal government'. As such, the reference to 'financial security' in the judicial suggestions promotes and justifies the 'matching' of the exercise of judicial power and the national governance in a broad sense. See China Court (2013).

[65] China Court (2018).

[66] As to judicial economy, it is the efficient management of litigation so as to minimize the duplication of effort. It also avoids wasting the judiciary's time and resources. For example, a court may consolidate two cases for trial to save the court and parties from having two trials. It may also order a separate trial on certain issues for the purpose of avoiding a later trial that would be more complex and time consuming. The promotion of judicial economy is the primary reason that interlocutory review is not favoured. *Butorac v. Fuddruckers Inc.*, 1988 US Dist. LEXIS 11144 (D. Kan. Sept. 22, 1988).

[...] Without the approval of the State Council or the futures regulatory authorities authorized by the State Council, no entities or individual can set up a futures market or trade in futures in any other form. Because futures transactions are of a financial and risky nature, they concern economic and *financial security* and social stability, and they must be conducted on approved markets and follow rules and regulations. [The law] does not explicitly state that non-compliance would lead to the invalidity of the transaction. But if a transaction that is non-compliant and was conducted on a market that was not approved by the authorities is ruled as being valid, it is likely that it would make futures transactions disorderly and trigger financial risks and affect social stability [...].[67]

Similar wording also appeared in a Supreme People's Court judgment in an appellate case, namely, *Liu Qiong, Shanxi Metal Markets Ltd Sales Contract Dispute*.[68] Similarly, in the 77 defrauding loan transaction cases, almost all of the judges used the following wording and references to financial security:

The court rules that the defendant, by means of [...], defrauded the financial institution in the form of loans, disrupted financial order, harmed *financial security*, and caused the financial institution to suffer grave losses. Thus the defendant committed the crime of defrauding loans.

The 77 relevant cases occurred throughout a 12-year period. It is difficult to determine how the standard wording or reference came about in the first place. Judging by similar wording, it is likely that the term financial security was used by a particular judge and has been faithfully followed ever since.

5 Key Observations

Our research has shown that the term 'financial security' in Chinese judicial considerations remains opaque and unclear and its application appears to be based on a defined (or at least broad) policy basis rather than on any clear and consistent legal basis. The term has been used in cases ranging from bank card theft, investment contract disputes to operating a financial business without a licence, as well as the liquidation of a financial institution. The judges form their own views as to what amounts to financial security and its role in a particular case or situation. While most

[67] See example in *Zhong shuijing yu Hunan Jiufeng Guoji Shangpin Xianhuo Jiaoyi Shichang Youxian Gongsi Weituo Licai Hetong Jiufeng* (张水金与湖南久丰国际商品现货交易市场有限公司委托理财合同纠纷案) [Zhang Shui Jiang and Hunan Jiufeng International Goods Trade Ltd Wealth Management Contract Dispute] *Zhejiang Anji Renmin Fayuan* (浙江省安吉县人民法院) [People's Court of Zhejiang Province, Anji Municipality] *Minshi Panjue Shu* (民事判决书) [Civil Judgment] (2017) *Zhe 0523 Minch 5902* [Commercial Case, First Instance, No. 5902].

[68] *Zuigao Renmin Fayuan* (最高人民法院) [Supreme People's Court of China], *Minshi Caiding Shu* (民事裁定书) [Civil Order] (2014) *Zuigaofa Minshen 4790* (最高法民申4790号) [Civil case, Appeal Instance, No. 4790].

judges have understood financial security in the light of its national importance, some have also used the term in the context of the validity of a civil contract.[69]

There are two key provisional findings that emerge from this study to date.

5.1 *Differential Treatment of Private and State Property Rights*

The first main concern is whether the Chinese courts can extend the equal protection of different property rights. In 2014, the Supreme People's Court issued Guidelines on the Equal Protection of Non-state Property Rights and Encouraging the Development of the Non-state Economic Sector[70] which apply to 'adjudicating financial loans, financial leasing, private financing cases involving non-state entities by law, and encouraging non-state entity financing by law'. In 2019, the second meeting of the CCP's Rule by Law Committee emphasised the 'equal protection of different property right entities by law'.[71]

In 2017, the Minister for Finance made repeated references to the role of state-owned financial institutions and state-owned capital in maintaining national financial security. The Minister elaborated in one speech:

State-owned assets in financial institutions are the key guarantee to advance national modernization and to maintain national *financial security*. It is the important tangible political foundation for the development of the Party and the State. Stronger and superior and bigger state-owned financial corporations are the important force in promoting the national economy, supporting the implementation of the national strategy, and protecting national *financial security* [...]. Through providing capital to stated-owned large commercial banks, policy banks and financial development institutions, stated-owned capital is gravitating towards industries that are affecting the national economy and national *financial security*, and also increasing the ability of the state-owned financial institutions to serve the economy and avoid and mitigate risks.[72]

In 2018, the CCP and the State Council issued Guidelines on the Management of State-owned Capital (the Guidelines).[73] The Guidelines open with the statement that 'State-owned capital is a guarantee for national modernization and the maintenance

---

[69] *Shanghaishi Minhangqu Renmin Fayuan* (上海市闵行区人民法院) [People's Court of Minhang District, Shanghai Municipality], *Minshi Panjue Shu* (民事判决书) [Civil Judgment] (2011) *Minminwu (Min) Chuzi 905* (闵民五(民)初字第905号) [Civil case, First Instance, No. 905].

[70] *Zhuigao Renmin Fayuan Guanyu Yifa Pingdeng Baohu Feigongyouzhi Jingji Chujing Feigongyouzhi Jingji Jiankang Fazhang de Yijian* (最高人民法院关于依法平等保护非公有制经济促进非公有制经济健康发展的意见).

[71] Xinhua Net (2019).

[72] *Guowuyuan Guanyu 2017 Nian Jinrong Qiye Guoyou Zichan de Zhuangxiang Baogao* (国务院关于2017年度金融企业国有资产的专项报告).

[73] *Guanyu Wanshan Guoyou Jinrong Ziben Guanli de Zhidao Yijian* (关于完善国有金融资本管理的指导意见).

of national financial security, and is the material and political cornerstone of our Party and national development'.

This raises the question of whether state property rights receive preferential treatment. Some Chinese scholars believe that private property rights are the source of threats endangering national financial security.[74] The prevention of the privatisation of the financial sector and continued State control is the means employed in China to maintain national financial security. The Supreme People's Court has historically considered protecting state property rights as one of the judicial policies to promote national financial security. The then vice-President of the Supreme People's Court, Li Guoguang, stated that all courts, within the boundaries of judicial interpretation, should act to best protect state property rights in matters such as the validity of contracts and statutory limitations.[75]

This raises the question of how does the equal protection of different property rights apply in cases involving the use of 'financial security'?

The study and the cases examined suggest that judges do not explicitly take different property rights into consideration in their legal reasoning. One of the findings of the study is that state-owned commercial banks have argued that a judgment unfavourable to or a judgment lien over the bank's assets would pose adverse effects for national financial security. There is no evidence that the courts have attached any weight to such arguments. National financial security has not been a factor in cases where the banks have been successful. Interestingly, on one occasion this national financial security argument was successfully used against a state-owned bank. In this case, the court ruled that:

China Agriculture Bank, a state-owned financial institution, representing national interests, should comply with rules and regulations, and maintain *financial security*. Due to its lax verification process and lax management, the bank should be responsible for the fact that it lost creditor rights as a result of the statute of limitations having expired.[76]

The equal protection of state and non-state property rights is mentioned in several judicial documents. In 2014, in the Guidelines on Courts Providing a Legal Avenue for Corporate Mergers and Acquisitions,[77] the Supreme People's Court stated that the equal protection of the non-state economy is a judicial goal as well maintaining financial security:

A corporate merger and acquisition does not only affect the company involved, but also impacts on a series of issues such as the equal protection of the state and non-state economy, the prevention of losses of national assets, and the maintenance of *financial security* [...] and social stability.

---

[74] Chinese Academy of Social Sciences (2016), pp. 35–41.

[75] Zhao (2002, p. 12).

[76] *Gansusheng Gaoji Renmin Fayuan* (甘肃省高级人民法院) [High People's Court of Gansu Province], *Minshi Panjue Shu* (民事判决书) [Civil Judgment] (2009) *Ganmin Zaizhongzi 4* (甘民再终字第4号) [Civil case, Appeal Instance, No. 4].

[77] *Zuigao Renmin Fayuan Guanyu Renmin Fayuan Wei Qiye Jianbingchongzu Tigong Sifa Baozhang de Zhidaoyijian* (最高人民法院关于人民法院为企业兼并重组提供司法保障的指导意见).

The study also reveals that in cases concerning the transfer of non-performing financial assets of state-owned commercial banks, the courts do resort to the term financial security and tend to treat state property rights differently.

In the 2009 case of *Shengyang Yinsheng Tiancheng Investment Management Ltd v. Shenyang Office of China Huarong Asset Management Ltd—Credit Rights Transfer Contract Dispute*, both the trial court and the appellant court ruled that one part of the contract was invalid because the underlying creditor rights were non-existent. The Supreme People's Court overruled the decisions of the lower courts on the basis that:

The purchase and disposal of non-performing loans of banks by financial asset management companies is crucial to national *financial security* and is of a strong policy nature. The transfer agreement in this case is not the same as the one between parties in a civil law relationship. The transfer in question is characterized by high risks, high returns, and is different from transactions that are ordinarily subject to market rules.[78]

A similar reasoning can be seen in the 2010 case of *Qinhai Kuilun Paint Chemical Ltd v. Qinhai Himalaya Biological Projects Ltd— Loan Dispute* case.[79] In a 2018 case, in the context of an asset management company disposing of a bank's non-performing assets, the court was faced with the issue of whether a public notice in a newspaper by the asset management company to its debtor would suspend the statutory limitation period. According to Article 85 of the Civil Procedure Law, the notice should be directly served on the debtor.[80] The court used 'financial security' in its reasoning to uphold the validity of the notice in the newspaper. The court observed:

[…] to support national financial reforms, to avoid losses of state-owned assets, to ensure the disposal of non-performing assets, and to lower costs, […] for all those purposes, the asset management company shall be allowed to use more flexible and less costly means to collect debts.[81]

The public notice in a newspaper was accepted as a valid means of serving the debtor which was otherwise not lawfully allowed.

---

[78] *Zuigao Renmin Fayuan* (最高人民法院) [Supreme People's Court], *Minshi Panjue Shu* (民事判决书) [Civil Judgment] (2009) *Mintizi 129* (民提字第125号) [Civil case, Appeal Instance, No. 125].

[79] *Qinghaisheng Gaoji Renmin Fayuan* (青海省高级人民法院) [High People's Court of Qinghai Province], *Minshi Panjue Shu* (民事判决书) [Civil Judgment] (2010) *Qing Miner Zhongzi 6* (青民二终字第6号) [Civil case, Final Instance, No. 6].

[80] According to Art. 92 of the Civil Procedure Law, a public notice is only applicable where the whereabouts of the person to be served is unknown or the service of process is not possible by other means as set out in the law. In this case, the debtor's whereabouts was known. See *Zhonghua Renmin Gongheguo Minshi Susong Fa* (中华人民共和国民事诉讼法) [Civil Procedure Law of the People's Republic of China], first promulgated by the Standing Committee of the National People's Congress on 9 April 1991.

[81] *Yibinshi Zhongji Renmin Fayuan* (宜宾市中级人民发现) [Intermediate People's Court of Yibin Municipality], *Minshi Panjue Shu* (民事判决书) [Civil Judgment] (2018) *Chuan 15 Minzhong 323 Hao* (川15民终323号) [Civil case, Final Instance, No. 323].

The courts' approach in differentiating state property rights from non-pubic rights can be better understood in a historical context. In 1999, the State Council decided to establish four state-owned asset management companies to address non-performing loan problems facing banks.[82] In 2001, in order to assist asset management companies in collecting debts, the Supreme People's Court issued rules concerning the validity of contracts and the statutory limitation concerning this process.[83] The

---

82 *Guowuyuan Bangongting Zhuanfa Renmin Yinhang, Caizhengbu, Zhengjianhui Guanyu Zujian Zhongguo Xinda Zichan Guanli Gongsi Yijian de Tongzhi* (国务院办公厅转发人民银行、财政部、证监会关于组建中国信达资产管理公司意见的通知) [Notice of the General Office of the State Council Forwarding the Opinion of the People's Bank of China, Ministry of Finance, China Securities Regulatory Commission on Establishing China Cinda Asset Management Co., Ltd. (People's Republic of China) State Council], issued by the State Council on 21 July 1999.

See also, *Guowuyuan Bangongting Zhuanfa Renmin Yinhang, Caizhengbu, Zhengjianhui Guanyu Zujian Huarong Zichan Guanli Gongsi, Zhongguo Changcheng Zichan Guanli Gongsi he Zhongguo Dongfang Zichan Guanli Gongsi Yijian de Tongzhi* (国务院办公厅转发人民银行、财政部、证监会关于组建中国华融资产管理公司、中国长城资产管理公司和中国东方资产管理公司意见的通知) [Notice of the General Office of the State Council Forwarding the Opinion of the People's Bank of China, Ministry of Finance, China Securities Regulatory Commission on Establishing China Huarong Asset Management Co., Ltd., China Greatwall Asset Management Co., Ltd. and China Orient Asset Management Co., Ltd], issued by the State Council on 21 July 1999.

83 These rules include: *Guanyu Shenli Sheji Jinrong Zichan Guanli Gongsi Shougou, Guanli, Chuzhi Guoyou Yinhang Buliang Daikuan Xingcheng de Zichan de Anjian Shiyong Falv Ruogan Wenti de Guiding* (关于审理涉及金融资产管理公司收购、管理、处置国有银行不良贷款形成的资产的案件适用法律若干问题的规定) [Rules of the Supreme People's Court of China on the Application of Law in Hearing Cases Relating to Assets from the Financial Asset Management Companies' Acquiring, Managing and Disposing of State-owned Banks' Non-performing Loans], issued by the Supreme People's Court on 3 April 2001.

See also, *Guanyu Guoyou Jinrong Zichan Guanli Gongsi Chuzhi Guoyou Shangye Yinhang Buliang Zichan AnjianJiaona Susong Feiyong de Tongzhi* (关于国有金融资产管理公司处置国有商业银行不良资产案件交纳诉讼费用的通知) [Notice of the Supreme People's Court of China on Litigation Payment in Cases of State-owned Financial Asset Management Companies Disposing of State-owned Banks' Non-performing Loans], issued by the Supreme People's Court on 25 October 2001.

See also, *Dui <Guanyu Guanche Zhixing Zuigao Renmin Fayuan 'Shier Tiao' Sifa Jieshi Youguan Wenti de Han> de Dafu* (对<关于贯彻执行最高人民法院'十二条'司法解释有关问题的函>的答复) [Reply of the Supreme People's Court of China to <Letter on Relevant Questions Regarding Carrying out the Supreme People's Court of China's 'Twelve Provisions' Judicial Explanation>], issued by the Supreme People's Court on 7 January 2002.

See also, *Guanyu Jinrong Zichan Guanli Gongsi Shougou, Chuzhi Yinhang Buliang Zichan Youguan Wenti de Buchong Tongzhi* (关于金融资产管理公司收购、处置银行不良资产有关问题的补充通知) [Supplementary Notice of the Supreme People's Court on the Purchase and Disposal of Non-performing Assets by Financial Asset Management Companies], issued by the Supreme People's Court on 30 May 2005.

See also, *Guanyu Yanchang Guoyou Jinrong Zichan Guanli Gongsi Chuli Guoyou Shangye Yinhang Buliang Zichan Anjian Jianban Jiaona Susong Feiyong Qixian de Tongzhi* (关于延长国有金融资产管理公司处理国有商业银行不良资产案件减半缴纳诉讼费用期限的通知) [Notice of the Supreme People's Court on Extending the Period of the Waiver of Court Costs by 50% for Cases Involving the Disposal of Distressed Assets of State-Owned Commercial Banks by State-Owned Financial Assets Management Companies], issued by the Supreme People's Court on 13 April 2006.

Supreme People's Court has reiterated that the applicability of these rules is limited.[84] These rules are only applicable to situations where asset management companies purchase, manage and dispose of the non-performing loans of state-owned banks.[85] In 2009, in the Minutes of the meeting on Hearing Cases about the Assignment of Non-performing Debts Involving Financial Institutions (the Minutes), the Supreme People's Court emphasised that the rules promulgated in 2001 are only applicable in cases where the transferors of non-performing loans to state-owned asset management companies are state-owned banks.[86]

In a 2015 case, *Huaxin Tiancheng Investment Ltd v. Li Hongping* etc., *Non-performing Loan Dispute*, the court rejected the plaintiff's request to use the 2001 rules on the basis that those rules were not applicable given the circumstances of the case in question:

The introduction of the Minutes is to resolve historical issues, namely, to standardize transfers of non-performing loans, to maintain social and corporate stability, to prevent the loss of state assets and to safeguard national *financial security*. The case in question involves two parties that are subject to market rules, and thus the Minutes do not apply.[87]

In 2008, the Supreme People's Court acknowledged that some entities receive favourable treatment in the context of state-owned banks disposing of non-performing loans.[88] This has been the only exception where state property rights

---

[84] Li (2002).

[85] *Guanyu Shenli Sheji Jinrong Zichan Guanli Gongsi Shougou, Guanli, Chuzhi Guoyou Yinhang Buliang Daikuan Xingcheng de Zichan de Anjian Shiyong Falv Ruogan Wenti de Guiding* (关于审理涉及金融资产管理公司收购、管理、处置国有银行不良贷款形成的资产的案件适用法律若干问题的规定) [Rules of the Supreme People's Court of China on the Application of Law in Hearing Cases Relating to Assets from the Financial Asset Management Companies' Acquiring, Managing and Disposing of State-owned Banks' Non-performing Loans], issued by Supreme People's Court on 3 April 2001.

[86] *Guanyu Shenli Sheji Jinrong Buliang Zhaiquan Zhuanrang Anjian Gongzuo Zuotanhui Jiyao* (关于审理涉及金融不良债权转让案件工作座谈会纪要) [Notice of the Supreme People's Court on Issuing the Summary of Minutes of the Symposium on Hearing Cases on the Assignment of Distressed Claims Involving Financial Institutions], issued by the Supreme People's Court on 30 March 2009.

[87] *Beijingshi Dier Zhongji Renmin Fayuan* (北京市第二中级人民法院) [Second Intermediate People's Court of Beijing], *Minshi Caiding Shu* (民事裁定书) [Civil Order] (2015) *Erzhong Min (Shang) Zhongzi 05792* (二中民(商)终字第05792号) [Civil case, Final Instance, No. 05792].

[88] The Supreme People's Court explained the policy considerations underpinning such treatment 'to best protect state-owned financial property, to reduce and dispose of non-performing loans of state-owned commercial banks and to ensure the competitiveness and repayment capacity of state-owned commercial banks, the CCP and the State Council had implemented strategies to strip and dispose of non-performing loans. From 1999 to the second half of 2008, the big four banks had stripped non-performing loans (NPLs) of the astonishing amount of up to more than RMB 2 trillion. All levels of the judiciary shall follow the Supreme People's Court's Rules of 2001 on Adjudicating cases involving financial asset management companies purchasing, managing and disposing of the NPLs of the state-owned banks and other relevant rules, and to provide protection for national financial assets (credit rights). These rules include: *Guanyu Shenli Sheji Jinrong Zichan Guanli Gongsi Shougou, Guanli, Chuzhi Guoyou Yinhang Buliang Daikuan Xingcheng de Zichan de Anjian Shiyong Falv Ruogan Wenti de Guiding* (关于审理涉及金融资产管理公司收购、管理

were treated differently from those of private property rights. The Supreme People's Court explained its reasoning:

The stripping and disposal of national financial assets (creditors' right) in the range of billions is not a simple dispute among private parties. It is a matter concerning the mobility of national assets and the redistribution of interests. Whether this can take place in a transparent, fair and just manner concerns the interests of the nation and every citizen, it concerns the people's confidence in the Party and the government, and it concerns the reform of the national financial system and the management of state-owned assets. This a contemporary national issue that is of public interest. Thus it would be unfair to assess these transfers of property rights on the basis of the principles of party autonomy and the protection of private property rights.[89]

、处置国有银行不良贷款形成的资产的案件适用法律若干问题的规定) [Rules of the Supreme People's Court of China on the Application of Law in Hearing Cases Relating to Assets from the Financial Asset Management Companies' Acquiring, Managing and Disposing of State-owned Banks' Non-performing Loans], issued by the Supreme People's Court on 3 April 2001.

See also, *Guanyu Guoyou Jinrong Zichan Guanli Gongsi Chuzhi Guoyou Shangye Yinhang Buliang Zichan AnjianJiaona Susong Feiyong de Tongzhi* (关于国有金融资产管理公司处置国有商业银行不良资产案件交纳诉讼费用的通知) [Notice of the Supreme People's Court of China on Litigation Payments in Cases of State- owned Financial Asset Management Companies Disposing of State-owned Bank Non-performing Loans], issued by the Supreme People's Court on 25 October 2001.

See also, *Dui <Guanyu Guanche Zhixing Zuigao Renmin Fayuan 'Shier Tiao' Sifa Jieshi Youguan Wenti de Han> de Dafu* (对<关于贯彻执行最高人民法院'十二条'司法解释有关问题的函>的答复) [Reply of the Supreme People's Court of China to <Letter on Relevant Questions Regarding Carrying out the Supreme People's Court of China's 'Twelve Provisions' Judicial Explanation>], issued by the Supreme People's Court on 7 January 2002.

See also, *Guanyu Jinrong Zichan Guanli Gongsi Shougou, Chuzhi Yinhang Buliang Zichan Youguan Wenti de Buchong Tongzhi* (关于金融资产管理公司收购、处置银行不良资产有关问题的补充通知) [Supplementary Notice of the Supreme People's Court on the Purchase and Disposal of Non-performing Assets by Financial Asset Management Companies], issued by the Supreme People's Court on 30 May 2005.

See also, *Guanyu Yanchang Guoyou Jinrong Zichan Guanli Gongsi Chuli Guoyou Shangye Yinhang Buliang Zichan Anjian Jianban Jiaona Susong Feiyong Qixian de Tongzhi* (关于延长国有金融资产管理公司处理国有商业银行不良资产案件减半缴纳诉讼费用期限的通知) [Notice of the Supreme People's Court on Extending the Period of the Waiver of Court Costs by 50% for Cases Involving the Disposal of Distressed Assets of State-Owned Commercial Banks by State-Owned Financial Assets Management Companies], issued by the Supreme People's Court on 13 April 2006.

At the same time, within the boundaries of the law and judicial interpretation, the courts shall protect, to the best of their ability, national financial assets (creditor rights) concerning matters such as the validity of contracts and statutory limitation periods—See *Zuigao Renmin Fayuan Yinfa <Guanyu wei Weihu Guojia Jinrong Anquan he Jingji Quanmian Xietiao Kechixu Fazhan Tigong Sifa Baozhang he Falv Fuwu de Ruogan Yijian> de Tongzhi* (最高人民法院印发《关于为维护国家金融安全和经济全面协调可持续发展提供司法保障和法律服务的若干意见》的通知) [Notice of the Supreme People's Court on Issuing Several Opinions on Providing Judicial Guarantees and Legal Services for the Maintenance of National Financial Security and Comprehensive, Coordinated and Sustainable Economic Development], issued by the Supreme People's Court on 3 December 2008.

[89] Wu (2009).

It can be concluded that there is no case to be made that state property rights have been differentiated from private rights and that state property rights have been given preferential treatment. On the occasion that state property rights were treated differently, financial security formed part of the legal reasoning of the courts to justify extending more protection to state property rights than to private rights.

5.2 Policy Implementation in Judicial Decision-Making

Public policy has long been incorporated in judicial decision-making in China.[90] The Supreme People's Court has issued various directives such as the Guidelines on Providing Legal Services to the Transitioning Economy, Guidelines on Assisting New City and Village Development, Guidelines on Proving Services for the Development of Beijing, Tianjing and Hebei, Guidelines on Providing Services to the Changjian Economic Zone, and 10 Classic Insolvency Cases on Supply-demand Economic Reforms. The titles of these directives suggest the presence of public policy considerations. The theme of financial security in those directives supports the courts in implementing this public policy agenda.

An example which aptly illustrates the nature and extent to which financial security has been utilized can be found in a speech by the then Vice President of the Supreme Court, Xi Xiaoming. In 2009, at the Adjudicating Commercial Cases After the Global Financial Crisis Conference, Xi gave a speech entitled 'Proactively Providing Services in Maintaining National Financial Security and Economy Development',[91] in which he noted that one of the principles in adjudicating commercial cases is to maintain national economic security. The Vice President explained:

Financial security is the key to national economic security. People's Courts must follow the state's macro management of the national economy and the surveillance of economic security. Guided by the principles of standardizing the activities of the financial markets, mitigating financial risks, maintaining financial stability, and protecting economic security, the courts adjudicate cases in a fair and just manner, thus preventing harm that financial crises might cause to the national economy, and ensure national *financial security* and economic safety.

One can see differences between the directives of the Supreme People's Court and the judgments of lower levels of the courts in that, instead of public policy, judges in adjudicating individual cases are inclined to highlight regulatory rules imposed by the regulatory authorities. This raises a question as whether breaching regulatory rules could render contracts invalid.

---

[90] Public policy could be interpreted broadly including the law, regulations, rules etc. See Kilpatrick (2000).

[91] *Zuigao Renmin Fayuan Fuyuanzhang Xi Xiaoming Zai Renmin Fayuan Yingdui Jinrongweiji Shangshi Shengpan Gongzuo Zuotanhuishang de Jianghua-Jijiyingdui, Gongkeshixian, Weiweihui Guojia Jinrong Anquan he Jingji Pingweng Jiaokuai Fazhan Tigong Youli Sifa Baozhang* (最高人民法院副院长奚晓明在人民法院应对金融危机商事审判工作座谈会上的讲话–积极应对,共克时艰,为维护国家金融安全和经济平稳较快发展提供有力司法保障).

When it comes to the validity of contracts, pursuant to section 52 of the Contract Law, one of the conditions that renders a contract void is when a party has breached a law and/or a regulation imposed by the State Council. It is unclear whether contravening a regulation issued by regulatory authorities would render a contract void.

In the case of *Yang Jinguo and Lin Jinkun Investment Dispute* in 2018, it was held that a contract under which dormant shareholders held shares in listed companies had contravened the rules issued by the China Security Regulatory Commission (CSRC), the securities markets regulator. It was therefore ruled that '[the contract] was detrimental to the interests of public retail investors, to the order of a capital market, to trade security, and to financial security and social stability, and was therefore contrary to the public interest'. The contract was thus held to be invalid. In its legal reasoning the court referred to two regulations issued by the CSRC to the effect that there was a contravention of a regulation. However, the ruling on the invalidity of the contract ultimately hinged on the fact that the contract was detrimental to the public interest, which is one of the conditions prescribed by section 52 of the Contract Law to render a contract void. The court stated:

The contracts between Yang Jinguo and Lin Jinsheng are in breach of the listed company regulation. Although they are a departmental regulation, they are made under the authorization of the law and must be consistent with the law. This is also a well-understood rule in the industry. The rule was adopted to protect the interest of public retail investors, and to protect the public interest. Therefore, pursuant to the sub-section 4 of section 52 of the *Con*tract Law, these contracts are void.

Similarly, in the case of *Zhou Meiseng and Jiangshu Fengyu Liangyou Shiye Group Transfer of Shares Dispute*,[92] the court held that Zhou Meiseng was not qualified to be a shareholder of Huaihai Rural Commercial Bank. The court invalidated a share transfer contract between Zhou Meisheng and Jiangshu Fengyu Liangyou Shiye Group on the basis that the shareholding in commercial banks related to national financial security, and the transfer of such shares needed to comply with the requirements of the regulatory authorities. The court reasoned:

Huaihai Rural Commercial Bank is a financial institution and is not a private company. In order to maintain *financial security* and stability, the government regulates banks under the principle of prudential regulation. Thus there are more stringent requirements regarding the qualifications of shareholders, the procedures for the transfer of shares, and percentage shareholding limits than for other companies. In this case, Huaihai Rural Commercial Bank did not agree with Zhou Meiseng becoming a shareholder of the bank. Also, Zhou Meiseng was not able to provide evidence to the effect that the board of the bank had discussed and agreed that Zhou Meisheng should become a shareholder. He failed to meet the conditions stipulated in the constitution of the Huaihai Rural Commercial Bank. As a result, Zhou's request

[92] *Jiangsu Province Gaoji Renmin Fayuan* (江苏省高级人民法院) [High Court of Jiangsu Province], *Minshi Caiding Shu* (民事裁定书) [Civil Order] (2015) *Sushangzongzidi(*2015)苏商终字第00542号 [Civil Case, Final Instance, No. 00542].

to confirm his shareholder status and register him as a shareholder of the bank is denied.

In this case, the court cited the CSRC's Rural Medium and Small Financial Institutions Administrative Licencing Rules and Guidelines on the Corporate Governance of Commercial Banks.[93] These two instruments are the rules that the regulator strictly imposes to regulate the conduct of banks. The court made particular reference to section 14 of the Guidelines on the Corporate Governance of Commercial Banks and highlighted the requirement that the board of a non-listed bank should be informed prior to the transfer of shares by majority shareholders. It left unresolved whether to invalidate a transfer transaction if this requirement is not satisfied. As was highlighted in the judgment in *Zhou Meiseng*, despite the fact that a contravention of a regulation does not necessarily invalidate the transaction, the court nevertheless held that the transaction was invalid by resorting to the term 'financial security'.

There are also instances where the courts have validated transactions that are in breach of rules issued by the regulatory authorities. This study has identified examples where the court relied on 'financial security' to support its reasoning to validate certain transactions. In the context of negotiable instruments, section 12 of the Law on Negotiable Instruments[94] states that a holder who contravenes the law due to substantial errors is not entitled to the rights of a holder. In some cases, in the process of refinancing negotiable instruments, banks have not complied with regulations imposed by the People's Bank of China. These non-compliances were not considered by the courts to be 'substantial errors' due to national financial security concerns, otherwise a 'substantial errors' ruling would deprive the banks of their rights as holders.[95]

In addition, in the 2014 case of *Hunan Changzhutan Financial Services Company and Hunan Xinlieying Education Company, Zhang Moyi* etc. *Loan Contract*

---

[93] *Zhongguo Yijianhui Nongcun Zhongxiao Jinrong Jigou Xingzhengxuke Shixiang Shishi Banfa he Shangye Yinghang Gongsi Zhili Zhiying* (中国银监会农村中小金融机构行政许可事项实施办法) 和(商业银行公司治理指引).

[94] *Piaoju Fa* (票据法).

[95] Among the examples, there are three decisions that have resorted to this line of reasoning. They are: *Zuigao Renmin Fayuan* (最高人民法院) [Supreme People's Court], *Minshi Panjue Shu* (民事判决书) [Civil Judgment] (2016) *Zuigaofa Minzai 66* (最高法民再66号) [Civil case, Appeal Instance, No. 66].

See also, *Zuigao Renmin Fayuan* (最高人民法院) [Supreme People's Court], *Minshi Panjue Shu* (民事判决书) [Civil Judgment] (2016) *Zuigaofa Minzai 68* (最高法民再68号) [Civil case, Appeal Instance, No. 68].

See also, *Zuigao Renmin Fayuan* (最高人民法院) [Supreme People's Court], *Minshi Panjue Shu* (民事判决书) [Civil Judgment] (2017) *Zuigaofa Minzai 116* (最高法民再116号) [Civil case, Appeal Instance, No. 116].

Dispute,[96] the court confirmed the validity of a loan contract between the companies although the regulatory rules and judicial interpretation still in place prohibited borrowing activities among companies:

The plaintiff Changzhutan had extended credit to the defendant Xinlieying on a short-term basis in order to help the latter with its liquidity difficulties. This conduct did not contravene the law since it did not endanger the national *financial security* and financial order. On the contrary, it assisted the financing needs of the company. Thus the rights of the plaintiff should be protected.

The court in the *Dapeng Securities and Shanghai Auto Group Insolvency Creditor Rights Dispute*[97] was also candid in its views regarding activities that contravened rules issued by the regulatory authorities:

The transaction was conducted over the counter which was not compliant with the Rules on National Inter-bank Bond Market Transactions (which was issued by the banking regulatory authority). This was a procedural defect. Although it deviated from the regulatory rules, the parties to the contract and the substantive aspect of the transaction were compliant with the law and the relevant regulations. The defect identified had no bearing on the parties and the nature of the transaction. It had no detrimental effects on national *financial security* and order. Thus it should not affect the validity of the transaction.

It is apparent throughout the cases examined in this study that a contravention of the regulations will not necessarily result in the transaction been held to be invalid. The term 'financial security' provides judges with a convenient means to support their reasoning either way. Among the cases discussed, the courts were reliant on regulations to form their legal reasoning. To some extent, regulations are broadly interpreted so as not only to cover the ones explicitly manifested in specific rules but also ones that are implicit such as financial security. The courts have resorted to financial security as a means to support and implement policy agendas such as encouraging asset mobility and liquidity as well as financial product innovation.[98]

---

[96] *Hunan Changsha Zhongji Renmin Fayuan* (湖南省长沙市中级人民法院) [Hunan Province Changsha City Intermediate Court] *Minshi Panjue Shu* (民事判决书) [Civil Judgment] (2014) *Changzhong minchu 00,890*(2014)长中民二初字第00890号 [Civil Case, Second Instance, No. 00890].

[97] *Guangdong Sheng Gaoji Renmin Fayuan* (广东省高级人民法院) [Guangdong Province People's High Court] *Minshi Panjue Shu* (民事判决书) [Civil Judgment] (2010) *Changzhong minchu 00,890*(2010)[Civil Case, Second Instance, No. 114].

[98] For example, the courts in Shanghai have adopted the view of encouraging financial innovation. A senior judge and the Chief Judge of the financial division at the High People's Court of Shanghai stated that 'financial innovation is something that the courts should encourage. On occasions when financial innovation and the interests of financial consumers come into conflict, we need to achieve a balancing act. We need to consider how to encourage financial innovation. See Lujiazui Forum (2013).

However, such judicial opinions are subject to change. In recent years, strict regulation and risk avoidance have featured more dominantly in judicial documents. For example, the High People's Court in Shanghai stated that 'disputes involving financial innovative products must be adjudicated cautiously [...] including financial innovative trading methods that are non-compliant with regulatory rules and the spirit thereof, and financial transactions that, under the disguise of financial

The courts actively bridge the gap between the law (the legislature) and public policy (the government).[99] When the relevant law is insufficient and/or vague, the courts are required to intervene. In addition, it also appears that judges have an active political agenda.[100] The courts are effectively advancing the intent of the government. In doing so, public policy forms part of the language of the courts. The implementation of public policy by the Chinese judiciary in this context has its drawbacks, however. The study highlights, as discussed above, that it is unclear whether a contravention of a regulation issued by regulatory authorities would render a contract void, and the courts are able to interpret it in a way that is reflective or supportive of the public policy of the day. There seems to be a recipe for uncertainty and inconsistency as, despite the similar facts of these cases, the findings of the courts may well be different due to the changing and variable application of public policy. All in all, the judiciary in China reflects the nature of the political structure that shapes the role of the state apparatus in its entirety.[101]

6 Final Remarks

After analysing 31 judicial documents of the Supreme People's Court and 242 judicial decisions of all levels of the judiciary, the chapter seeks to investigate the way in which and the extent to which the term financial security is used. The findings are as follows. First, the precise definition and application of financial security is elusive. Financial security is a term that has been left undefined, whether intentionally or unintentionally. This unsurprisingly leads to a situation where this term has been interpreted or utilized in many different ways. There are various reasons as to why this term is deployed by the judiciary which include the role of the judiciary within the state apparatus, the courts' exercise of judicial discretion, and the courts' own rule-making for financial activities. This term also allows the judges to render probative

innovation, understate financial risks, evade financial regulation'. See *Shanghaishi Gaoji Renmin Fayuan Guanyu Luoshi Jinrong Fengxian Fangfan Gongzuo de Shishi Yijian* (上海市高级人民法院关于落实金融风险防范工作的实施意见) [Implementation Opinions of the Higher People's Court of Shanghai on the Implementing the Prevention of Financial Risks], issued by the High People's Court of Shanghai on 25 June 2018.

99 Lu (2006) p 107.

100 This is in contrast to the roles of the courts in the US where the courts see their role as an interpreter of legislation, and are not willing to act as a super-legislature to weigh the wisdom of legislation, see *Ferguson v. Skrupa*, 372 US 726 (1963).

101 In the US, only the Supreme Court has a role to play in national policy making. See Casper (1976, pp. 50–63). And also quoting Oliver Wendell Holmes, Jr. in *Ferguson v. Skrupa*, 372 US 726, 731–732 (1963) that 'we emphatically refuse to go back to the time when courts used the Due Process Clause "to strike down state laws, regulatory of business and industrial conditions, because they may be unwise, improvident, or out of harmony with a particular school of thought" […] [n]or are we able or willing to draw lines by calling a law "prohibitory" or "regulatory". Whether the legislature takes for its textbook Adam Smith, Herbert Spencer, Lord Keynes, or some other is no concern of ours'. By contrast, the courts at all levels in China implement the government's policy.

significance to certain evidence, to make judicial recommendations, and provides them with an avenue to achieve a degree of judicial uniformity in judgments.

The manner in which the term is used in these judicial decisions also sheds some light on the way new judgments are rendered in similar cases. With one unusual exception, private and state property rights are generally treated similarly by the courts. In addition, those cases are also illustrative of the role of the courts in China's state apparatus in carrying out and furthering government policy objectives.

Therefore, the term is analogous to the ancient Greek myth of the Delphic Oracles. In Ancient Greece, when the oracle was consulted, Delphi produced answers that 'may not be instantly comprehensible answers, although "none of them is deliberately ambiguous".'[102] The consulting city would decide for itself what the oracle actually meant or what Apollo wanted them to do.[103] In the context of financial security, the Chinese courts are similarly able to decide what it ought to mean, how it ought to be used in judicial reasoning or what the government wants them to do.

References

Ai J (2008) Zhongguo Faguan Zuidahua Shenme (中国法官最大化什么) [What China's judges should maximise]. Falv he Shehui Kexue (法律和社会科学) [Law and Social Science] 2008(3):98–151

Borghard E (2018) Protecting financial institutions against cyber threats: a national security issue. Working Paper, Carnegie Endowment for International Peace

Bowden H (2005) Classical Athens and the Delphic Oracle: divination and democracy. Cambridge University Press, Cambridge

Casper JD (1976) The Supreme Court and national policy making. Am Political Sci Rev 70(1):50-63

Chenguang W (2006) Law-making functions of the Chinese courts: judicial activism in a country of rapid social changes. Frontiers of Law in China 1(4):524–549

China Court (2013) Yancheng: Yize Sifa Jianyi Yinqi Quanshi Jinrong Zhixu Guifan (盐城:一则司法建议引发全市金融秩序规范) [Yancheng: judicial advice triggered city-wide normative financial order]. http://rmfyb.chinacourt.org/paper/images/2013-03/08/04/2013030804_pdf.pdf. Accessed 20 Feb 2020

China Court (2018) Sifa Jianyishu (最高人民法院司法建议书) [People's Supreme Court of China, Judicial recommendations]. https://www.chinacourt.org/article/detail/2018/03/id/3249187.shtml. Accessed 23 July 2019

China Court (2019) Jianchi Dang dui Renmin Fayuan Gongzuo de Juedui Lingdao (坚持党对人民法院工作的绝对领导) [Adhering to the CCP's leadership of the People's Courts]. https://www.chinacourt.org/article/detail/2019/02/id/3736207.shtml. Accessed 13 Aug 2019

China Insolvency Law (2014) Zuigao Renmin Fayuan Fuyuanzhang Xi Xiaoming zai Quanguo Bufen Zhonggaoji Renmin Fayuan Shenli Zhengquan Gongsi Pochan Anjian Zuotanhui shang de Jianghua—Jiexuan (最高人民法院副院长奚晓明在全国部分中、高级人民法院审理证券公司破产案件座谈会上的讲话-节选) [Excerpts from the Speech by Xi Xiaoming, the Vice President of the Supreme People's Court, at the Securities Firm Insolvency Forum with attendees from some nationwide intermediate and High People's Courts nationwide]. http://syclaw.sjtu.edu.cn/pochan/show.aspx?info_lb=766&flag=753&info_id=155. Accessed 20 Feb 2020

[102] Bowden (2005, p. 49).

[103] Bowden (2005, p. 51).

China News (2014) Zhouqiang: Yao Ganyu Xiang Xifang Cuowu Sichao Liangjian (周强:要敢于向西方错误思潮亮剑) [Zhou Qiang: We should have the courage to show the sword to Western erroneous notions]. http://www.chinanews.com/gn/2017/01-14/8124300.shtml. Accessed 20 Feb 2020

Chinese Academy of Social Sciences (2016) Zhongguo Shehui Kexueyuan 'Pushi Jiezhi' Lun Pipan Wenxuan (中国社会科学院'普世价值'论批判文选) [Critical digest of 'universal value' by the Chinese Academy of Social Sciences]. Zhongguo Shehui Kexue Chubanshe (中国社会科学出版社) [Chinese Academy of Social Sciences Press] 2016 6:35–41

Coffee Jr JC (2001) The rise of dispersed ownership: the roles of law and the state in the separation of ownership and control. Yale Law J 111(1):1-82

Court.gov.cn (2016) Zuigao Renmin Fayuan Guanyu Shenhua Sifa Gongkai, Cujin Sifa Gongzheng Qingkuang de Baogao (最高人民法院关于深化司法公开、促进司法公正情况的报告) [Report of the Supreme People's Court on extending judicial publicity and promoting judicial fairness]. http://www.court.gov.cn/zixun-xiangqing-30161.html. Accessed 20 Feb 2020

Deckert SK, Vikers CH (2011) An introduction to sociolinguistics: society and identity. Bloomsbury, New York

Guo S (2018) Sifa Wenjian de Zhongguo Tese yu Shijian Kaocha (司法文件的中国特色与实践考察) [The Chinese characteristics and a practical review of judicial documents]. Huanqiu Falv Pinglun (环球法律评论) [Global Law Review] 2018 4:170–192

He W (2018) The regulation of securities markets in China. Palgrave Macmillian, New York

Huang T (2012) Zuigao Renmin Fayuan de Sifa Wenjian: Xianzhuang, Wenti yu Qianjing (最高人民法院的司法文件:现状、问题与前景) [Judicial documents from the Supreme People's Court: current status, problems and prospects]. Faxue Luntan (法学论坛) [Legal Forum] 2012 4:124–129

Ji W (2006) Zuigao Renmin Fayuan de Juese Jiqi Yanhua (最高人民法院的角色及其演化) [Role of the Supreme People's Court and its adaptation]. Qinghua Faxue (清华法学) [Tsinghua University Law Journal] 2006 1:4–20

Kilpatrick DG (2000) Definitions of public policy and the law. https://mainweb-v.musc.edu/vawprevention/policy/definition.shtml. Accessed 20 Feb 2020

Kuester J (2013) Transnational influences on financial crime. National Security and Armed Conflict Law Review 4:71-79

La Porta R, Lopez-de-Silanes F, Shleifer A, Vishny RW (1998) Law and finance. Journal of Political Economy 106(6):1113-1155

Li G (2002) Renqing Xingshi, Tigao Renshi, Nuli Shijian Gongzheng yu Xiaolv Shiji Zhuti, Kaituo Minshangshi Shenpan Gongzuo Xinjumian—Zai Quanguo Fayuan Minshangshi Shenpan Gongzuo Huiyi de Jianghua (认清形势 提高认识 努力实践公正与效率世纪主题 开拓民商事审判工作新局面—在全国法院民商事审判工作会议上的讲话) [Understanding the situation, improving recognition, hardly practising the century-old theme of fairness and efficiency, exploring the new situation of civil and business justice—speech at the National Working Conference of Civil Courts and Business Justice]. Renmin Fayuan Chubanshe (人民法院出版社) People's Court Press, Beijing

Lu L (2006) Lun Zuigao Fayuan zai Hongguan Tiaokong zhong de Juese Dingwei (论最高法院在宏观调控中的角色定位) [Role and position of the Supreme People's Court in macro-control]. Xiandai Faxue (现代法学) [Modern Law Science] 2006 6:107–121

Lujiazui Forum (2013) Shanghaishi Gaoji Renmin Fayuan Jinrong Shenpanting Tingzhang, Gaoji Faguan Yanglu Fayan Shilu (上海市高级人民法院金融审判庭庭长、高级法官杨路发言实录) [Speech given by Yang Lu, Senior Judge and the Chief Judge of the Financial Division at High People's Court of Shanghai, 2013 Lujiazui Forum Series]. http://sh.eastday.com/m/2013ljz/u1a7487288.html. Accessed 20 Feb 2020

Malkawi BH (2011) Balancing open investment with national security: review of US and UAE laws with DP World as a case study. University of Notre Dame Australia Law Review 13:153-192

Mattila H (2006) Comparative legal linguistics. Ashgate, Aldershot

Merryman H (1985) The civil law tradition: an introduction to the legal systems of Western Europe and Latin America. Stanford University Press, Stanford

OpenLaw (2016) Dashuju Jiedu 2014 Nian Zhongguo Caipan Wenshu Gongkai (大数据解读2014年中国裁判文书公开) [Using big data to analyse the publicity of judgments in China in 2014]. http://openlaw.cn/research/15253c218332830dca02eb150d800870. Accessed 20 Feb 2020

People.com.cn (2013) Mengjianzhu Tongzhi Jianli (孟建柱同志简历) [Brief biography of Meng Jianzhu]. http://cpc.people.com.cn/n/2012/1115/c351757-19594462.html. Accessed 20 Feb 2020

People.com.cn (2019) Xi Jinping: Quanmian Shenru Zuohao Xinshidai Zhengfa Gexiang Gongzuo, Cujin Shehui Gongping Zhengyi Baozhang Renmin Anju Leye (习近平:全面深入做好新时代政法各项工作 促进社会公平正义保障人民安居乐业) [Xi Jinping: Comprehensively and profoundly ensuring political and legal work, promoting societal fairness and justice and guaranteeing that people live and work in peace]. http://cpc.people.com.cn/n1/2019/0117/c64094-30560032.html. Accessed 20 Feb 2020

Posner R (1973) Economic analysis of the law. Little Brown and Company, Chicago

Rehman SS (2011) National security challenges and the global financial crisis. Florida International University Law Review 7:119-148

Rodriguez RV (2010) Economic terror: market manifestations of terror attacks. National Security Law Brief 1:129-136

Sarnikar S, Johnsen DJ (2009) Cyber security in the national market system. Rutgers Business Law Journal 6:1-28

Sina News (2014) Xi Jinping zai G20 Fenghui Diyi Jieduan Huiyi shang de Fayan—Quanwen (习近平在G20峰会第一阶段会议上的发言—全文) [Xi Jinping's speech at the G20 Summit first stage meeting—full text]. http://news.sina.com.cn/c/2014-11-16/153331152863.shtml. Accessed 20 Feb 2020

Wu X (2009) 'Jinrong Buliang Zhaiquan Zhuanrang' Zhun Sifa Jieshi Fuyu Difang Zhengfu Youxian Goumaiquan—Zuigaoyuan Minerting Youguan Fuzeren Huiying Gejie Zhiyi ('金融不良债权转让'准司法解释赋予地方政府优先购买权—最高院民二庭有关负责人回应各界质疑) [The anticipated judicial interpretation of 'Financially distressed debt assignment' gives local government prior purchase rights—responsible person from Civil Division II of the Supreme People's Court, Responses to Questions from the Public]. Fazhi Ribao (法制日报) [Legal Daily], 14 May 2009

Xinhua Net (2014) Jianchi Zongti Guojia Anquanguan, Zou Zhongguo Tese Guojia Anquan Daolu (坚持总体国家安全观 走中国特色国家安全道路) [Adhering to national security, and following national security with Chinese characteristics]. http://www.xinhuanet.com//politics/2014-04/15/c_1110253910.htm. Accessed 20 Feb 2020

Xinhua Net (2019) Xi Jinping Zhuchi Zhaokai Zhongyang Quanmian Yifa Zhiguo Weiyuanhui Dierci Huiyi (习近平主持召开中央全面依法治国委员会第二次会议) [Xi Jinping hosts the Second Conference of the Central Commission for Comprehensively Ruling the Country by Law]. http://www.xinhuanet.com/2019-02/25/c_1124161654.htm. Accessed 20 Feb 2020

Zhao F (2002) Fahui Shenpan, Zhixing Zhineng Zuoyong, Baozhang Guojia Jinrong Anquan—Fang Zuigao Renmin Fayuan Fuyuanzhang Li Guoguang (发挥审判、执行职能作用 保障国家金融安全—访最高人民法院副院长李国光) [Making use of judicial and enforcement functions and safeguarding national financial securities—interview with Li Guoguang, Vice President of the Supreme People's Court]. Renmin Sifa (人民司法) [People's Judicature] 2002 8:12–15

Chapter 6
The Closed Door of Courts: Selective Adjudication on Financial Disputes

Abstract In China, courts may refuse to accept certain disputes involving financial matters without any solid or explicit legal grounds. An analysis of such a phenomenon should help to understand the functioning logic of China's judicial power. This chapter suggests that there are a number of reasons behind the selective adjudication phenomenon, including a lack of applicable legal rules, a weak ability of the courts to understand complicated financial matters, the background of the economic system transition, the political consideration of "maintaining social stability" and judiciary self-interest. Selective adjudication has inevitably had a negative effect on China's financial markets, and reform is thus necessary.

1 Introduction

In the modern financial world, courts play an undeniably important role in shaping market order.[1] To understand this role, we must observe the behavior of judges in individual case trials, and based on their combined judgments determine how judicial power reacts to certain types of litigation and influences the conduct of market participants. In general, this chapter considers cases that were brought before and judged by courts. The efforts of courts can only be reviewed based on cases that have gone through the legal process. If a dispute did not enter into the judicial cycle, judges were not given an opportunity to announce their opinions, and we could not count that dispute as part of our judicial performance research sample.[2]

---

[1] See Ibrahim F. I. Shihata, "The Role of Law in Business Development," 20 Fordham International Law Journal 1577, 1997; Luc Laeven and Giovanni Majnoni, "Does Judicial Efficiency Lower the Cost of Credit?", World Bank Working Paper 3159, 2003, and Rafael La Porta, Florencio Lopez-de-Silanes, Andrei Shleifer & Robert W. Vishny, "Law and Finance," Journal of Political Economy, 1998.

[2] This does not mean that we pay no attention to disputes outside the judicial system. Indeed, non-legal mechanisms (e.g., private negotiation) are equally important in the financial community, and deserve a place in academic research. This chapter simply suggests that when parties do not choose legal solutions, the role of courts is very limited, and scholars cannot persuasively use such a scenario to comment on judicial efficiency.

T. Huang and W. He, *Politics Meets Markets*, Contemporary Chinese Civil and Commercial Law, https://doi.org/10.1007/978-981-97-9176-7_6

Although the academic attention paid to on-going and concluded cases has been proper in most places, the same may not be true in China. One feature makes the Chinese judicial system appear special. Chinese courts sometimes refuse to respond to claims related to certain conduct or transactions in the financial market, despite there being no legal bar (e.g., jurisdiction) that precludes a party from initiating legal proceedings. In practice, trials are denied due to a number of explicit policies or implicit conventions, which are not express law provisions[3] but are nevertheless firmly followed by judges. In contrast, it is unthinkable for a Western court to reject hearing a petition without a solid statutory basis.[4] Such a difference may problematize the case-based research method. For example, scholars may conduct case studies to detect trends among those who are using legal action to resolve certain kinds of disputes. However, statistics may prove unreliable. Although a calculation may reflect that no case was ever raised in a court and this may imply harmony in the financial market, this harmony may simply be the result of shutting cases out of the courtroom. Scholars would not be able to reveal the truth if they turned a blind eye to cases denied by courts (although the number of these cases may be relatively low or constitute only a small percentage[5]). Put another way, people who have a research interest in the Chinese judicial system should not restrict their insights to a narrow group of cases accepted by courts, but rather expand them to disputes in which parties' pleas for judgment are turned down. Investigating which category of claims are denied trial and why courts avoid taking on these claims could reveal some of the unique characteristics of the current Chinese judicial system. More importantly, via this perspective, we may better realize the relationship between courts and the financial market in China.

In contrast to the common case-based empirical study, this chapter reviews financial disputes that the judicial power has been unwilling to deal with in an effort to consider the willingness of Chinese courts to accept an action. We expect that analyzing such disputes in detail and summarizing their common ground could reveal the inherent logic of the judicial power exerted in China and possibly indicate the role of courts in developing the Chinese financial legal system. This chapter includes three parts. Part I outlines the instances in which financial disputes are denied the

[3] Here, the term "law" refers to all statutes made by legislative bodies (i.e., the National People's Congress (NPC) in China) and by competent authorities under the authorization of the NPC in accordance with relevant provisions in the statutes.

[4] E.g., Article 4 of the French Civil Code: "A judge who refuses to give judgment on the pretext of legislation being silent, obscure or insufficient, shall be prosecuted for being guilty of a denial of justice".

[5] It is an impossible task to calculate the number of disputes refused for trial. Despite the request of the Civil Procedure Code, Chinese courts usually do not make any written ruling to declare their denial decision, and outsiders may thus not discover the number by reviewing court documents. However, some commentators have estimated that as such incidents often involve "the serious social contradiction [that has] emerged and accumulated since the reform in late 1970s," their number may indeed be "a very high figure" and "not less than the [number of] cases accepted by the courts." See Jingwen Zhu, "Data Analysis of Flow of Litigation into Different Channels in China," SOCIAL SCIENCE IN CHINA [English], Volume 1, 2009, at 110.

chance to enter into the legal process. Although the courts accept some cases, litigation parties can later encounter procedural obstacles that are deliberately installed by the courts themselves. Part II explains why the judicial mechanism of selective adjudication of financial cases has been established in Chinese courts. Various reasons for the filtration are suggested, including a lack of applicable legal rules, a weak ability of the courts to understand complicated financial matters, the background of the economic system transition, the political consideration of maintaining social stability and judiciary self-interest. Finally, Part III indicates the negative effect imposed by this judicial filtration upon the Chinese financial market.

2 WHICH Financial Disputes Are Subjected to Selective Adjudication?

Two types of disputes are commonly considered financially oriented. The first is between market actors (e.g., a customer may challenge a bank on an unfair charge) and initiates civil lawsuits. The other relates to contentions between regulatory bodies and market actors (e.g., a listed company may appeal against a penalty imposed by the authority upon it), which may ultimately fall under the jurisdiction of administrative law. This chapter has no ambition to enter both kinds of disputes into a comprehensive discussion. Instead, it focuses on financial litigations between market actors for three reasons. First, as the lawsuits filed against regulatory authorities face many more statutory restrictions, the courts have no discretion over whether to accept an action. Article 12 of the Administrative Procedure Code (CAPC) of 1990 provides that certain categories of administrative action (e.g., the act of making decisions and orders with general binding force) cannot be sued in courts,[6] a prohibition that is not found in the civil procedure. Second, litigations between market actors and regulatory authorities inevitably relate to the controversial topic of governmental pressure on judicial independence in China. Such a problem deserves a comprehensive review in a separate paper rather than a brief consideration. Further, most financial litigations occur between market actors. Individuals and companies are not inclined to challenge regulatory authorities due to the worry that China's courts, which are presumed absent of independence, may disfavor their claims.

As long as relevant parties file their claims to the courts, judges are called to make a decision on whether to accept such actions. Chinese law has set clear standards for court decisions. The country's Civil Procedure Code (CCPC) of 2012 provides that "an action to be instituted must meet all of the following conditions: (1) the plaintiff is a Chinese citizen, legal person or any other organization with a direct interest in the case; (2) there is an identifiable defendant; (3) there are specific claims, facts

[6] Later in 2000, the Supreme Court of China issued a guideline related to the interpretation of CAPC provisions. The guideline expanded the scope of administrative actions precluded by Article 12. See Section 2, "Interpretation on some issues concerning the implementation of Administrative Procedure Law" (March, 2000).

and reasons; (4) the case is within the scope of civil actions acceptable by the courts and under the jurisdiction of the court in which the action is instituted."[7] Failure to comply with these conditions would lead to a ruling to refuse to accept an action.[8] One could come to the preliminary conclusion that unless explicitly excluded by the CCPC, any civil lawsuit must be accepted by the courts as long as it has satisfied the formality standards prescribed by the Codes. (The courts are not required to review the substance of cases at this stage.)

This conclusion may be abandoned in some circumstances. In practice, the courts are used to deny the acceptation of certain financial litigation groups, disregarding that these actions have properly complied with the CCPC rules and are not within the scope of exclusion provisions. We are thus faced with a strange legal circumstance. There are some financial cases that in accordance with the law are supposed to be accepted and heard by the courts, but ultimately fail to enter the courtroom and thus lose their opportunity to be resolved by judicial procedures. This is as strange as a scenario in which a police officer refuses to answer a 911 call despite his or her duty to respond. Our objective is thus to look deeply into the nature of such an ironic self-conflict. Before discussing the reasons why Chinese courts turn down such litigations, it is necessary to have a clear understanding of the kinds of financial litigations that Chinese courts have turned down.

2.1 The "Denied" Actions in the Field of Financial Disputes

Due to its reform and opening-up policies, China transitioned from a planned economic system to a market economy. Modern financial industries were gradually established in the country during this transition. Rapid market growth is inevitably accompanied by conflicts and disputes. Some of these arguments knock at the doors of the courts as a last resort for justice or relief. In response to such demand, the courts are willing to hear complicated financial cases and deliver their opinions.[9] However, with this willingness comes caution. When many stock exchanges were founded around the country in the 1990s, many private firms raised capital and the general public took the opportunity to invest. Nevertheless, most of the exchanges were established without authorization,[10] and the transactions conducted through these exchanges were highly unregulated. The courts predictably came under great

[7] Article 119, the Civil Procedure Code of 2012 (CCPC).

[8] Article 123 of the CCPC. Of course, the plaintiff may appeal against the ruling of refusal.

[9] In a guideline drafted by the Supreme Court in 1980, it was first affirmed that courts at any level could accept cases related to financial products, e.g., insurance and commercial loans. (However, policy-related bank loans, e.g., lending to famers based on public policy, were excluded out of the acceptable group.) See Tribunal of Business Litigation (of the Supreme Court), "Preliminary opinions on the scope of actions acceptable by Tribunals of Business Litigation of Courts" (Aug. 8, 1980).

[10] The Securities Act of China makes it clear that a stock exchange can only be established with the authorization of the Central Government (i.e., the State Council). See Article 102, the Securities Act

pressure, as litigations were often initiated in connection with the transactions made on such "unauthorized" exchanges. In 1998, the Supreme Court finally decided to close the door on these actions. A directive notice sent by the Supreme Court to inferior courts declared that, in relation to cases involving disputes of illegal, over-the-counter stock trading, the courts shall (1) deny the acceptance of actions, if such actions had not been accepted yet; (2) suspend the trial, if such actions had been accepted and (3) suspend the execution, if a final judgment had already been handed down on the actions.[11]

Since then, the courts have tended to stay away from certain financial litigations. Judicial interpretation has played a significant role in allowing courts to justify their denial. The term "judicial interpretation" has a much broader sense in China than in typical common law systems, which define it simply as a theory or mode of thought that explains how the judiciary should interpret the law. In China, the term refers to a form of legal rules normally drafted by the Supreme Court that not only acts as a binding instruction to inferior courts on how to understand and apply the law, but is also an instrument that gives the Supreme Court a quasi-law-making function. This supplements the statutes to which the judicial interpretations relate when the statutes themselves are ambiguous (although China's courts are never formally recognized as having such law-making capabilities). Put another way, Chinese-style "judicial interpretation" is a product of quasi-legislation, and thus some commentators refer to it as "secondary law."[12] Among all of these interpretations, the most notorious came in 2001 when the courts refused to give investors a chance to fight against wrongdoings in the Chinese capital market. Investors had long suffered due to the misrepresentations committed by listed companies. At the boiling point, a large number of investors rushed to the courts for remedies. The courts hung back when confronted with the increasing number of lawsuits. The Supreme Court issued a judicial interpretation in response, i.e., the "Notice on temporary denial of acceptance of civil compensation actions in connection with securities."[13] In this Notice, it was explained that "subject to the limitations of legislation and judiciary conditions, (the courts) are not ready to accept and hear such cases; after careful consideration, (the Supreme Court) comes to a conclusion that (all inferior courts) shall temporarily not accept civil compensation actions against those prescribed wrongdoings (in connection with securities)." Later in 2002, the Supreme Court relaxed the ban to a certain extent and allowed

of 2005. The Shanghai Stock Exchange and Shenzhen Stock Exchange are currently recognized as authorized stock exchanges.

[11] See the Supreme Court, Fa [1998] No. 145 (Dec. 4, 1998).

[12] For a detailed analysis, see Li Wei, "Comment: Judicial Interpretation in China," 5 Willamette J. Int'l L. & Dispute Res. 87 (1997); Ronald C. Keith & Zhiqiu Lin, "Judicial Interpretation of China's Supreme People's Court as 'Secondary Law' with Special Reference to Criminal Law," China Information, Volume 23, No. 2, July 2009, 223–255.

[13] See the Supreme Court, Fa-Ming-Chuan [2001] No. 406 (Sept. 21, 2001).

investors to bring actions against the misrepresentations committed by listed companies.[14] The denial effect of the 2000 Notice still remains, as such misrepresentation lawsuits typically face obstacles in practice.[15] Indeed, it would be unfair to suggest that the Supreme Court consistently maintains a conservative attitude. In a 2007 speech, Supreme Court Vice-president Xi Xiaoming said the following:

"After the revision (in 2005), the Securities Act has introduced more definite rules about civil liabilities caused by inside dealing and market manipulation. As for relevant lawsuits brought by investors against wrongdoers, the courts shall now determine the acceptance of actions in line with the prerequisite rules set by the judicial interpretations (of the Supreme Court) applicable to misrepresentation, as well as in compliance with the jurisdiction rule of the law."[16]

These words sent a positive signal, and some local courts (e.g., courts in Beijing and Nanjing) have already taken steps to accept securities litigations.[17] However, for several reasons (discussed as follows), no investor plaintiff had ever received a favorable ruling until recently.

In addition to denying actions against market participants who commit wrongdoings, the courts have long been reluctant to accept cases in which investors sue stock exchanges for regulatory function failure. The "Rules on the issues of jurisdiction and acceptance of litigations in relation to regulatory functions of stock exchanges," a judicial interpretation drafted by the Supreme Court in 2005, required inferior courts not to accept cases in which investors challenged the regulatory actions of a stock exchange (e.g., condemning misconduct, suspension and termination of listing) against issuers and relevant parties "without directly involving investors' interest." Considering the key term of this rule, i.e., "without directly involving investors' interest," the Supreme Court did not give any explicit definition. Its silence has left a large amount of room for the discretion of inferior courts, and has thus allowed the courts to "comfortably" decide whether to accept these "troublesome" cases based on an ambiguous standard.[18]

[14] See the Supreme Court, "Notice on the relevant issues concerning the acceptance of cases of disputes over civil tort arising from misrepresentation in the securities market," Fa-Ming-Chuan [2001] No. 43 (Jan. 5, 2002).

[15] See Bing Peng, "Establishing the System of Securities-Related Administrative Liability to Compensate Investors: Targeting Inside Dealing and Market Manipulation" (Jianli Buchang Touzizhe de Zhengquan Xingzheng Zeren Jizhi: Zhendui Neimu Jiaoyi he Caozong Shichang Xingwei), PEKING UNIVERSITY LAW JOURNAL [China], Volume 5, 2004.

[16] See "The speech of the vice president of the Supreme Court, XI Xiaoming, in the national working conference on civil and commercial Trial" (May 30, 2007).

[17] See Yixin SONG, PROTECTION OF INTEREST IN STOCK MARKETS (Gushi Weiquan) (Shanghai Academy of Social Science Press, 2009) [China], at p. 10.

[18] For example, the courts in Shanghai (the location of one of China's two stock exchanges) view disputes caused by managing acts (e.g., declaring a transaction as void, or deferment of settlement) of the Shanghai Stock Exchange as not "directly involving investors' interest" and thus maintain a negative attitude toward accepting relevant cases. For a detailed analysis, see Wendao LU, THEORY OF SELF-REGULATION OF STOCK EXCHANGES (Zhengquan Jiaoyisuo Zilu Guanli Lun) (Peking University Press, 2008), at pp. 179–185.

In addition to official judicial interpretations, the courts use many informal measures to delay litigation acceptance and suspend trials and executions. As a practical tradition, China's local-level Higher Courts usually refer the complicated problems met in dealing with specific litigations to the Supreme Court. The answers of the Supreme Court are then published in written form, and not only instruct the decisions of the Higher Courts that asked the questions, but bind any inferior courts that are facing similar cases. For example, in 2005, as a response to the report of the Higher Court of Hubei (in relation to a dispute between two local branches of Agricultural Bank of China and China Great Wall Asset Management Corporation[19]), the Supreme Court set a clear rule that the courts shall not accept contractual dispute actions related to policy-based financial asset transmission between any asset management corporation and state-owned commercial bank.[20] Furthermore, under the request of the authorities or for the purpose of collaboration with administrative actions, it is common for courts to issue informal notices to close their doors on cases in which a financial institution is involved. The first recorded instance of the Supreme Court sending a Notice to inferior courts occurred in 1995, in the form of a request to suspend any pending execution procedure against a trust company (subsidiary to the Bank of China).[21] Similar measures were regularly applied later in the disposition of several distressed financial institutions (e.g., trust and investment corporations, urban credit associations and brokerage firms).[22]

To be sure, the rules of action denial are not just limited to the aforementioned judicial documents (e.g., those formal judicial interpretations, informal "Notices" or even "Summaries of Working Conference"). In some circumstances, even the statement of a Supreme Court judge may create a principle, although his or her words can in no way be recognized as any formal source of law. For example, in a 1998 speech, former Supreme Court Vice-president Guoguang Li said that the courts shall not accept certain financial cases (e.g., cases related to individuals or companies conducting a deposit-taking business without proper authorization) but leave them to be settled by relevant regulatory bodies or local governments.[23] A more

[19] In 1999, four asset management corporations (i.e., Great Wall Asset Management Corporation, Cinda Asset Management Corporation, Huarong Asset Management Corporation and Orient Asset Management Corporation) were established under the direct leadership of the State Council with the specific purpose of dealing with non-performing loans of stated-owned commercial banks. These asset management corporations would normally purchase non-performing loans from the banks at a price equal to the book value of such loans.

[20] See the Supreme Court, [2004] Min-Er-Ta-Zi No. 25 (Jun. 16, 2005). Later in 2009, in the "summary of working conference on the trial in relation to cases of toxic financial asset transmission" passed by the Supreme Court to all inferior courts, the scope of denial was further extended, e.g., the courts shall not accept an action brought by creditors against a state-owned firm in bankruptcy due to an arrangement of state policy.

[21] See the Supreme Court, Fa [1995] No. 209 (Dec. 21, 1995).

[22] See Tao HUANG, "The Bankruptcy of Financial Institutions and 'Triple-Suspension' Decisions of the Courts" (Jinrong Jigou Tuishi yu Fayuan de 'San Zhongzhi' Jueding), SHANGHAI FINANCE [China], Volume 9, 2009.

[23] See Guoguang LI, "The Speech in the National Working Conference on Trial of Commercial Cases" (Nov. 23, 1998).

recent instance is the address of former Second Tribunal of Civil Trials Vice-director Xiaoming Song, who communicated the attitude of the Supreme Court toward actions caused by the liquidation of financial institutions. It was announced that during a financial institution's bankruptcy procedures, a creditor who is unsatisfied with the liquidation result shall refer his or her dissent to the authorities for resolution, rather than bringing litigation before the courts.[24] This unwritten rule was subsequently confirmed by a Notice of the Supreme Court in 2009.[25]

It would be incorrect to conclude that only the Supreme Court can frustrate the acceptance of litigation in connection with financial matters. Indeed, denial occasionally occurs even at the local-court level. For example, the Higher Court of Shanghai released a guideline in 2003[26] that provided that the courts in Shanghai[27] shall not accept litigations when the shareholders of a listed company file a petition to invalidate a resolution of a general meeting or board of directors. Further, in 2006, the Higher Court of Shanghai published a guideline that requested every local inferior court not to hear cases involving over-the-counter transactions of unlisted company stocks.[28] Similar incidents also appeared in the Guangxi Zhuang Autonomous Region, where the Higher Court of Guangxi passed a controversial notice to inferior courts that classified 13 types of cases as "temporarily unacceptable" (e.g., securities litigations related to inside dealing and market manipulation).[29]

Other than on the basis of explicit rules or policies, local courts may sometimes preclude certain litigations by implicit convention. For example, in 2007, after the listed company Hangxiao Steel Structure Inc. was punished by the China Securities Regulatory Commission (CSRC) for misrepresentation, investors filed lawsuits before the Intermediate Court of Hangzhou (capital of Zhejiang Province). Instead of accepting and hearing the cases, the Intermediate Court refused to decide whether to accept it (regardless of the statutory time limit set by the CCPC that a court must make such a decision within 7 days). Instead, it kept delaying the decision, claiming that it required guidance from the Higher Court and Supreme Court.[30] These actions are quite common for courts dealing with securities litigations around the country. In terms of the legal disputes caused by the "warrant" (a financial product that

---

[24] See Xiaoming SONG, "The Summary in the Symposium about the Courts' Disposal of Bankruptcy Cases of Financial Institutions" (Nov. 10, 2004).

[25] See the Supreme Court, Fa-Fa [2009] No. 35.

[26] See the Higher Court of Shanghai, "Disposal opinion on the issues in relation to the trial of corporate litigations (Volume 1)," Hu-Gao-Fa [2003] No. 216 (Dec. 18, 2003).

[27] The guideline may have a direct effect only on the Higher Court itself and lower courts in the district of Shanghai. The courts in other areas and the Supreme Court are not bound by it.

[28] See the Higher Court of Shanghai, "Response to the issues on the trial of corporate litigations," Hu-Gao-Fa-Min-Er [2006] No. 8 (Jun. 6, 2006).

[29] See "Notice of the Higher Court of Guangxi on temporarily not accepting certain types of cases at the present time," Gui-Gao-Fa [2003] No. 180 (Sept. 2003).

[30] See Yixin SONG, *supra.* note 17, at p. 67.

recently appeared in the Chinese securities market),[31] most courts frequently choose an "ostrich policy" and struggle to close their doors on disputes.[32]

2.2 *Restrictions Set by the Courts During the Trials*

As stated previously, the courts may reject the entrance of certain financial disputes into judicial procedures. However, in broadening our perspective, we may find that a "gray zone" of academic interest in addition to these clear "denial of trial" incidents. Although there is no visible obstacle in the way that precludes financial litigations from being accepted, the courts may nevertheless establish all sorts of restrictions during a trial, making it more difficult for plaintiffs to pursue their claims.

First, the plaintiffs may be told that they can only raise lawsuits before designated courts. For example, through a judicial interpretation,[33] the Supreme Court dictated that only the intermediate courts in Shanghai or Shenzhen could respectively hear cases in which the Shanghai or Shenzhen Stock Exchanges were named as defendants (or third parties) due to a dispute in connection with their self-regulatory functions. In another judicial interpretation by the Supreme Court,[34] it was provided that all lawsuits against the misrepresentations of listed companies must be filed to the intermediate courts where the companies are incorporated. The principle established by the CCPC, i.e., "a lawsuit can be under the jurisdiction of the court at the place where the tort occurs,"[35] is thus explicitly deprived of applicability. An inevitable consequence of such an arrangement is that most investors have no choice but to bring litigation before a court thousands of miles from their residences. This inconvenience naturally has a negative influence on investors' motivations to seek judicial remedies.

Second, the courts may impose some restrictive preconditions before the party can raise a legal action. For example, the Supreme Court makes it clear that "[i]n a case of civil compensation arising from misrepresentation, which is accepted by the court, such misrepresentation must have been investigated by CSRC or its dispatched office, and an effective penalty decision shall have been made by it. Only when the party files a lawsuit by relying on the investigation result as the factual basis may the court accept this case in accordance with the law."[36] Furthermore, inferior courts are required to seek approval from the Higher Court and Supreme Court for accepting

---

[31] A warrant is a security that is similar to an option that entitles the holder to buy the underlying stock of the issuing company at a fixed exercise price until the expiry date.

[32] One exception was the First Intermediate Court of Shanghai's confirmation in its judgment on a 2009 case (Liqiang XING v. Shanghai Stock Exchange) that "warrant" disputes are within the courts' jurisdiction. This judgment was later published in a bulletin by the Supreme Court, implying its changing standpoint on the issue. See "Bulletin of Supreme Court," Volume 7, 2010.

[33] See the Supreme Court, Fa-Shi [2005] No. 1.

[34] See *supra*. note 14.

[35] See Article 28 of CCPC.

[36] See *supra*. note 14.

cases related to investment bank bankruptcies.[37] For such cases, the Supreme Court specifies eight conditions for the acceptance of an action, such as the CSRC and Supreme Court's approval of the bankruptcy and the proper treatment of employees. Only when all of the conditions have been satisfied can the court allow the case to be accepted. A similar reporting procedure is also requested when dealing with the bankruptcy case of a listed company.[38] To justify this policy, the Supreme Court explains that "the bankruptcy of a listed company is very sensitive and complicated, involving many interested parties," and that "although the Bankruptcy Code has provided a more effective instrument for the revival of a listed company, the courts still need to maintain cautious in accepting cases relating to the bankruptcy of listed companies until other relevant policies (e.g. a proper framework of disposition of corporate employees and properties) are introduced."[39]

Third, a restriction may commonly be applied to the form of a lawsuit. In accordance with the CCPC, although many people may respectively bring their claims to court and a commonality may be found in their subject matter, the courts may consolidate every suite into a "joint action" provided every party agrees.[40] When a "joint action" is brought forward in which the exact number of plaintiff parties is high to the point of uncertainty, the court may publish a notice to inform qualified persons to register within a certain period. The parties that have registered with the court may choose one or more representatives to participate in the litigation on their behalf. (If no representative is chosen, the court may determine a representative or representatives after consulting with the registered parties.) The judgment or ruling made by the court in the "joint action" shall then bind all of the registered parties, and apply to any similar action brought forward by any party that has not registered with the court.[41] This is referred to in China as the "representative action with an uncertain number of parties." This kind of "representative action" obviously provides a cost-effective procedural solution to a scenario in which a large group of people suffers significant losses from securities fraud or misconduct such as misrepresentation. Investors may be more capable of protecting their interests if they band together to confront a strong opponent (a well-known example of such an arrangement is the U.S.-style class action). However, despite the explicit provision in the CCPC, courts have almost never applied the "representative action" in practice. Chinese judges have long declined to fully embrace a notion similar to the U.S.-style class action[42]

---

[37] See *supra.* note 16.

[38] Ibid.

[39] See Xiaoming XI, "Some Issues on Application of Law that Shall Be Paid Attention in Civil and Commercial Trials at the Present Time" (Dangqian Minshangshi Shenpan Gongzuo Yingdang Zhuyi de Jige Falv Shiyong Wenti), APPLICATION OF LAWS [China], Volume 7, 2007.

[40] See Article 52 of the CCPC.

[41] See Article 54 of the CCPC.

[42] It was also explicitly mentioned in the "Notice on the relevant issues concerning the acceptance of cases of disputes over civil tort arising from misrepresentation in the securities market" that "with regard to misrepresentation cases, the courts shall accept such cases in the form of individual action or joint action, but shall not accept them in the form of group action.".

on the basis that the time to introduce this form of litigation has never arisen.[43] Courts usually limit the number of plaintiffs in joint actions, sometimes by splitting one joint action into a number of smaller groups.[44] Further, the Supreme Court makes it clear that the number of plaintiffs in a joint action shall be determined before the trail begins.[45] Anyone who has an incentive to organize a joint action must determine and communicate with all (or most) of the victims to prepare a list of named plaintiffs.[46] This is fundamentally different from a U.S.-style class action, in which lead plaintiffs can represent claimants who do not specifically appear before the courts. Such claimants may be bound to the litigation unless they choose to exclude themselves.[47]

In summary, not every financial dispute that has sufficiently satisfied the CCPC's requirements may be accepted by the courts and resolved through judicial procedures. On the contrary, Chinese courts often install a number of roadblocks, making it difficult for parties to seek remedies. In this sense, an important task of the courts is to exercise their power and screen out cases in which they do not want to intervene.

3 WHY Financial Disputes Are Subjected to Selective Adjudication?

This section considers the reasons why case filtration occurs within the judicial system. The short answer is that China's courts are not independent.[48] Although this is true, major financial institutions such as state-owned commercial banks are favored due to their strong connections with the authorities (e.g., shareholdings and personnel appointments), and some large corporations can easily lobby for support from local governments due to their contribution to the local economy (e.g., job creation and tax payment). To avoid seeing these parties defeated in litigations, the courts may refuse to accept their cases in the first place. However, this answer only partly explains the presence of case filtration at best. Why do the courts refuse to accept financial litigations, rather than simply take on cases and deliver judgments

---

[43] See Walter Hutchens, *Private Securities Litigation in China: Material Disclosure about China's Legal System?*, 24 U. Pa. J. Int'l Econ. L. 599 (2003), 643–644.

[44] See "A New Problem in Securities Civil Litigation: The Number of Plaintiffs in Joint Actions are Limited" (Zhengquan Minshi Susong Xinwenti, Gongtong Susong Yuangao Renshu Shouxian), in SECURITIES TIMES (Apr. 9, 2003) [China]. Available at: http://www.people.com.cn/GB/jinji/35/159/20030409/966783.html.

[45] See *supra*. note 13.

[46] Given that the Chinese securities market is dominated by small retail investors, this task may be much more exhausting. Each victim has only a small damages claim, and thus the organizers of the joint action must find a sufficiently large number of plaintiffs to aggregate a massive amount of claims (to justify the huge costs of searching and communication).

[47] U.S. Federal Rules of Civil Procedure, Rules 23(a) and 23(c)(3).

[48] On the topic of the Chinese judicial system's independence, see Qianfan Zhang, "The People's Court in Transition: The Prospects of the Chinese Judicial Reform," Journal of Contemporary China, Volume 12, Issue 34, 2003, pp. 69–101.

in favor of "beloved" parties? Why do the courts accept one group of financial cases and deny others? There are other complicated factors that influence the behavior of China's courts and judges, and five possible factors are identified in this section.

3.1 Lack of Legal Rules in China's Financial Markets

A simple explanation may be that the supply of legal rules in emerging financial markets normally falls short on meeting the growing demand to resolve market disputes. In modern society, a basic role of the courts is to apply legal rules to judge cases. Therefore, a lag in legislation and rule making is detrimental to the efficiency of a judicial function. This is an exact definition of the financial world. To maximize self-interest, tens of thousands of market participants are continually trying their best to "create" or "invent" all kinds of innovative products and instruments. At the same time, these innovations may give rise to disputes never before seen in the markets. If lawmakers and regulatory agencies cannot catch up to the speed of innovation by producing workable legal rules, judges may soon find themselves unable to locate applicable rules to resolve disputes. After all, the market would not stop to wait on the perfection of the legal system, and neither would disputes disappear until proper legal rules were properly designed.

The authorities in China remain accustomed to the traditional planned economy and are not highly responsive to changes in the financial markets. Instead, they prefer to focus on resolving existing problems, and rarely consider the future development of markets or adjust their working agendas in advance. The field of securities litigation offers an appropriate example. China's first Securities Act was passed in the 1990s against the background of the Asian financial crisis. As they witnessed the collapse of stock markets in the area, it is understandable that Chinese lawmakers were very concerned about the importance of financial risk control during the enactment.[49] In contrast, the legislature gave little consideration to protecting investor interests, and the Securities Act offered no relevant provisions on the issue. As a result, when investors later rushed to the courts to bring lawsuits against listed companies, the courts were understandably uncomfortable and confused, as no applicable rules were available to ensure a ruling. In this circumstance, the Supreme Court issued the Notice in 2001 and disallowed inferior courts to handle securities litigation.[50]

In other cases, although a law or regulation has already introduced general principles on a certain issue, the courts may nevertheless find applying such principles problematic due to the absence of detailed guidelines and procedural rules in the legal sources. For instance, in 2003, an investor who held 24.56% of the units of a close-end fund made a proposal to the fund management company, and called for

[49] See General Office of the NPC (National People's Congress) Standing Committee, APPLICATION GUIDELINE OF SECURITIES ACT OF PEOPLE'S REPUBLIC OF CHINA (Zhonghua Renmin Gongheguo Zhengquanfa Yingyong Zhinan) (Jan. 1999) [China], pp. 377.

[50] See *supra.* note 13.

a general meeting of the fund holders to consider a resolution to change the fund to an open-end fund. However, the fund management company refused to sign the proposal statement and to convene the general meeting. The investor then raised the argument to a district court in Shanghai, basing his claim on a provision in the Securities Investment Fund Act that "fund holders who represent more than 10% of the fund units are entitled to require the convening of the general meeting of fund holders (with respect to a matters within the authorities of general meeting)."[51] However, this provision did not follow any rule on how such a right could be enforced in a judicial way. Given the silence of the Act, the court finally decided not to accept the case, as it was unsure whether the law actually granted judges any authoritative power to force the fund management company to call a general meeting in accordance with the requirement of a qualified investor.

3.2 *The Courts Are Incapable of Hearing Complicated and Innovative Financial Disputes*

Although the lack of a supply of legal rules may factor into a court's "denial of trial," it cannot constitute the whole answer. It is worth bearing in mind that the courts themselves are also playing the role of rule-maker. Through the issuance of documents such as judicial interpretations, the courts and especially the Supreme Court have become de facto participants in China's legislation structure. In theory, even if the legislature and regulatory bodies failed to produce the rules, the courts could fill the gap by themselves. However, when confronted with challenging cases, the courts regularly turn their back on "troubles" rather than actively use their rule-making power to remove the uncertainty.[52]

Why is this so? The courts may reject or restrict the acceptance of certain financial cases because they are short on the knowledge and experience necessary to hear financial disputes. The courts usually give some explanation in legal documents to justify their decisions not to accept certain financial litigations. Through an analysis of these documents, we observe that to a certain extent the courts are not too shy to admit their weaknesses. For example, the Supreme Court issued a judicial interpretation in 2003 entitled "Certain provisions on trial of civil compensation cases arising from misrepresentation in the securities market."[53] In accordance with this document,

[51] See Article 72 of the Securities Investment Fund Act of 2003 (now Article 84 of the Act due to the amendment in 2012).

[52] By comparison, the role of American courts are not absent in the history of securities regulation in the U.S. For example, the definition of the term "securities" was largely shaped by the U.S. Supreme Court in *SEC v. Howey Co.* (328 U.S. 293 (1946)) and in other cases. See James Cox, Robert Hillman & Donald Langevoort, SECURITIES REGULATION: CASES AND MATERIALS (3rd ed.) (Aspen Law & Business, 2001), pp. 117–203.

[53] See the Supreme Court, Fa-Shi [2003] No. 2 (Jan. 9, 2003). This was also confirmed in the "Notice on the relevant issues concerning the acceptance of cases of disputes over civil tort arising from misrepresentation in the securities market." See *supra.* note 13.

the courts could only accept lawsuits in which the plaintiff investors' claims were based on an administrative sanction decision made by a relevant authority (e.g., the CSRC) or a penal sentence instrument of the courts. The Supreme Court confessed that the restriction is in place because "without no such a precondition as buffer, the courts would very likely be flooded with a large number of these cases."[54] In other words, the restriction reflects the worry related to the courts' resource and capability deficiencies.

Nevertheless, it is not convincing that the courts avoid certain financial cases simply because the judges think themselves incapable of understanding and handling their complexity. For a long time, the courts repeatedly held back on accepting misrepresentation cases, pleading that "they are not ready" or that "the conditions are not mature" enough for them to hear the disputes. Further, although the outside world questions the integrity of financial statements, some listed companies may turn out to be aggressive and sue those critics for defamation. In contrast to the conservative attitude they hold in misrepresentation cases, the courts rarely hesitate in taking on libel cases. This difference raises a question: faced with a case that targets the accuracy of corporate information, why do the courts stop claiming themselves incapable when listed companies are seated in the plaintiff position?

3.3 Background of a Market Economy in Transition

The behavior of the judicial system cannot be understood without considering China's financial markets. Unlike most countries, the so-called "socialist market economy"—an economic model implemented by China after the reform beginning in 1978—is not accurately described as a "spontaneous social order,"[55] i.e., an evolution of the economic system initiated and driven by the market force. Rather, it was artificially "constructed" as a replacement for the centrally planned economy of the prior 3 decades. In other words, the market economy was introduced out of the Chinese government's determination and effort, and was not a choice pushed forward by an invisible hand. This was especially true during the development of the financial markets. In the past, the central government relied on its superior authority over an administrative hierarchy to organize the country's economic system. Financial institutions, which had the central bank serving as an exclusive nexus, used to be subsidiary to the treasury. Under this system, no financial market existed in the modern sense. With the reform and opening up, the importance of financial markets became apparent and the government began to actively instruct the establishment of these markets on its own initiative (e.g., opening the stock market even though

[54] See Guoguang LI, UNDERSTANDING AND APPLICATION OF JUDICIAL INTERPRETATIONS OF THE SUPREME COURT ON TRIAL OF MISREPRESENTATION CASES IN THE SECURITIES MARKET (Zuigao Renmin Fayuan Guangyu Shenli Zhengquan Shichang Xujia Chenshu Anjian Sifa Jieshi de Lijie yu Shiyong) (People's Court Press, 2003) [China], pp. 128–131.

[55] See Friedrich A. Hayek, THE CONSTITUTION OF LIBERTY (University of Chicago Press, 1978).

the concept of the "stock limited company" had been abandoned for nearly half a century[56]). This impulse has introduced rapid growth to China's financial markets in the last 30 years. However, an inevitable side effect is that the government has enjoyed a high level of control over the operation of the financial markets. In China, for instance, no securities can be offered to the public without permission from the authorities (in contrast to the Western model in which a registration is sufficient for the public offering of securities). Further, it is up to regulators to draw an upper limit on the interest rate that a commercial bank can charge its clients. Put another way, the government maintains a tight grip on China's financial market, which continues to be shadowed by the old-fashioned planned economy.[57]

In a sense, when the financial markets defer to the planning of a centralized authority, the role of the courts is limited or even redundant. As the domination of such a planner goes unchallenged, the market participants may simply be told to follow instructions rather than enter into contracts with one other like independent entities in a pure market economy. For example, the Supreme Court correctly pointed out that the only reason why asset management corporations (AMCs) take in non-performing assets from state-owned commercial banks is because they are required by public policy to do so. As such, "it is only a transfer of state-owned property (between two state-owned financial institutions) under governmental directive," and not a result of business negotiation driven by the desire to maximize self-interest.[58] In this situation, it is understandable that if any dispute were to occur between two parties, they would be more willing to refer the problem to the government that arranged the transaction in the first place. Further, if the disputed parties were to call for judicial resolution, the courts may feel powerless because they have no authority to settle the argument. Given these observations, it is no wonder that the Supreme Court finally chose not to accept cases of toxic asset transfer but instead to let the government solve them.[59] In 1993, the Supreme Court closed the door on cases related to special loans awarded by the government to alleviate poverty based on the reason that "it is proper to let the administrative bodies handle the disputes."[60] It appears that the courts are very careful not to trespass too far into the government's domain in the financial system.

---

[56] For a consideration of the structural change of China's capital market and financial system, see Yao Guangye, "The Process, Objectives and Patterns of Investment System Reform in China," Journal of Contemporary China, Volume 11, Issue 32, 2002, pp. 573–579.

[57] For observations on the historical development of China's banking industry and its regulatory system, see Jun Ma, "China's banking sector: From administrative control to a regulatory framework," Journal of Contemporary China, Volume 5, Issue 12, 1996, pp. 155–169. See also Minxin Peia, "The political economy of banking reforms in China, 1993–1997," Journal of Contemporary China, Volume 7, Issue 18, 1998, pp. 321–350 (discussing the defective features of China's banking system).

[58] See *supra.* note 20.

[59] Ibid.

[60] See the Supreme Court, Fa-Fu [1993] No. 7 (Aug. 28, 1993).

3.4 Political Considerations on Maintaining the Stability of Society and Financial Markets

"Maintaining stability" is currently a top priority for Chinese politics.[61] The ruling Communist Party has long declared that a stable social order is crucial for the economic development of the country.[62] To meet this purpose, every part of the regime must take every necessary measure to prevent major chaos and dislocation. The judiciary cannot be an exception to this principle.[63] Thus, the courts must take seriously any litigation that may affect the interests of large groups of people. The financial markets are certainly a source of such intractable issues. Considering the huge number of depositors, policyholders and retail investors in China, it is obvious that any disputes that occur in the market could trigger public outrage. This outrage could be further stimulated when investors around the country become organized through lawsuits (i.e., a joint action) and united as a strong power. Such an outcome would intensify societal conflict and pose a threat to the authority of the Party. In this circumstance, the courts may be inclined to stay away from certain controversial financial litigations to minimize the potential risk to social stability.

Let us take securities litigation as an example. As mentioned previously, the Supreme Court presents an obstacle to misrepresentation cases by establishing a precondition (i.e., the plaintiff can only bring the lawsuit forward when an administrative sanction or criminal penalty has already been imposed against the alleged misrepresentation) because the courts are deficient in the resources necessary to deal with these cases. However, this raises an interesting question. If the Supreme Court has already designed the "water gate" to keep out a "flood" of securities litigations, why does it set up an additional restriction on the form of the lawsuit by disallowing the plaintiff investors to initiate a "representative action with an uncertain number of parties"? It is clear that such a form of "representative action," which is explicitly provided in the CCPC, has a cost-saving benefit for the courts, as hearing thousands of cases with similar facts and subjects one after the other could amount to a waste of time. Why would the courts choose a more difficult path? The answer may no longer be a judicial issue, but extend to a political concern. The Supreme Court confessed that "as China's securities market is now in a course of transition relying on stability and progress, if (the courts) remove all limitations to the acceptance of misrepresentation cases, it would not be beneficial for keeping a balance between establishing a proper market order (through the gradual elimination of misconducts)

---

[61] See "China Vows to Address Public Complaints to Maintain Social Stability," in BEIJING REVIEW (Mar. 3, 2009). Available at: http://www.bjreview.com.cn/NPC&CPPCC2009/2009-03/05/content_182748.htm.

[62] See Feng Chen, *Order and Stability in Social Transition: Neoconservative Political Thought in Post-1989 China*, China Quarterly, No. 151, Sep. 1997, pp. 593–613; Xinping Guan, *China's Social Policy: Reform and Development in the Context of Marketization and Globalization*, Social Policy & Administration, Volume 34, Issue 1, Mar. 2000, pp. 115–130.

[63] See "Maintaining stability: top priority for Chinese judiciary, police in 2012," in XINHUA NEWS (Dec. 23, 2012). Available at: http://news.xinhuanet.com/english/china/2011-12/23/c_131324108.htm.

and maintaining the market stability, neither would it be good for achieving the goal of capital raising and investment in the market."[64] This shows that the Supreme Court is determined to place the mission of "maintaining stability" (i.e., to suppress any large-scale lawsuit that may turn into a public movement beyond the government's control) far above its fundamental judiciary function (i.e., to firmly and rationally apply the law).

The words "maintaining stability" have been explicitly referred to on other occasions. For example, the government has called the disposition of illegal over-the-counter stock trading a topic of crucial importance to the stability of social and market order.[65] It is thus not surprising that the Supreme Court avoided stepping into the fray at the risk of disturbing the government's effort to "maintain stability."[66] Confronted with a wave of distressed investment banks' bankruptcy applications, the Supreme Court put the principle of "maintaining social stability" first on its agenda and instructed inferior courts to keep it firmly in mind. Moreover, at the local level, the courts are actively watching out for potential community instability. The Higher Court of Shanghai released a guideline in 2006, asking the inferior courts under its jurisdiction to pay "serious" attention to lawsuits in which the validity of the resolutions of a general meeting or board meeting of listed companies are in question (i.e., the investors petition to the courts to declare a resolution void).[67] As the Higher Court explained, because such cases may trigger the problems of mass litigation and instability in the securities markets, "the courts must be cautious in accepting these cases, and if necessary, report to the Higher Court for approval of acceptance."[68] In sum, given the present political philosophy and structure, it is understandably certain that judicial power must follow the overwhelming demand to "maintain stability" while sacrificing the aims to protect investors and resolve disputes.

3.5 Self-interest of Judiciary

Finally and probably most importantly, the courts deny the acceptance of certain financial litigations because the filtration may serve their own interest. Like most individuals and organizations, the courts and judges are likely to be rational actors looking to maximize their self-interest by "calculating" the cost/return of their actions and performing the actions in a way that achieves the optimal expected outcome.[69]

---

[64] See *supra.* note 54.

[65] See "Notice of General Office of the State Council," Guo-Fa-Ban (1998) No. 10 (Mar. 25, 1998).

[66] See *supra.* note 11.

[67] See *supra.* note 29.

[68] Ibid.

[69] See Gary S. Becker, THE ECONOMIC APPROACH TO HUMAN BEHAVIOR (University of Chicago Press, 1978), and Joyce S. Osland, David A. Kolb, Irwin M. Rubin & Marlene E. Turner, ORGANIZATIONAL BEHAVIOR: AN EXPERIENTIAL APPROACH 8th ed. (Prentice Hall, 2006).

In the preceding sections, this chapter interprets judicial behavior from an outside perspective, and implies that the courts may be influenced by external pressures such as an undeveloped legal system and a political obligation to refuse hearing cases in an effort to "maintain social stability." However, such a suggestion is misleading, as we have thus far failed to consider judiciary incentive.

At times, China's courts do not want to become involved in troublesome litigation. Put another way, denying a trial is a strategy for returning a problem back to the territory of another authority. Anyone interested in understanding China's political system must realize that China does not apply the "*trias politica* principle" (i.e., the doctrine of separation of powers). The judiciary in China is not in a position independent of the administration. Rather, along with other branches of the state, it is a component of a supreme political machine under the control of the Communist Party to organize economic, social and political affairs. Under this superior-authority arrangement, state governance functions are divided into several parts and allotted to different branches (including the judiciary). Each branch has almost exclusive power to regulate and judge any relevant affair. For example, in financial markets, the dominant power is awarded to regulatory bodies (often referred to in China as the "one bank and three commissions," including the Central Bank of China, China Securities Regulatory Commission, China Banking Regulatory Commission and China Insurance Regulatory Commission), which have a large say in making rules and fixing problems. Courts are normally accustomed to endorsing and executing the decisions of regulatory bodies.[70] In some ways, the structure resembles that of a corporation in which a marketing department is mainly responsible for setting the marketing strategy, while other departments do not directly interfere.

As long as we understand this political "conventional wisdom," the evasive attitude of courts is easily explained. Because shaping the order of a financial market is the responsibility of regulatory bodies, courts may be comfortable concluding that it is none of their business to take part in the resolution of financial disputes. For example, at a national conference, former Supreme Court Vice-president Guoguang Li said that "in general, as for the disputes relating to unauthorized public solicitation for fund raising…they shall be left to the relevant authorities for settlement."[71] This obviously expresses the judiciary's standpoint, i.e., "do not put my finger into another person's pie." In other words, the courts believe it unnecessary to clean up the "mess" caused by the incompetence of other bodies. Regulatory agencies or local governments

[70] This is exactly the case in the government's effort to crack down on unapproved and illegal public solicitation for raising funds (i.e., crowdfunding). In 2007, the State Council agreed to organize a joint conference institution by holding irregularly scheduled meetings of senior officers from different departments to give advice on how to work together against illegal crowdfunding. The China Banking Regulatory Commission (CBRC) was made the leading actor of the meetings, and the Chairman of the CBRC was made the convener. See "Reply by the State Council," Guo-Han [2007] No. 4 (Jan. 8, 2007). In practice, the CBRC's conclusion is often considered decisive in determining the legality of a crowdfunding activity. As long as an activity is considered illegal by the CBRC, the courts will almost always accept its opinion and convict the individuals who raised the funds. This indicates the strong position of the financial regulatory bodies.

[71] See *supra.* note 23.

should take responsibility for the emergence and deterioration of financial disputes. It is no good for judges to get involved in such trouble, as they could draw the fire onto themselves and turn their courts into targets of media coverage and public anger.

The judiciary incentive must also be carefully assessed in the courts' restrictions on the forms of lawsuits when a large number of investors are involved (e.g., rejecting the notion of "representative action"). In fact, the current organizational structure of China's judicial system produces a stimulus to encourage courts to place all kinds of obstacles in the way of accepting these cases. The performance of the courts in China and particularly inferior courts is under very rigid annual assessment against a series of statistics[72] such as the number of cases being reversed by a superior court during the appeal and the number of cases that are not ruled within the time limit. The income and promotion of judges rely greatly on these assessment results. This pressure thus has some influence on judiciary behavior. First, although the "representative action" model is convenient for investors in a misrepresentation scenario, the courts may hold the opposite view and believe that the cost outweighs the benefit. A court must devote a significant amount of time, energy and personnel to hear a representative action. Even if the case were judged smoothly, the court would not gain any additional credit in its annual assessment. In the assessment, the performance of the court in each case, regardless of their individual differences, is given an equal score. Therefore, it would not matter if the court made a judgment on a securities litigation or a small-claim tort case. In sum, the courts cannot benefit from playing an active and successful role in resolving disputes over financial matters (to offset the court's input of recourse). Second, if the trial became stuck and could not be completed within the prescribed period,[73] it could cause trouble. Failing to complete the trial in time would certainly be detrimental to the court's assessment results. If the court's ruling did not satisfy the investors, it may create a public relations disaster. Of course, there is no guarantee that investors will always win a legal battle or that a judgment will make every party happy. Considering the political sensitivity to "maintaining stability," a court's ruling may be labeled by the supreme authority as a disappointing "mistake." This would have a negative influence on the annual assessment results, and the court's efforts for the entire year may be destroyed by that single "mistake." Such a conclusion would be based simply on the subjective feeling of the superior, rather than on any objective standard. Consequently, it is difficult to say why a court would have any incentive to take on a case with high risk but little return.

---

[72] The assessment is carried out at both internal and external levels. The internal assessment is normally organized by a special committee that evaluates the personal performance of judges in the court. A superior court is in charge of the external assessment of the performance of the inferior courts under its jurisdiction. In accordance with the law, "the judicial work of the courts at lower levels is subject to supervision by the courts at higher levels." See Article 17(2), Organic Code of the People's Courts of the People's Republic of China (2006).

[73] E.g., Article 149 of the CCPC: "A court shall complete the trial of a case under formal procedure within six months after the case is docketed. If an extension of the period is necessary under special circumstances, the period may be extended for six months with the approval of the president of the court; and any further extension shall be subject to the approval of the superior court".

4 Final Remarks

As discussed previously, this chapter considers how and why Chinese courts use a filtration system to avoid subjecting certain financial litigations to judicial procedures. Our analysis helps us better understand the actual role of the courts in dispute resolution against the background of China's rapidly growing financial markets. At the same time, it gives us an opportunity to identify the inside and outside incentives and limitations that influence the behavior of the judiciary. Indeed, we sympathize with the courts, as the judicial power in China is typically surrounded by a number of barriers. However, our sympathy does not justify the filtration system, as doing so would underestimate its negative effects. What is reasonable for the courts (i.e., refusing to accept an action) may not be good for society, as it deprives some people of a chance of remediation. In the modern world, constitutions guarantee the fundamental human right to bring a lawsuit before a court for the purpose of enforcing a right or redressing a wrong. It is a rational claim for justice, and serves the principle of economic efficiency in the sense that it maximizes social welfare. A fair, proper and timely system of dispute resolution that relies on the judicial cycle can effectively decrease negotiation and transaction costs in the financial markets, and thus sustain the confidence of investors and encourage future innovation. To the contrary, filtration prevents disputes from being resolved through litigation. It may also cause confusion among the parties in a transaction, as no one can be sure how an unexpected argument will be settled in the future. Such uncertainty may affect the perspective of market participants toward expected returns and decrease their willingness to reach deals. Put another way, the filtration system imposes an additional cost on every party, which may damage the prosperity of the financial markets in the long term.

In China, the blockage of this channel of judicial remedy may distort the functioning of financial regulation. Because it deprives investors of a chance to sue wrongdoers in the markets, the notion of "private enforcement" becomes unworkable.[74] As a result, most of the responsibilities of investigating and redressing violations are placed on the shoulders of regulatory agencies such as CSRC. Leaving behind the controversy over whether private enforcement is preferable in the securities markets,[75] one thing is certain: an exclusive reliance on a public enforcer is not feasible. First, although a regulator could impose a heavy penalty on the offender, it may not compensate for the loss suffered by investors due to the misconduct. As long as investors realize such risks, they will be reluctant to either put their savings into the markets or ask for a discount on securities prices. Of course, this may raise the capital cost of financing and suppress the activity of financial markets. Second, regulatory agencies may be short on resources and staff. It is very likely that some

74 See William M. Landes & Richard A. Posner, "The Private Enforcement of Law," 4 J. Legal Stud. 1 (1975).

75 See Howell E. Jackson & Mark J. Roe, "Public and Private Enforcement of Securities Laws: Resource-Based Evidence," Journal of Financial Economics, Volume 93, Issue 2, 2009, 207–238, and Amanda M. Rose, "Reforming Securities Litigation Reform: Restructuring the Relationship between Public and Private Enforcement of Rule 10B-5," 108 Colum. L. Rev. 1301 (2008).

cases are not on the regulatory radar, or must endure a long investigation process, as investigating a case and reaching a conclusion typically takes years. Third, although regulatory agencies monopolize the enforcement power, the risk of "rent seeking"[76] is increasing as financial institutions try their best to lobby for a friendly regulatory environment. These agencies may thus be "captured" to advocate for the concerns of interest groups rather than safeguard the public investors in a process known as "regulatory capture."[77] Furthermore, it is obvious that disputes would not just disappear simply because the courts refused to hear them. When the courts close their doors, the regulatory agencies may be the only choice left for investors to petition. However, this arrangement cannot always produce a reasonable answer. It is necessary to realize that a regulator may sometimes be directly involved in a dispute with investors, or be blamed for the emergence of the dispute. Given the conflict of interest, it would be hard to ensure that the regulator redresses such problems and grievances. If the disputes could not be solved smoothly (i.e., if the regulator either dealt with the issue unfairly or rejected addressing it outright), the disappointment and indignation would accumulate and spill over, creating an inevitably destructive effect. In this sense, we may witness a ridiculous situation in which a court's choice to "maintain stability" and social order by refusing to accept certain financial litigations actually creates a much more serious instability in the market and society.

The warning signal should not be ignored. As long as the courts keep neglecting their function of dispute resolution, the regulatory failure and social tension deadlock may never be broken. The status quo must be changed. The judiciary must adjust its behavior model to meet the needs of the real world. The courts are expected to act as intermediaries to cushion the collision between disputed parties. Some Chinese judges fortunately appear to be ready to face the trend of change: "(against the background of the transition of an economic system) all disputes amongst entities or individuals can only be solved by legal measures or litigations; this is exactly the consequence caused by the establishment of market economy."[78] Further, market participants are losing patience over judiciary inaction. People never cease demanding change when defending their interests. For example, after suffering great losses in a number of misrepresentation scandals, many investors, well-known economists and legal scholars expressed their strong disappointment and protested against the Supreme Court's ban on accepting actions connected to securities transactions. The public pressure finally forced the Supreme Court to make a concession and partly remove its prohibition in 2003. This shows that the scope for the courts to resist change is becoming smaller.

---

[76] See Gordon Tullock, RENT SEEKING (Edward Elgar, 1993), and Anne O. Krueger, "The Political Economy of the Rent-Seeking Society," *American Economic Review*, Volume 64, No. 3, Jun. 1974, 291–303.

[77] See Lawrence G. Baxter, Understanding Regulatory Capture: An Academic Perspective from the United States (June 27, 2012). THE MAKING OF GOOD FINANCIAL REGULATION, pp. 32–34 (Stefano Pagliari, ed., 2012). Available at SSRN: http://ssrn.com/abstract=2094659.

[78] Xiaoming XI, "China's market economy and Trails of Civil and Commercial Cases," a speech in the Law School of Renmin University of China (Oct. 23, 2007).

Nevertheless, change is never easy. The courts must give up its filtration of financial cases. This goal relies on a systematic reformation of China's social and political structure. Enhancing judicial independence is an indispensable step over the long term. Under the present political institution, the judiciary is largely subject to interference from the other branches of government.[79] This lack of independence is harmful to the reputation of China's judicial system, and will shake the confidence of parties who walk into the courtroom to resolve disputes. To reverse the state of things, the government must seriously review and reshape the function of the judiciary, and consider it as more than merely a "tool" that can be easily manipulated. Instead, the government must respect the independence of courts and recognize them as places to settle disputes. As long as the political fetter is relished, the courts will be more comfortable taking on the financial litigations they formerly feared, and judges will become more experienced at understanding and handling financial disputes. At that moment, China's courts will play an important role in shaping financial market order as the theory suggests.

[79] See Carl F. Minzner, "China's Turn against Law," 59 Am. J. Comp. L. 935 (2011).

Chapter 7
A Return to Adam Smith? Bigtechs Versus *Status Quo* Financial Law and Regulation

Abstract In the past decades, the rise of Bigtechs in finance has taken place at a time of declining public trust in governments and traditional financial institutions. In addition to the changes they brought to finance, the chapter outlines that Bigtechs, leveraging on technological advances, challenge the *status quo* financial law and regulation, thus the financial systems. Technology has the potential to fill the void of trust left by *status quo* financial system. The chapter in turn raises the question as to whether the functions or the roles of the State in financial markets perhaps should be reconsidered and the possibility that technology may provide a means to fill the void of trust left by the governments and financial institutions.

1 Introduction

Trust is a fundamental part of a society and a financial system. Since the removal of the gold standard in 1931 in the UK,[1] we have placed trust in a system where the state would make good on their promises and a ten-dollar note would get you a loaf of bread. The fundamental role of trust in financial institutions should not be underestimated: financial products and services are inherently personal and potentially have a significant impact on the lives of customers. Financial law and regulation essentially promote and maintain trust in the system; as a result, participants participate.

In the past decades, the rise of Bigtechs in finance has occurred at a time of declining public trust in governments and in traditional financial institutions. By leveraging new technology, 'Bigtechs'[2] have entered and made themselves a visible

---

[1] James Morrison, 'Shocking Intellectual Austerity: The Role of Ideas in the Demise of the Gold Standard in Britain' (2016) 70(1) *International Organization* 175, 176.

[2] The term bigtech was defined as large globally active technology firms with a relative advantage in digital technology, See Basel Committee on Banking Supervision, Sound Practices: Implications of fintech developments for banks and bank supervisors (Consultative Document (August 2017) https://www.bis.org/bcbs/publ/d415.pdf BigTech firms are major technology companies that have expanded into financial services. They are part of a broader category of 'TechFin' companies that leverage their existing technologies and customer bases in a non-financial service industry to subsequently enter the financial sector: see, e.g., Alessandra Tanda and Cristiana-Maria Schena,

T. Huang and W. He, *Politics Meets Markets*, Contemporary Chinese Civil and Commercial Law, https://doi.org/10.1007/978-981-97-9176-7_7

player operating in the global financial sector. Their access to vast amounts of data combined with computational capacities to analyse that data has led to the enormous strides Bigtechs are achieving in their market performance.[3] In the US, Bigtechs such as Amazon, Google, and Facebook have developed considerable footprints in finance. Similarly, in China, three bigtech companies, namely Alibaba, Tencent, and Baidu, have made their presence prominent in China's financial sector. Bigtechs are not only engaging in traditional financial services, but are also expanding the boundaries of financial services.

Bigtechs have pursued a strategy of progressively broadening their financial activities—starting with payment infrastructure and expanding into 'the provision of credit, insurance, and savings and investment products, either directly or in cooperation with financial institution partners'.[4] Bigtechs are distinctive in the financial sector because of the breadth of their networks and the complexity of their data technology.[5] By using their various products and services as an 'entry point to other products or markets', Bigtechs are able to challenge incumbent firms[6] and exert significant control over markets.[7]

The effects of Bigtechs have been most prominent in China, which has witnessed significant changes in national financial systems after the emergence of Bigtechs. Bigtechs in China have market capitalisations 'comparable to those of the world's largest financial groups'.[8] Alipay and WeChat Pay 'account for 94% of the mobile payments market',[9] expanding their payment services to cover 'hundreds of millions' of customers within the span of a decade.[10] Bigtech mobile payments reached 16% of Chinese GDP in 2017.[11] Bigtechs have continued to diversify their offerings, setting

---

'BigTech Strategic Approaches: Worrying Competition?' in *FinTech, BigTech and Banks* (Palgrave Pivot, 2019) 37, 37; Dirk A Zetsche et al., 'From Fintech to Techfin: The Regulatory Challenges of Data-Driven Finance' (2018) 14(2) *New York University Journal of Law and Business* 393.

[3] Sands, Mike. 2017. Customer Data Is the Secret To Silicon Valley's Success." Forbes, November 29,

2017. Accessed May 22, 2019. https://www.forbes.com/sites/mikesands1/2017/11/29/customerdata-is-the-secret-to-silicon-valleys-success/#135386886c3b.

[4] Jon Frost et al., 'BigTech and the Changing Structure of Financial Intermediation' (BIS Working Paper No 779, April 2019) 2.

[5] Jon Frost et al., 'BigTech and the Changing Structure of Financial Intermediation' (BIS Working Paper No 779, April 2019) 2.

[6] Alessandra Tanda and Cristiana-Maria Schena, 'BigTech Strategic Approaches: Worrying Competition?' in *FinTech, BigTech and Banks* (Palgrave Pivot, 2019) 37, 47.

[7] Lucia Pacheco Rodriguez and Pablo Urbiola Ortun, 'From FinTech to BigTech: An Evolving Regulatory Response' (2020) 75(229) *Boletin de Estudios Economicos* 119, 129.

[8] Financial Stability Board, *BigTech in Finance: Market Developments and Potential Financial Stability Implications* (Report, 9 December 2019) 4.

[9] Jon Frost et al., 'BigTech and the Changing Structure of Financial Intermediation' (BIS Working Paper No 779, April 2019) 6.

[10] Long Chen, 'From Fintech to Finlife: The Case of Fintech Development in China (2016) 9(3) *China Economic Journal* 225, 227, 231.

[11] Jon Frost et al., 'BigTech and the Changing Structure of Financial Intermediation' (BIS Working Paper No 779, April 2019) 6.

up online banks, consumer credit, and insurance products.[12] Such products tend to be more limited than payment services, but are actively growing.[13] The influence and competitiveness of Bigtech is particularly significant because they are uniquely able to service niches unmet by incumbent banks. For instance, underprivileged customers in China who previously may not have been able to provide sufficient documentation to access traditional bank credit have gained access to financial services from Bigtechs, which have offered them digital services to produce and score transactions data in lieu of documentation.[14]

Changes to finance are increasingly visible internationally and are likely to intensify in the future,[15] accelerated through the rise of Amazon, Apple, Facebook and Google.[16] These companies have already developed extensive networks capable of building economies of scale, enabling the creation of 'a data-driven, international market presence' that can accelerate the growth of financial ventures.[17] These companies have the capacity to rapidly expand into the consumer financial marketplace by purchasing smaller companies and monopolising markets. The companies have considerable financial firepower, with each having 'over $500 million in market capitalization'.[18] These factors, in conjunction with established customer networks and brand recognition, will allow Bigtechs to expand into financial services very rapidly.[19] In doing so, they will continue to develop as major players in financial markets. In 2018, financial services represented about 11% of the revenues of Bigtechs.[20]

The literature has so far predominantly focused on the effects of technology and Bigtechs in particular on incremental and structural changes in finance and financial markets. What has rarely been discussed is the fact that the presence and expansion

---

[12] Alessandra Tanda and Cristiana-Maria Schena, 'BigTech Strategic Approaches: Worrying Competition?' in *FinTech, BigTech and Banks* (Palgrave Pivot, 2019) 37, 44.

[13] Ant Financial offers insurance and investment products. Yu'ebao reached RMB 1.7 trillion AUM in five years: Jon Frost et al., 'BigTech and the Changing Structure of Financial Intermediation' (BIS Working Paper No 779, April 2019) 8.

[14] Jon Frost et al., 'BigTech and the Changing Structure of Financial Intermediation' (BIS Working Paper No 779, April 2019) 7.

[15] Lucia Pacheco Rodriguez and Pablo Urbiola Ortun, 'From FinTech to BigTech: An Evolving Regulatory Response' (2020) 75(229) *Boletin de Estudios Economicos* 119, 130.

[16] Dirk A Zetsche et al., 'From Fintech to Techfin: The Regulatory Challenges of Data-Driven Finance' (2018) 14(2) *New York University Journal of Law and Business* 393, 396–7. For example, Facebook announced plans for the stablecoin Libra in 2019: Financial Stability Board, *BigTech in Finance: Market Developments and Potential Financial Stability Implications* (Report, 9 December 2019) 7.

[17] Dirk A Zetsche et al., 'From Fintech to Techfin: The Regulatory Challenges of Data-Driven Finance' (2018) 14(2) *New York University Journal of Law and Business* 393, 414.

[18] Michael B Landau, 'The Astounding Growth of "Big Tech" and the Lack of Enforcement of the Intellectual Property, Antitrust, and Contract Laws (2020) 30(3) *Albany Law Journal of Science and Technology* 1, 1.

[19] Financial Stability Board, *BigTech in Finance: Market Developments and Potential Financial Stability Implications* (Report, 9 December 2019) 3.

[20] Bank for International Settlements, Annual Economic Report 2019 (Report, June 2019) https://www.bis.org/publ/arpdf/ar2019e3.pdf 56.

of these Bigtechs presents a challenge for financial regulation and ultimately for the State, and has the potential to reshape interactions between financial markets and the State. One such recent battle was between Facebook and the *status quo* financial system. On 18 June 2019, the Libra Association announced its plans to introduce Libra as a blockchain-based global digital currency which is similar to Bitcoin but is more stable. The proposal proved contentious and in the face of immense pressure, Libra was repositioned as a more traditional coin which will be tied to fiat currencies in April 2020.[21] Most recently, on 23 October 2020, Ma Yun, the founder of Alibaba and the controller of Ant Finance, criticized financial regulation and stated that Basel is an old folks club.[22] He held the view that security (mortgage and guarantee) is an outdated way to manage risks; data should be the basis for credit management.[23] Soon after his speech, *Internet Micro-credit Business Regulation (Provisional)* was issued for public consultation on 24 October which would restrict the business of Ant Finance in a significant way.[24] On 2 November, regulatory authorities "had a chat" with key personnel of Ant Group.[25] On 3 November, the IPO of Ant Group was suspended by the Shanghai Stock Exchange.

The aim of this chapter is to investigate whether technology has the capacity or demonstrated capacity to change the manner in which financial markets have been regulated over the past few decades, with particular attention directed towards Bigtechs such as Amazon, Google, Facebook, Alibaba, Tencent and Baidu. The *status quo* financial market was established after the Wall Street Crash of 1929, which led to a series of reforms instigated by the Roosevelt Government in the US. This series of

---

[21] 'Libra: The Path Forward', *Libra Association* (Blog Post, 18 June 2019) https://libra.org/en-US/blog/the-path-forward/.

[22] The speech was deleted soon after and not available on official webpages. Zhou Yanyan, 'Ma Yun: Chinese finance does not have systemic risks, but still lacks the risks of a healthy financial system', 21 Jingji (Web Page, 24 October 2020).

https://m.21jingji.com/article/20201024/herald/6fde8932bd811ddb7f887a24bf96e99b.html.

[23] Zhou Yanyan, 'Ma Yun: Chinese finance does not have systemic risks, but still lacks the risks of a healthy financial system', 21 Finance and Economics (Web Page, 24 October 2020) https://m.21jingji.com/article/20201024/herald/6fde8932bd811ddb7f887a24bf96e99b.html.

[24] In Nov 2020, the PBoC and the China Banking and Insurance Regulatory Commission issued Internet Micro-credit Business Regulation (Provisional) for public consultation: People's Bank of China Legal Affairs Department, 'Announcement of the China Banking and Insurance Regulatory Commission and the People's Bank of China on the "Interim Measures for the Administration of Online Small Loans (Draft for Comment)"' (Web Page, 2 November 2020) http://www.pbc.gov.cn/tiaofasi/144941/144979/3941920/4119958/index.html, under which stringent prudential regulation is imposed. First of all, micro credit companies are not allowed to finance 100% more than its net assets ARTICLE 12. micro credit companies should contribute no less than 30% for individual loans. Article 15 (3) In other words, internet financing platforms are not intermediaries any more. They must be the lenders themselves which would subject them to tighter prudential rules. These measures would dampen the business mode of ant financial for example. in the first half of 2020, ant financial made approximately RMB 46 billion in profit via "digital finance technology platform" which accounted for 63.4% of its profit. Ant group co., ltd., h share ipo, 27 October 2020, 13.

[25] China Securities Regulatory Commission, 'Four departments jointly arrange talks with relevant personnel of Ant Group' (Web Page, 2 November 2020) http://www.csrc.gov.cn/pub/newsite/zjhxwfb/xwdd/202011/t20201102_385514.html.

reforms in the US included the introduction and implementation of the *Banking Act* of 1933, the *Securities Act* of 1933, and the *Securities Exchange Act* of 1934. These reforms largely established the rules under which financial markets have operated since. Prior to that, there were no specific rules concerning the state and the markets with regards to the financial sector. The previous rules were predominantly based on the law concerning property, contracts and torts. The primary redress for disputes arising or in relation to financial markets was court action. After the reforms adopted by the Roosevelt government were emulated around the world, it has become the norm for the state to intervene in markets in its capacity as the market regulator. This chapter queries the basis for state intervention in financial markets. In turn, this chapter questions the interventionist role of the state in the markets, and whether is it subsequently possible for the state to return to what Adam Smith describes as a night watchman state.[26]

While the focus of this chapter is on Bigtechs in particular, including Amazon, Google, and Facebook in the US and Alibaba, Tencent, and Baidu in China, this chapter will also refer to technology in general. The remainder of the chapter is organized as follows. Part II will map out Bigtechs' inroads into the financial sector in the US and China. Bigtechs have established themselves as all-rounder financial services providers in financial markets. Furthermore, they are able to expand into areas or territories that other financial institutions are not equipped to reach. Part III will review the implications of the rise of Bigtechs in finance for financial regulation and the state. By doing so, Bigtech challenges *status quo* financial regulation as well as financial systems themselves. The issue of trust on the part of the public in *status quo* financial systems is also examined in Part III. Either through prudential regulation or information disclosure, the system operates on the basis of belief or trust. It is a matter of whether or to what extent technology is able to fill the void of trust left by *status quo* financial systems. Part IV concludes that, whilst acknowledging there is potential in technology, it is likely that the State ultimately would still wield the power of regulation, i.e. imposing the parameters within which Bigtechs operate.

[26] Adam Smith once believed that government's proper roles should be confined to: the provision of national defence, the administration of justice, and public goods (transportation and education). Adam Smith's Roles for Government and Contemporary U.S. Government Roles: Is the Welfare State Crowding Out Government's Basic Functions? Lipford, Jody W; Slice, Jerry. The Independent Review; *Oakland Volume* 11, Iss. 4, (Spring 2007): 485–501.

2 Bigtechs: Bring Technology and Finance Together

2.1 Traditional Banking and Financial Markets

To date, the focus of the US Bigtechs has mostly been on payment services. Their cooperation with the traditional banking industry is also observable.[27] Payment services is an area where Bigtechs are able to employ their advantages with technology. Amazon's first known payment product was "Pay with Amazon", launched in 2007.[28] Since 2011, Amazon has built up its financial ecosystem with the introduction of a number of services like Amazon Pay and Amazon Cash. Amazon Pay is a digital wallet enabling users to pay for goods from vendors other than Amazon. Amazon is licensed and regulated in the US as a money transmitter, and due to the US federal legal system, it has obtained licences from all different states' financial or monetary regulators.[29] Another product, Amazon Cash, allows people to add money into their Amazon Balance, allowing consumers to use the product when making purchases from convenience stores or grocery stores.[30]

In comparison, Google, as a search engine technology company, does not have organic advantages in the financial services industry like Amazon does. This makes its advances in finance even more notable. Google's most well-known product is Google Pay, largely due to the company's Android system, which is the operating system on a large number of smartphones, tablets and watches.[31] Generally speaking, Google Pay is a digital wallet platform and online payment system that empowers in-app and tap-to-pay purchases on mobile devices.[32] Google Pay is branded as "pay for whatever, whenever" and "card benefits, without the cards.[33] As for licenses, similar to Amazon payment services, Google has obtained money transmitter licenses from

---

27 Financial Stability Board, BigTech in Finance, Market developments and potential financial stability implications, 9 December 2019. Page 1.

28 'Everything You Need To Know About What Amazon Is Doing In Financial Services', CBInsights (Web Page, 31st January 2019) https://www.cbinsights.com/research/report/amazon-across-financial-services-fintech/.

29 'Money Transmitter Licenses', Amazon (Web Page, 31st March 2020) https://pay.amazon.com/help/82972.

30 'Amazon Cash', Amazon (Web Page, 31st March 2020) https://www.amazon.com/b?ie=UTF8&node=14583169011.

31 Google Pay was reformed in 2018 as a merger and internal consolidation of Google Wallet which was launched in 2011 and Android Pay which enabled transaction by the usage of near field communication technology; 'Big Tech in Finance: A Deep Dive into the Future of FinTech', Norman Alex (Web Page, 10th Febuary 2020) https://www.normanalex.com/2020/02/10/big-tech-in-finance-a-deep-dive-into-the-future-of-fintech/.

32 'Google Pay', Australian FinTech (Web Page, 31st March 2020) https://australianfintech.com.au/Company/google-pay/.

33 'About', Google Pay (Web Page, 31st March 2020) https://pay.google.com/intl/en_au/about/. Google Pay app also adds support for boarding passes and event tickets on mobile devices 'Google Pay', Australian FinTech (Web Page, 31st March 2020) https://australianfintech.com.au/Company/google-pay/.

all states in the US[34] and has obtained different licenses globally to support its global expansion—for example, it has an e-money licence in the EU[35] and an Australian Financial Services License in Australia for non-cash payment products.[36] Globally, Google Pay's market share surpassed all other local payments in India and comprises up to one third of the Indian mobile payment market.[37] In Singapore, Google Pay has cooperated with the country's local big banks, like DBS and OCBC, to enhance seamless payment and inter-bank transaction experiences for users.[38] In the UK, Google Pay has integrated with the UK-based banking platform Curve to work with all banks and cards on Mastercard and Visa networks.[39]

Compared to Amazon and Google, Facebook's entry into payment services markets was comparatively late. Facebook Pay was launched in late 2019 to enable Facebook users to use this new payment system for a number of Facebook-owned platforms such as Facebook, Messenger, WhatsApp and Instagram.[40] But currently it is only available in the US with limited functionality, and has not been introduced on a global basis.[41]

In addition to payment services, Bigtechs also entered into other traditional areas of banking and financial services. Through Amazon Lending and Amazon Prime, Amazon is engaged in the deposit-taking and lending business. Amazon Prime plays an important role in attracting savings from consumers.[42] It has been in cooperation with Visa to introduce a new type of membership card where consumers can obtain a 5% cash back on the purchase price of goods bought on the Amazon site.[43] This

---

[34] 'Google Payment Corp. Money Transmitter Licenses', Google (Web Page, 31st March 2020) https://support.google.com/pay/answer/7160765?hl=en.

[35] 'Google granted e-money licence for EU', Payments Cards & Mobile (Web Page, 7th January 2019) https://www.paymentscardsandmobile.com/google-granted-e-money-licence-for-eu/.

[36] 'Product Disclosure Statement', Google (Web Page, 31st March 2020) https://payments.google.com/payments/apis-secure/u/0/get_legal_document?ldo=0&ldt=buyertos&ldr=AU#.

[37] S&P Global Market Intelligence, 2020 India Mobile Market Report (Report, 2020) 8; Digbijay Mishra, '30% UPI Market Share Cap to Hit E-Pay Adoption: GPay', *Times of India* (online, 7 November 2020).

[38] 'Google Ties Up with DBS and OCBC to Enhance Google Pay in Singapore', FinTech News (Web Page, 12nd November 2019) https://fintechnews.sg/35049/mobilepayments/google-ties-up-with-dbs-and-ocbc-to-enable-googlepay-singapore/.

[39] 'UK FinTech Curve announces Google Pay integration', IBS Intelligence (Web Page, 31st March 2020) https://ibsintelligence.com/ibs-journal/ibs-news/uk-fintech-curve-announces-google-pay-integration/.

[40] 'What is Facebook Pay, where is it available, and how does it work?', Pocket-lint (Web Page, 13rd November 2019) https://www.pocket-lint.com/apps/news/facebook/150058-what-is-facebook-pay-where-is-it-available-and-how-does-it-work.

[41] 'Home', Facebook Pay (Web Page, 31st March 2020) https://pay.facebook.com.

[42] Natalie Berg and Miya Knights, *Amazon: How the World's Most Relentless Retailer Will Continue to Revolutionize Commerce* (Kogan Page, 2019) 31–2; 'About Amazon Prime', *Amazon* (Web Page) https://www.amazon.com.au/gp/help/customer/display.html?nodeId=201910360#:~:text=As%20an%20Amazon%20Prime%20member,gives%20you%20access%20to%202.

[43] 'About 5% Back on Amazon Prime Rewards Visa Signature Card', Amazon (Web Page, 31st March 2020) https://www.amazon.com/gp/help/customer/display.html?nodeId=202109390.

is offered in the form of a new type of Visa credit card that particularly attracts online shoppers. According to a survey by Bain, if Amazon offers a free online banking account with a 2% cash back benefit, it will attract 70% of users from the 18 to 34 age group, which indicates that Amazon has wide traction with the younger generation.[44] Moreover, Amazon Prime users usually belong to the well-financed middle class with a higher loyalty to the Amazon brand and service, which are also the target demographic of traditional banks. In late 2019, Google further enhanced its presence by announcing the launch of a checking account and personal banking product in conjunction with Citigroup that will be available through the Google Pay app.[45]

In China, Bigtechs have also made their presence in the financial markets felt. An online shopping platform Taobao.com was founded in May 2003.[46] Alibaba' Alipay, was initially introduced to support transactions on Taobao.com, launching in December 2004 as a third-party online payment platform.[47] In October 2014, Ant Financial was established as part of the Alibaba Group[48] and further entrenched Alibaba's presence in the financial sector.[49] Ant Financial's main business includes wealth management and lending. In May 2015, Ant Financial also gained a banking license when it set up MyBank as its largest shareholder (30%).[50] As one of the first few private banks in China, MyBank is the first bank in China that builds its system on a cloud platform, which enables the capability to process large amounts of data and provide more small-to-medium enterprises with suitable financial services.[51]

---

[44] 'Can Amazon Take Customer Loyalty to the Bank?', Bain & Company (Web Page, 18th September 2018) https://www.bain.com/insights/can-amazon-take-customer-loyalty-to-the-bank/.

[45] 'Google to offer personal banking accounts in partnership with Citigroup', The Guardian (Web Page, 13rd November 2019) https://www.theguardian.com/technology/2019/nov/13/google-checking-accounts-cache-citigroup-bank.

[46] Alibaba Group ("Alibaba") was founded in 1999 by 18 people led by Jack Ma focusing on global wholesale business. With the development of internet, by December 2001, Alibaba.com surpassed 1 million registered users. 'History and Milestones', Alibaba Group (Web Page, 1st March 2020) https://www.alibabagroup.com/en/about/history?year=2003.

[47] 'History and Milestones', Alibaba Group (Web Page, 1st March 2020) https://www.alibabagroup.com/en/about/history?year=2004. Alibaba completed its initial public offering on the Main Board of Hong Kong Stock Exchange in November 2007,then listed on New York Stock Exchange in September 2014, and was back to Hong Kong stock market in November 2019.

[48] 'History and Milestones', Alibaba Group (Web Page, 1st March 2020) https://www.alibabagroup.com/en/about/history?year=2014.

[49] However, Ant Financial is quoted by Alibaba as "an unconsolidated related party, provides payment and financial services to consumers and merchants on Alibaba's platforms" in Alibaba's recent Annual Report and Ant Financial's financial status was not consolidated in Alibaba's financial statements, 'Item 4 Information of the Company', Investis Digital (Web Page, 6th May 2019) https://otp.investis.com/clients/us/alibaba/SEC/sec-show.aspx?Type=page&FilingId=13476929-313107-570104&CIK=0001577552&Index=11400.

[50] 'About MyBank', MyBank (Web Page, 1st March 2020) https://www.mybank.cn/about.htm.

[51] 'About MyBank', MyBank (Web Page, 1st March 2020) https://www.mybank.cn/about.htm.

Alibaba has also obtained relevant licenses directly or indirectly in other financial businesses.By partnering with Ant Financial's subsidiary, Tianhong Asset Management, and other third-party fund management companies, Alibaba provides a money marketplace under the name of Yu'ebao.[52] Alipay obtained a Third-party Payment License in May 2012, granting it eligibility to access existing fund companies for their service for consumers. Following the launch of Yu'E Bao and the subsequent acquisition of 51% equity in Tianhong Asset Management in February 2015 and 60.8% equity in Shumi Fund in April 2015, Ant Financial obtained its Fund Sales License.

Another Bigtech in China, Tencent, also entered the financial sector. Tencent's LiCaiTong was launched together with Wechat Red Packet as a wealth management platform based on Wechat. Furthermore, Tencent's CaiFuTong obtained the Third-party Payment License at the same time as Alipay. Tencent its obtained Fund Sales License by acquiring the majority shareholding in HowBuy Fortune so that it indirectly obtained the Fund Sales License.[53] In June 2018, Teng An Fund, a wholly owned subsidiary of Tencent, obtained its own Fund Sales License and formally marched into the territory of consumer-facing purchases and sales.[54]

With both QQ and Wechat, Tencent is the most important social network giant in China. Unlike Alibaba, which interacts with the financial sector by way of online B2B and B2C, Tencent's progressive entry into the financial sector was reliant on its social network base.[55] Tencent aimed to "connect people and finance, to explore the power of human connections and to establish an open economy to provide innovative financial services to users".[56] Tencent entered the financial sector through Wechat Pay and Red Envelope.[57]

In December 2014, WeBank was co-founded by Tencent[58] as a "disruptor" of the traditional banking industry. According to its 2018 Annual Report, WeBank has a

[52] 'Item 4 Information of the Company', Investis Digital (Web Page, 6th May 2019) https://otp.investis.com/clients/us/alibaba/SEC/sec-show.aspx?Type=page&FilingId=13476929-313107-570104&CIK=0001577552&Index=11400.

[53] 'Tencent in Offensive: All Financial Licenses Equiped, Fighting for the Fund Market', PE Daily (Web Page, 5th January 2018) https://m.pedaily.cn/news/425664.

[54] 'Txfund Waiting for Open, Tencent Entering Third Party Fund Sales', JRJ (Web Page, 12nd June 2018) http://fund.jrj.com.cn/2018/06/12042724666174.shtml.

[55] Tencent was founded in Shenzhen in 1998 and its initial product was instance message services, namely QQ. By February 2001, its peak concurrent user accounts exceeded 1 million; The company was listed on the main board of Hong Kong Stock Exchange in June 2004. In January 2011, Weixin (Wechat) was launched and thereafter Wechat Pay was launched in August 2013. By December 2018, the daily transaction volume of Tencent's mobile payment services exceeded 1 billion'Milestones', Tencent (Web Page, 1st March 2020) https://www.tencent.com/en-us/about.html#about-con-3.

[56] 'Connect Ecosystem', Tencent (Web Page, 1st March 2020) https://www.tencent.com/zh-cn/business.html.

[57] In January 2014, WeChat Red Packet was launched and nearly 20 million "packets" were exchanged on 2014 Chinese New Year's Eve. This number increased to 1 billion on the same day in the following year 2015.

[58] 'Milestones', Tencent (Web Page, 1st March 2020) https://www.tencent.com/en-us/about.html#about-con-3. WeBank was founded by Tencent holding 30%, Baiyeyuan, Liye Group and unnamed

variety of business operations, including consumer lending, wealth management, a credit provider service or guarantee, foreign currency exchanges and transfers and insurance.[59] WeBank obtained permission to be established as a private bank in July 2014, marking Tencent's entry into the banking industry in the area of micro financing.[60]

Similar to Google, Baidu Inc (Baidu), which was founded in 2000, was initially purely a search engine.[61] Unlike Alibaba and Tencent, Baidu's operations did not include a strong financial services focus until recent years. Baidu's efforts in the financial sector are primarily distributed via Du Xiaoman Financial, formally known as Baidu Finance, which was initially launched in December 2015.[62] Du Xiaoman was demerged from Baidu in 2018 and started to operate independently, following Baidu's internal restructuring in its financial services groups. At that time, the CEO of Du Xiaoman, Guang Zhu, described Du Xiaoman as a "FinTech company" that "is not very good at financial assets", but focuses on "how to open AI technologies to financial institutions' use".[63]

Despite its relatively late start, Du Xiaoman made progress in obtaining well-rounded financial licenses in different areas of finance, including payment services,

---

others. See 'Preparation Department of Webank Got Approval', WeBank (Annual Report, 1st March 2020) https://www.webank.com/announcement/news-detail04.html.

[59] '2018 Annual Report', WeBank (Annual Report, 1st March 2020) https://www.webankcdn.net/s/hjupload/app/pdf/annual_report_2018.pdf.

[60] 'Preparation Department of Webank Got Approval', WeBank (Annual Report, 1st March 2020) https://www.webank.com/announcement/news-detail04.html.

[61] 'Company Overview', Baidu (Web Page, 1st March 2020) http://ir.baidu.com/company-overview/.

[62] 'Du Xiaoman Financial' (Web Page, 1st March 2020) https://www.duxiaoman.com/index. In May 2019, Tencent's joint venture in Hong Kong received virtual banking license from Hong Kong Monetary Authority 'Milestones', Tencent (Web Page, 1st March 2020) https://www.tencent.com/en-us/about.html#about-con-3. In the latest news, on 7 January 2020, Tencent's subsidiary Sea, a tech start-up in Singapore, has submitted an application to Monetary Authority of Singapore for a Singapore Digital Bank Licence: 'Sea Supported by Tencent Applying for Singapore Digital Bank License', Economic and Commercial Office of the Embassy of the People's Republic of China in the Republic of Singapore (Web Page, 9th January 2020) http://sg.mofcom.gov.cn/article/dtxx/202001/20200102928947.shtml).

Tencent's revenue increased by 21% year-on-year, primarily driven by commercial payment services and other FinTech services or digital products. '2019 Interim Report', Tencent (Interim Report, 14th August 2019) http://cdc-tencent-com-1258344706.image.myqcloud.com/storage/uploads/2019/11/09/7536055957ef88a09712fc5c5c24abab.pdf. Recently on 24 February 2020, Wechat Pay HK's cross-border payment service was permitted which provides smooth cross-border payment service for Wechat users in HK, Macau and mainland China: Chen Peng, 'WeChat Hong Kong Wallet Got Approval of Opening Hong Kong and Macao Cross-Border Payment Services', The Beijing News (Web Page, 24th Febuary 2020) http://www.bjnews.com.cn/finance/2020/02/24/694337.html. With large number of QQ and Wechat users amongst Chinese community globally, Tencent is expected to explore more in cross-border financial services.

[63] Cai Pengcheng, 'Review of Baidu Financial: How was the first AI graduate born under Robin Li's Lead?', TMT Post (Web Page, 13th July 2018) https://www.tmtpost.com/3351824.html.

banking and micro finance.[64] In terms of payment services, Du Xiaoman Wallet, formally known as Baidu Wallet, received its Third-Party Payment license in July 2013.[65] However, its market coverage was 0.27% by the first quarter of 2018,[66] showing that Du Xiaoman is still not comparable with Alibaba and Tencent. In terms of banking business, Baidu and China CITIC Bank co-founded aiBank in 2017, marking Baidu's entry into internet banking. However, in contrast to other internet banks like MyBank and WeBank, aiBank deploys a "direct bank" mode which also relies on a traditional bank, namely CITIC.[67]

2.2 New Territories in Banking and Financial Services

2.2.1 "Know Your Customer" Technology

In addition to traditional businesses such as payment, lending and wealth management, Bigtechs are also able to venture into new territories in financial markets by virtue of advantages in technology and data. The changes brought by Bigtechs have incrementally changed the ways in which banking is conducted.

The 'Know Your Customer' technology provides a powerful example. Through customer identification and authentication technology, Bigtechs are privy to customer data which is generally not accessible to traditional financial institutions on the scale and comprehensiveness of the Bigtechs. They have the potential to disintermediate traditional intermediaries such as banks.[68] Amazon's most recent eye-catching product is probably Alexa. It is one of the most cutting-edge voice recognition assistants available for helping people to manage their life by asking for assistance and

---

[64] There are some commentary that Baidu's march into the insurance industry is "always slower" than other big tech companies like Alibaba, Tencent and JD: 'Obtaining Insurance Licenses, Why is Baidu always Slower', Iyiou Insurance Technology (Web Page, 20th October 2018) https://www.iyiou.com/p/83713.html. In August 2019, CEO Guang ZHU left Du Xiaoman, which, together with other senior management's departure, shed some doubts on the future prospects of Du Xiaoman. the downsliding of Du Xiaoman is partly due to the downhill-trend of Baidu, and partly due to the ignorance of a comprehensive understanding of users' needs, and also the scenario of an internet "search" being not as closely connected with financial services as online shopping or social networks; HONG Ruoxin: 'Du Xiaoman's History of Lost in Financial Market', Sina Finance (Web Page, 5th August 2019) https://finance.sina.cn/zl/2019-08-05/zl-ihytcitm7073957.d.html?from=wap.

[65] Jing Yu, 'PBOC Issued More Third-party Payment License, Sina, Baidu were Included', 36kr.com (Web Page, 10th July 2013) https://36kr.com/p/204512.

[66] 'Review of Baidu Financial: How was the first AI graduate born under Robin Li's Lead?', TMT Post (Web Page, 13th July 2018) https://www.tmtpost.com/3351824.html.

[67] 'One Year Anniversary of Baidu Bank: an Emerging 'Internet Bank', 01 Caijing.com (Web Page, 29th November 2018) http://www.sinotf.com/GB/consumerfinance/2018-11-29/2OMDAwMDMyNzQ2OA.html.

[68] Mobey Forum Digital ID Expert Group, How to Make Digital Identity a Success: Insights and Learnings from Seven Digital ID Schemes: A Report from Mobey Forum's Digital ID Expert Group (Report, February 2020) https://mobeyreport.com/digital-id-report20200213/#introduction.

initiating requests with the simple statement "Alexa, please...". Notably, financial skills and payment processing skills are a large part of "Alexa". Amazon has cooperated with PayPal, Amex, Store Card, and other financial technology companies to enable Alexa to help support people's financial needs with quick voice assistance.[69] This technology, together with other biometric technology like fingerprinting and eye-pattern scans, has challenged traditional payment security methods as well as the current regulatory framework.[70] While biometric recognition is subject to security and privacy concerns in the US and other developed economies, Bigtechs are not so constrained in providing such services elsewhere. For instance, Amazon uses its facial recognition technology to provide banking services in West Africa via a mobile app for identify verification purposes.[71] Individuals have access to banking services based on income verification by using biometric and employer data.[72] Similarly, since 2015, Alibaba has introduced 'Smile to Pay' facial recognition payment services such as Alipay in China.

While traditional financial institutions are integrating recognition technology into their operations to fulfil their 'know your customer' obligations, Bigtechs are privy to 'know your customer' information-data. Data allows Bigtechs to create quasi-personal credit systems. For example, Zhima Credit, also known as Sesame Credit, was introduced to the public in 2015 in China by Ant Financial.[73] By using algorithmic systems, Zhima Credit offers a personal credit score which integrates data through Alipay and Alibaba's various services to assess a user's credit history and ability to meet contractual obligations. It assesses identification information including education, occupation and current employer, driver's licence, proof of assets such as property ownership, financial investment activities through Alibaba's Yu'E Bao, or even social connections.[74] Zhima Credit assesses the creditworthiness of a user and can be a very powerful tool for personal or commercial transactions. As a result, a high-score user may check into some hotels without paying a hotel deposit

---

69 'Alexa Skills: Business & Finance', Amazon (Web Page, 31st March 2020) https://www.amazon.com/Alexa-Skills-Business-Finance/b?ie=UTF8&node=14284819011.

70 Facebook's facial recognition feature became the centre of a lawsuit in Illinois. In breaching Illinois' Biometric Information Privacy Act, Facebook stored biometric data without users' consent see Patel v. Facebook No. 18-15982 (9th Cir. 2019); According to some third-party testing (e.g. testing done by secrss.com), the successful rate of face scan payment remains questionable because the result can be different when a person closes his eyes or opens his eyes: Si Yue, How safe do you think facial recognition mobile payments are? We measured that the accuracy rate was less than 70%, Secrss (Web Page, 15 April 2019) https://www.secrss.com/articles/9971.

71 Amazon, The Facts on Facial Recognition with Artificial Intelligence, https://aws.amazon.com/rekognition/the-facts-on-facial-recognition-with-artificial-intelligence/.

72 Kaiser Laisen, 'Aella Credit empowers underbanked individuals by using Amazon Rekognition for identity verification', *Amazon Web Services* (Blog Post, 15 August 2018) https://aws.amazon.com/blogs/machine-learning/aella-credit-empowers-underbanked-individuals-by-using-amazon-rekognition-for-identity-verification/.

73 Ant Financial, 'Ant Financial launches Sesame Credit, China's first personal credit service system' (Press Release, 28 January 2015) https://www.alibabagroup.com/cn/news/press_pdf/p150128.pdf.

74 Ant Financial, 'Ant Financial launches Sesame Credit, China's first personal credit service system' (Press Release, 28 January 2015) https://www.alibabagroup.com/cn/news/press_pdf/p150128.pdf.

or may receive swift loan approvals. It also enables access to other services, such as the use of a shared bike or a shared car without any requirement to pay a deposit.[75] Traditional banks have gradually taken up Zhima Credit in the course of business. The Guangdong Development Bank used Zhima Credit in assessing the creditworthiness of its customers,[76] as did the China Merchants Bank.[77] In a market where there was no effective official or formal personal credit system,[78] quasi systems, such as Zhima, have proved to be of good market utility, enabling more efficient decision-making in banking.

2.2.2 Inclusive Finance

Bigtechs are also making strides in inclusive finance. The idea of inclusive finance is to make credit accessible to individuals and small businesses who might otherwise not have access to traditional forms of credit. Inclusive finance is a long-standing concept that dates back to the Grameen Bank in Bangladesh, founded by Muhammad Yunus in 197 to help customers who were otherwise unable to access credit. It took Ant Finance five years to reach its customers in the rural areas in China in numbers that were five times greater than those of the Grameen Bank.[79]

Bigtechs again leverage technology to provide increased access to financial services. One reason that historically impeded inclusive finance is the fact that traditional banks tend to have only limited or non-cost effective means to make risk assessments of marginalised potential customers. These problems could be overcome by fintech. Commercial banks' risk assessments were traditionally reliant on information provided by a third party, for instance a credit rating agency, as well as financial information provided by the applicant enterprise. Data analytics is able to capture information in a more comprehensive and efficient manner. As a result, the lender would have a better understanding of the applicant's credit profile. In a way, data would again improve the information asymmetry issue. As a result of technology, people who did not previously have access to banking services due to geographical and other barriers could gain better access to credit.

Bigtechs improve the credit access of small and medium sized enterprises. The cost of transactions is accordingly reduced through the existence of transaction trails and

---

[75] Si Yue, 'How safe do you think facial recognition mobile payments are? We measured that the accuracy rate was less than 70%', Secrss (Web Page, 15 April 2019) https://www.secrss.com/articles/9971.

[76] Zhima credit related products were suspended by the bank: China Guangfa Bank, 'Announcement of the suspension of China Guangfa Bank services' (Announcement, 26 October 2016) http://www.cgbchina.com.cn/Info/20819733.

[77] Liu Peng, 'In 2019, you only need a Zhima Credit Score to secure a loan! So unexpectedly easy!', Csai (Web Page, 12 March 2019) https://www.csai.cn/loan/1288141.html.

[78] The central bank backed official personal credit system, Baihang Credit has not taken off. Index, Baihang Credit (Web Page) https://www.baihangcredit.com/#/index.

[79] Long Chen, From Fintech to Finlife: the case of Fintech Development in China, China Economic Journal, 2016, VOL. 9, NO. 3, 225–239.

records. Technology, such as AI, could be utilized to better assess the creditworthiness of borrowers. Instead of giving a score as envisaged by the traditional approach, data, such as trended data in conjunction with machine learning, is able to provide a more accurate assessment of a borrower's creditworthiness.

The notion of Decentralized Finance (Defi) enabled by blockchain is still an evolving idea. Access to blockchain-based programs could be potentially universal. The ideal is deceptively simple but effective; Defi enables a world where financial services are accessible to anyone with a smartphone and internet connection.[80]

There are examples where technology supported economic developments in east European countries, India and Africa.[81] Since 2013, financing enabled by phone services and the internet has reached and assisted the development of the rural economy in China.[82] The ready availability of credit improves the living standards of farmers.[83]

Crowd-funding enabled by technology is a good example of inclusive finance. Crowd-funding can be categorized into donation crowd-funding, reward crowd-funding, peer-to-peer lending, and equity-based crowd-funding.[84] In a strict legal sense, the latter two types of fund-raising activities would be subject to regulation. However, in the US, the *Jumpstart Our Business Startups Act* exempted some of those activities from regulation.[85] Under s 4(a)(6) of the newly added *Securities*

---

[80] Sid Coelho-Prabhu, 'A Beginner's Guide to Decentralized Finance', *Coinbase* (Blog Post, 7 January 2020) https://blog.coinbase.com/a-beginners-guide-to-decentralized-finance-defi-574c68ff43c4.

[81] Regional development of financial innovation in eastern European countries. by: Sumedrea, Silvia. Bulletin of the Transilvania University of Brasov. Series V: Economic Sciences. 2019, Vol. 12 Issue 2, pp. 133–142. 10p.https://doi.org/10.31926/but.es.2019.12.61.2.17. Mobile money for unbanked in India. By: Niyogi, Aditi; Niyogi, Syon. International Journal of Finance & Policy Analysis. Autumn2012, Vol. 4 Issue 2, p26-35. 10p. Technology-driven information sharing and conditional financial development in Africa. By: Asongu, Simplice A.; Anyanwu, John C.; Tchamyou, Vanessa S. Information Technology for Development. Oct2019, Vol. 25 Issue 4, p630-659. 30p. 12 Charts. https://doi.org/10.1080/02681102.2017.1311833.

[82] Md. Morshadul Hasan, Lu Yajuan, Appel Mahmud, Regional Development of China's Inclusive Finance Through Financial Technology 10(1) SAGE Open 1–16.

[83] An empirical analysis of rural farmers' financing intention of inclusive finance in China: The moderating role of digital finance and social enterprise embeddedness; Gulizhaer Aisaiti, Luhao Liu, Jiaping Xie, Jun Yang; Industrial Management & Data Systems, v 119 issue 7.

[84] Pierrakis and Liam Collins, Banking on Each Other: Peer-to-Peer Lending to Business: Evidence from Funding Circle. (Project Report) London, U.K.: NESTA, 2013, p. 43.

[85] Pub. L. No. 112–106, 126 Stat. 306 (2012). Jeremy Britton Whitbeck, The JOBS Act of 2012: The Struggle Between Capital Formation and Investor Protections (Research Paper, 15 June 2012) available at http://ssrn.com/abstract=2149744. The US Securities and Exchange Commission announced the final rules for Section 4 of the JOBS Act (or Regulation A +) on 25 May 2015. See US Securities and Exchange Commission, "SEC Adopts Rules to Facilitate Smaller Companies' Access to Capital" (Press Release, 25 March 2015) available at: http://www.sec.gov/news/pressrelease/2015-49.html.

Act (also called Regulation A+), an exemption from registration for certain crowdfunding transactions is provided, effective from June 19, 2015.[86] In the approximately 16 months since the introduction of the new exemption, Regulation A+ securities offerings have outpaced the past rate of the old regime.[87]

In the traditional paradigm, small investors had to be active in seeking out information about a particular issue or issuers. For retail investors, considerable resources would be required to achieve such a task. These investors would normally rely on institutional investors. In the context of crowd funding, technology allows crowdfunding platforms to prominently display the current level of funding and the number of backers, which has an effect of sending signals about the quality of an issue.[88] The investors could access and share information via the platform and reach "a state of wisdom of crowd".[89] For example, after about $4000 had been raised in an $80,000 crowdfunding campaign for an action video game on Kickstarter, two potential investors identified the project as fraudulent and notified other investors.[90] Technology enables investors to share and access information. Reputational penalties are consequential for companies.[91] In the age of the internet, reputations regarding an issue or an issuer are consequential for the success of crowdfunding activities.[92] Despite its own challenges, crowdfunding is a successful attempt to minimize information asymmetry in the marketplace.[93]

Alibaba was considered a market leader in inclusive finance. As discussed above, from Alipay to Yu'E Bao, Alibaba has emerged from providing financial services to businesses in Taobao.com, to a company which provides all kinds of financial services

[86] US Securities and Exchange Commission, *Regulation Crowdfunding: A Small Entity Compliance Guide for Issuers* (Guide, 13 May 2016) https://www.sec.gov/info/smallbus/secg/rccompliance guide-051316.htm.

[87] Anzhela Knyazeva, Regulation A + : What Do We Know So Far? (White Paper, 7 December 2016) https://www.sec.gov/dera/staff-papers/white-papers/18nov16_knyazeva_regulat ion-a-plus-what-do-we-know-so-far.html.

[88] The Role of Information Signals in Determining.

Crowdfunding Outcomes Jin-Hyuk Kim ∗ Peter Newberry† Calvin Qiu, (Conference Paper, 14 August 2018) https://www.tse-fr.eu/sites/default/files/TSE/documents/ChaireJJL/Digital-Econom ics-Conference/Conference/kim_jin-hyuk.pdf; also see Signaling in Equity Crowdfunding, Gerrit K.C. Ahlers, Douglas Cumming, Christina Günther, Denis Schweizer 39(4) *Entrepreneurship Theory and Practice* 955.

[89] James Surowiecki, The Wisdom of Crowds: Why the Many Are Smarter Than the Few and How Collective Wisdom Shapes Business, Economics, Societies and Nations, Anchor Press 2004.

[90] Ajay K. Agrawal, Christian Catalini, and Avi Goldfarb, "Some Simple Economics of Crowdfunding", NBER Working Paper No. 19133, June 2013; 28.

[91] Jonathan M. Karpoff and John R. Lott, Jr., The Reputational Penalty Firms Bear from Committing Criminal Fraud, Journal of Law & Economics, Vol. 36, No. 2 (Oct., 1993), pp. 757–802.

[92] For example, in the US, likes on the crowdfunding facebook page would affect the success of the fund-raising. See Alexey Moisseyev, "Effect of Social Media on Crowdfunding Project Results" (2013), Dissertations and Theses from the College of Business Administration. Paper 39, available at http://digitalcommons.unl.edu/businessdiss/39.

[93] Seth Freedman and Ginger Zhe Jin, Do Social Networks Solve Information Problems for Peer-to-Peer Lending? Evidence from Prosper.Com, 2008, NET Institute Working Paper No. 08-43, available at SSRN: http://ssrn.com/abstract=1304138.

that are available to the masses.[94] Alibaba works with different levels of local government in China to promote "financial inclusion". For instance, in December 2017, the government of the Shandong Province signed a strategic cooperation agreement with Alibaba and Ant Financial to promote financial inclusion in Shandong Province.[95] More recently, in January 2020, the Pingliang Municipality in Gansu Province signed a cooperation agreement with Alibaba, resulting in the launch of the "Financial Inclusion + Smart County" project, which promotes e-commerce and financial services, eliminating poverty by utilizing big data technology.[96]

The Libra Association has made 'inclusiveness' one of its vision statements with the Libra project.[97] It also aimed to establish 'a more inclusive ... financial system' when it announced the Libra project in June 2019.[98] According to Mark Zuckerberg, "the Libra project is about promoting financial inclusion through a safe, low-cost and efficient way of sending and receiving payments around the world'.[99] In 2017, Partnering up with PayMaya, Facebook launched Facebook Messenger Pay in the Philippines, which is a market with limited banking services penetration.[100] Amazon is also setting up a global map mainly engaging developing economies like India and Mexico. For instance, Amazon has set up a well-equipped business structure in India that includes payment technology, a lending platform and micro-insurance.[101]

As demonstrated, Bigtech companies are not only capable of providing better and more efficient services in the arena of traditional banking and financial services, they also have the means to extend new territories and forge new frontiers of finance. Via technology, Bigtech companies offer new ways to provide existing services as

---

[94] The main requirement for such an exemption is that the maximum offering amount is limited to $1,070,000; US Securities and Exchange Commission, *Regulation Crowdfunding: A Small Entity Compliance Guide for Issuers* (Guide, 13 May 2016) https://www.sec.gov/info/smallbus/secg/rccomplianceguide-051316.htm.

[95] Yuan Tao and Li Zilu, 'Shandong Province Government Signed a Comprehensive Strategic Cooperation Agreement with Alibaba Group and Ant Financial Group, Liu Jiayi Met with Jack Ma', CPC News (Web Page, 29th December 2017) http://cpc.people.com.cn/n1/2017/1229/c117005-29735921.html.

[96] Lan Tian, 'Pingliang Municipality Government Signed a Comprehensive Cooperation Agreement with Alibaba Group', Gansu Daily (Web Page, 3rd January 2020) http://gansu.gansudaily.com.cn/system/2020/01/03/017324892.shtml.

[97] Libra, The Libra project is for the world (Web Page) https://libra.org/en-US/vision/.

[98] Libra, Libra White Paper (White Paper, April 2020) https://libra.org/en-US/white-paper/.

[99] Hearing before the united states house of representatives committee on financial services October 23, 2019, Testimony of Mark Zuckerberg, Founder, Chairman and Chief Executive Officer, Facebook; https://financialservices.house.gov/uploadedfiles/hhrg-116-ba00-wstate-zuckerbergm-20191023-u1.pdf.

[100] 'PayMaya and Facebook launch payment tools in Messenger', Philstar (Web Page, 26 September 2017) https://www.philstar.com/business/2017/09/26/1742864/paymaya-and-facebook-launch-payment-tools-messenger; Financial Inclusion in 2018: BigTech Hits Its Stride; Greta Bull, CGAP (Blog Post, 9 January 2018) https://www.cgap.org/blog/financial-inclusion-2018-bigtech-hits-its-stride.

[101] 'Everything You Need To Know About What Amazon Is Doing In Financial Services', CBInsights (Web Page, 31st January 2019) https://www.cbinsights.com/research/report/amazon-across-financial-services-fintech/#Mexico.

well as new services. In doing so, they pose challenge to the existing regulatory framework in the financial markets, but also indirectly challenges the role of the State in financial markets. In Part III, the advent of Bigtech companies no doubt challenges the *status quo* of the financial system. More importantly, in the age of the decline of trust on state institutions, potentially, using the case study of blockchain, BigTech companies would overcome information asymmetries which provided the basis for financial markets regulation, and provide alternative ways how financial services are conducted.

3 Alternative to Trust in *Status Quo* Financial Systems?

3.1 Status Quo *Financial Regulation and Financial Systems*

What Bigtechs confront is a financial system that has been subject to the regulation of the State since 1934. By and large, as illustrated via licensing systems, they are able to venture into existing financial markets and become prominent players. In China, Alibaba, Tencent, and Baidu have obtained licences to operate in banking, securities, and insurance. Similarly, Amazon, Google, and Facebook have been subject to licencing systems in the US.

Since the introduction of the *Securities Exchange Act* 1934 and the *Banking Act of 1933*, the regulation of securities markets has been largely intended to ameliorate the issue of information asymmetry. Prudential regulation has been the focus of banking regulation. Through intermediaries such as banks, exchanges and underwriters, these systems have operated over the past century. Technology brings new challenges to State regulation. So far, the State has made accommodations for such changes (though the success of such accommodations is debatable).

Alibaba operated Yu'E Bao, one of the biggest online money markets. Platforms such as Yu'E Bao are in fact money markets themselves. They bear the features of state sanctioned securities markets. Through these platforms, one would be able to raise funds in exchange for, *inter alia*, equity or debt from the general public. Traditionally, intermediaries such as securities companies and other professionals are normally associated with public fundraising activities and assume the responsibility of bridging the information gap between the issuer and investors. Nowadays, they are being replaced by the platform operators of Bigtech innovations. Bigtechs have also adopted their own information disclosure mechanisms which largely utilise online platforms. Some states have created conditional exemptions under the existing state laws and regulations. For example, in the US, within the limitations set by *the Jumpstart Our Business Startups Act*, securities traded via crowdfunding platforms are exempted from the registration requirements of s 12(g) of the *Securities Exchange Act* 1934.[102]

---

[102] SEC, Crowdfunding (Final Rule, 25 May 2015) https://www.sec.gov/rules/final/2015/33-9974.pdf.

The rise of Bigtechs is perceived by some as a challenge to existing financial markets. For example, in 2014, the Chinese government media mouthpiece CCTV's Securities Information Channel's editor-in-chief released an article titled 'Outlawing Yu'E Bao' in which Ye'E Bao was dubbed as a vampire in the banking sector and a threat to national economic security.[103] The responses from the State would normally involve stringent regulation. Third-party payment processor regulation in China offers an example. In China, until the introduction of the PBoC's *Rules on Non-financial Institutions' Third-Party Payment Processing Services* ('the *2010 Rules*') in 2010, third party payment processors were subject to little scrutiny and regulation. Under *the 2010 Rules*, processors are required to obtain a licence from the PBoC for providing such services. Existent processors, such as Alibaba, were given one year to obtain the licence. Under the *2010 Rules*, there were a few noticeable requirements. First, under art 9 of the *2010 Rules*, the minimum registered capital for an applicant that intends to operate services nationwide is 100 million yuan in the form of paid-in cash capital, while it is 30 million yuan for an applicant that intends to operate the payment business in a province. In addition, processors are required to pay no less than 10% of their daily average balance of clients' deposits as paid-in cash capital, which would be greater than the initial 100 million yuan paid-in cash capital for processors such as Alibaba.[104]

Clearly, as newcomers in well-established financial markets, Bigtechs undermine the *status quo* and present challenges to the existing order of financial markets. By way of adaptation, Bigtechs have been required to obtain licenses for their operations. On occasions, the struggle has manifested itself in a more public manner. Libra is illustrative in this regard. Facebook signalled that it would introduce Libra in June 2019. Libra was initially positioned as 'a simple global currency and financial infrastructure that can empower billions of people'.[105] Libra was initiated as a permissioned blockchain digital currency /token that is similar to Bitcoin but is more stable, i.e. in the form of stablecoin.[106] It was a coin that raised many social ideals such as sustainable development goals, financial inclusion and financial empowerment.[107] However, after the concept was introduced, it has encountered challenges not only from US regulators but also from regulators in other countries. For example, the French Finance Minister stated that France would not allow development of Libra because it might be a threat to the monetary sovereignty of nations in the EU, with potential risks accruing from the abuse of marketing dominance[108] and systemic financial

---

[103] Niu Wenxin, Outlawing Yuebao (Blog Post, 21 February 2014) http://blog.sina.com.cn/u/1192082717.

[104] When receiving payments online from buyers, as a third party, Alibaba, via Zhifubao would hold on to the payments for 15 days before disbursing funds to sellers.

[105] 'Introducing Libra', *Libra* (Media Release, 18 June 2019) https://libra.org/en-US/updates/introducing-libra/.

[106] Global trend toward stablecoins; Libra, 'Libra Association Response to G7' (Media Release, 1 October 2019) https://libra.org/en-US/updates/libra-association-response-to-g7/.

[107] 'Updates', *Libra* (Web Page) https://libra.org/en-US/updates/.

[108] Libra may also have anticompetitive consequences. The structure of Libra as a permissioned blockchain retains a centralised group of persons capable of driving anticompetitive behaviours.

risks.[109] Libra has the potential to shift control of monetary policy to the Libra Association.[110] By inserting a global, private entity between governments and citizens, Libra has the potential to substantially weaken the power of capital controls.[111] In Australia, the main regulatory agency, ASIC, warned in November 2019 that the proposed Libra ecosystem may pose many risks and threats including the proliferation of scams based on Libra via mobile apps.[112] In April 2020, the Libra Association repositioned Libra as a more traditional coin which will be tied to fiat currencies.[113] The change is indicative of the pressures that Libra Association had been under, including, but not limited to, the US House Committee on Financial Services, the Federal Reserve, and Securities and Exchange Commission. In July 2019, the Federal Reserve set up a working group to evaluate Libra.[114] It recommended that Libra not be introduced without US regulatory approval.[115] In July 2019 at a congressional hearing, issues concerning competition, addressing money laundering, protecting

---

Competition risks stem from the small group validating transactions, exclusive access to the Facebook ecosystem, and the ability to discretionarily select and change members, protocols, and networks. Thibault Schrepel, 'Libra: A Concentrate of "Blockchain Antitrust"' (2020) 118 Michigan Law Review 160, 166.Libra enhances Facebook's advertising market; and in turn Facebook provides user data, thereby concentrating market power Pedro Aranguez-Diaz, 'A New Opportunity for Digital Competition: Facebook, Libra, and Antitrust' (2020) 50 Stetson Law Review 199, 222.. This advantage may give rise to a monopoly as other stablecoins and digital financial competitors are no longer able to compete with the dominance of a digital currency integrated with social media and advertising submarkets Evidence to Committee on Financial Services, Examining Facebook's Proposed Cryptocurrency and Its Impact on Consumers, Investors, and the American Financial System, US House of Representatives, Washington, 17 July 2019, 83 (Robert Weissman). this position may be entrenched if Libra becomes a systemically significant payments and capital market infrastructure deemed 'too big to fail' Dirk A Zetzsche, Ross P Buckley and Douglas W Arner, 'Regulating Libra' (2021) 41(1) Oxford Journal of Legal Studies 80, 105.. The risk of this trajectory is multiplicative, because a blockchain requires the consensus of a majority of nodes—a condition that will become difficult to satisfy once Libra becomes more widespread, meaning that anticompetitive practices implemented early in Libra's lifespan are increasingly irreversible Thibault Schrepel, 'Libra: A Concentrate of "Blockchain Antitrust"' (2020) 118 Michigan Law Review 160, 168..

[109] Chhavianshika Singh, 'France Finance Minister Calls Facebook Libra a Threat to 'Monetary Sovereignty'', News 18 (Web Page, 13rd September 2019) https://www.news18.com/news/tech/france-finance-minister-calls-facebook-libra-a-threat-to-monetary-sovereignty-2307541.html.

[110] Dirk A Zetzsche, Ross P Buckley and Douglas W Arner, 'Regulating Libra' (2021) 41(1) *Oxford Journal of Legal Studies* 80, 107.

[111] Dirk A Zetzsche, Ross P Buckley and Douglas W Arner, 'Regulating Libra' (2021) 41(1) *Oxford Journal of Legal Studies* 80, 107.

[112] Casey Tonkin, 'ASIC warns of 'risks and threats' from Facebook crypto', ACS (Web Page, 7th November 2019) https://ia.acs.org.au/article/2019/asic-warns-of--risks-and-threats--from-facebook-crypto.html.

[113] 'Welcome to the official White Paper', *Libra* (Web Page, April 2020) https://libra.org/en-US/white-paper/#cover-letter.

[114] Clare Duffy, 'Facebook's Libra 'raises many serious concerns', Fed Chairman says', *CNN* (online, 10 July 2019) https://edition.cnn.com/2019/07/10/tech/facebook-libra-fed/index.html.

[115] Bill Huizenga, 'Mark Zuckerberg Confirms to Rep. Huizenga that Facebook's Libra Cryptocurrency must Receive U.S. Approval to move forward', *Congressman Bill Huizenga* (Press Release, 23 October 2019) https://huizenga.house.gov/news/documentsingle.aspx?DocumentID=400986.

data privacy, national and cybersecurity risks and the stability of the US dollar were raised.[116] Chairman of the Federal Reserve Jerome Powell noted that the size of Facebook's userbase distinguished Libra from other digital currency endeavours.[117] He argued that its threat to central banks was unique because of 'the potential for widespread adoption big enough to potentially displace the U.S. dollar as the world's reserve currency'.[118] Uptake of Libra may also have international effects: Securities and Exchange Commission Chair Gary Gensler stated that Libra would 'definitely disrupt the central banking and monetary policy' in developing countries if uptake was significant and diminished the role of the dollar.[119] Although the Head of Calibra at Facebook, David Marcus, argued that Facebook intended to coordinate with central banks to minimise the risk of interference,[120] Congressman Al Green criticised him for relying on Facebook's intention of non-interference without addressing potentially unforeseeable consequences of widespread implementation.[121] Under such pressures, several initial partners chose to leave the venture.[122] In April 2020, Libra formally initiated the payment system licensing process with the Swiss Financial Markets Supervisory Authority (FINMA).[123]

The progress of Libra so far and the significant opposition it has encountered demonstrates that the State will not lightly relinquish its traditional role in regulating financial services, including fintech-based services. Through licensing systems, technology-driven financial services, similar to traditional financial services, will ultimately continue to be subject to State regulation and subordinate to the will of the State.

---

116 Rebecca Heilweil, Facebook's Libra Gets a Second Day of Grilling in House Hearing, *Representative Carolyn B Maloney* (Media Release, 17 July 2019) https://maloney.house.gov/media-center/in-the-news/facebooks-libra-gets-a-second-day-of-grilling-in-house-hearing.

117 Evidence to Committee on Financial Services, *Examining Facebook's Proposed Cryptocurrency and Its Impact on Consumers, Investors, and the American Financial System*, US House of Representatives, Washington, 17 July 2019, 31 (Andy Barr).

118 Evidence to Committee on Financial Services, *Examining Facebook's Proposed Cryptocurrency and Its Impact on Consumers, Investors, and the American Financial System*, US House of Representatives, Washington, 17 July 2019, 31 (Andy Barr).

119 Evidence to Committee on Financial Services, *Examining Facebook's Proposed Cryptocurrency and Its Impact on Consumers, Investors, and the American Financial System*, US House of Representatives, Washington, 17 July 2019, 89 (Gary Gensler).

120 Evidence to Committee on Financial Services, *Examining Facebook's Proposed Cryptocurrency and Its Impact on Consumers, Investors, and the American Financial System*, US House of Representatives, Washington, 17 July 2019, 5 (David Marcus).

121 Evidence to Committee on Financial Services, *Examining Facebook's Proposed Cryptocurrency and Its Impact on Consumers, Investors, and the American Financial System*, US House of Representatives, Washington, 17 July 2019, 72 (Al Green).

122 Lauren Feiner and Kate Rooney, paypal withdraws from facebook's libra cryptocurrency, *Congresswoman Sylvia Garcia* (Media Release, 7 October 2019) https://sylviagarcia.house.gov/media/in-the-news/paypal-withdraws-facebook-s-libra-cryptocurrency.

123 Libra, Libra Association applies for payment system license from FINMA (Media Release, 16 April 2020) https://libra.org/en-US/updates/finma-payment-system-license/.

Overall, the State has too much at stake in the regulation of financial markets to simply reduce or even abdicate its role. The State does not only regulate financial markets but is also a key player and a beneficiary of the *status quo* financial system. For example, the major banking law reforms in the United States were driven by the government need to obtain public finance.[124] This is supported by an empirical study of usury laws in the nineteenth century, which suggests that financial regulation is the product of incumbents with political power seeking to further their own private interests.[125] In the US, 'economic interests within congressional districts are significant determinants of legislator voting behaviour with respect to financial legislation.'[126] Similarly, in China, the financial system serves the needs of the state. For example, the introduction of the Shanghai Stock Exchange and Shenzhen Stock Exchange was a matter of the government yielding to economic necessity.[127] By establishing securities markets, the government was able to raise capital from the public which was needed to pursue its economic agenda as well as to finance the government's budget deficit.[128]

3.2 *Stepping into the Trust Void?*

The rise of Bigtechs in finance has occurred at a time of declining public trust in governments and in traditional financial institutions. The State undertakes to protect private property and enforce contracts. It relies on trust or belief on the part of the public that the State acts in a manner which is principled and prompt. The fundamental role of trust in financial institutions should also not be underestimated: products and services are inherently personal and potentially have a significant impact on the lives of customers.[129]

---

[124] Stephen Haber, Douglass C North and Barry R Weingast (eds), *Political Institutions and Financial Development* (Stanford University Press, 2008) 49–50.

[125] Efraim Benmelech and Tobias J Moskowitz, 'The Political Economy of Financial Regulation: Evidence from U.S. State Usury Laws in the 19th Century' (2010) 65(3) *The Journal of Finance* 1029.

[126] Stephen Haber, Douglass C North and Barry R Weingast (eds), *Political Institutions and Financial Development* (Stanford University Press, 2008) 128–129.

[127] Weiping He, the Regulation of Securities Markets in China, Palgrave Macmillan, 2018, 15.

[128] Gong Haocheng, Shanghai Jinrong Gaige Wangshi, Financial Reform in Shanghai, Zhongxi Shuju (Zhongxi Publishing) 2013, 50; The World Bank, *China Between Plan and Market*, (1990) XVII.

[129] Governments, private actors can all supply trust. See discussions in M. Todd Henderson, Salen Churi, The Trust Revolution How the Digitization of Trust Will Revolutionize Business and Government (Cambridge University Press, 2019).

The 2008 GFC prompted a significant loss of trust in government[130] (and also the financial sector).[131] Though there has been some recovery to pre-crisis levels,[132] trust remains near historic lows in many countries.[133] This has proven problematic for liberal democracies, which are founded upon a delicate balance between trust and distrust to enable successful governance.[134] Therefore, without trust in governments—or other institutions such as markets—it is difficult to mobilise support for meaningful reforms and successful policy-making.[135]

Trust deficits are evident in the US (reflected in its toxic and divided political culture), where trust in the government remains near historic lows, with only 17% of Americans stating that they trust their government to do what is right 'just about always' or 'most of the time'.[136] The figure has not surpassed 30% since 2007 and stands in stark comparison to the high point of 77% in the 1960s.[137] The Financial Trust Index measures a similar decline. At the end of 2008, trust was measured at 15%, rising in mid-2009 to 27%, and then declining again and hovering around 20% between 2010 and 2019.[138] Many Americans (64%) believe that low trust in the federal government makes it harder to solve problems, and that it is very important to improve confidence in the government (68%).[139] At the end of 2008, American public trust in financial institutions was at 20%. Between 2009 and 2013 it oscillated between 18 and 28%, then rose steadily to 34% by the end of 2019.[140] Gallup measured the

---

[130] OECD, *Government at a Glance* (OECD Publishing, 2013) 20 https://www.oecd-ilibrary.org/docserver/gov_glance-2013-6-en.pdf?expires=1573720107&id=id&accname=guest&checksum=803C88C5DA2ED91A8F558BD38E401810.

[131] See, e.g., Robert Hurley, Xue Gong and Adeela Waqar, 'Understanding the Loss of Trust in Large Banks' (2014) 32(5) *International Journal of Bank Marketing* 348, 349; Timothy Earle, 'Trust, Confidence, and the 2008 Global Financial Crisis' (2009) 29(6) *Risk Analysis* 785, 785.

[132] OECD, *Government at a Glance 2019 Summary* (OECD Publishing, 2019) https://www.oecd-ilibrary.org/docserver/93a2269c-en.pdf?expires=1573788072&id=id&accname=guest&checksum=B8073F34E2756AB25BA611CACA394645.

[133] Richard Wike, Laura Silver and Alexandra Castillo, 'Many Across the Globe Are Dissatisfied With How Democracy Is Working', *Pew Research Centre* (Article, 29 April 2019) 1 https://www.pewresearch.org/global/2019/04/29/many-across-the-globe-are-dissatisfied-with-how-democracy-is-working/.

[134] Gerry Stoker, Mark Evans and Max Halupka, *Trust and Democracy in Australia: Democratic Decline and Renewal* (Democracy 2025 Report No. 1, December 2018) 49.

[135] Dora Gyorffy, *Institutional Trust and Economic Policy: Lessons From the History of the Euro* (Central European University Press, 2013) 13-4.

[136] 'Public Trust in Government: 1958-2019', *Pew Research Centre* (Article, 11 April 2019) https://www.people-press.org/2019/04/11/public-trust-in-government-1958-2019/.

[137] 'Public Trust in Government: 1958-2019', *Pew Research Centre* (Article, 11 April 2019) https://www.people-press.org/2019/04/11/public-trust-in-government-1958-2019/.

[138] Chicago Booth and Kellogg School, 'Wave 28 Results' *Financial Trust Index* (Web Page, 2019) http://www.financialtrustindex.org/resultswave28.htm.

[139] Lee Rainie, Scott Keeter and Andrew Perrin, 'Trust and Distrust in America', *Pew Research Center* (Web Page, 22 July 2019) https://www.people-press.org/2019/07/22/trust-and-distrust-in-america/.

[140] Chicago Booth and Kellogg School, 'Wave 28 Results' *Financial Trust Index* (Web Page, 2019) http://www.financialtrustindex.org/resultswave28.htm.

trust in banks in 2008 at 32%, dipping to 22% in 2009. Between 2009 and 2013, trust in banks fluctuated between 21 and 26%, then rose steadily to 32% in 2012, and dipped slightly to 30% in 2019.[141]

Since the introduction of the *Banking Act of 1933*, the *Securities Act of 1933*, and the *Securities Exchange Act of 1934*, regulatory authorities have exercised powers through regulation and have become an integral part of financial markets. In general, banks are subject to entry licensing and prudential requirements. In securities markets, the problem has been about information asymmetry. The State primarily employs either a registration or approval system that is underpinned by the need for information disclosure. Market players participate in the markets trusting the State's role and powers. Through regulation, the State is able to or has maintained the operation of financial systems.

A question arises as to whether Bigtechs could provide some alternative *status quo* financial system. As discussed, Bigtechs have brought changes to financial markets. Traditionally highly sought-after intermediaries such as banks and underwriters are missing from Bigtech transactions. Effectively, Bigtechs have weakened the centrality of banks through a process of 'disintermediation'.[142] We have seen new ways, *albeit* in an incremental manner, for technology to overcome the problem of information asymmetry.

Bigtechs are agents for technology and they are placed to see through the changes that can be potentially brought about by technology. One technology is blockchain. For example, in 2018, Google Venture invested in Veem,[143] which is a cross-border digital payment platform that enables users to transfer cryptocurrency between companies. Another example is that the strategies of Ant Financial can be summarized as "BASIC"—Blockchain, Artificial Intelligence, Security, Internet of Things, and Cloud Computing.[144] Alibaba also commits to blockchain-related technologies. In October 2018, Alibaba filed a patent application with the US Patent and Trademark Office for a blockchain-based system that allows third-party administrative intervention in a smart contract context,[145] demonstrating Alibaba's efforts in blockchain-powered transaction solutions.

---

[141] 'Confidence in Institutions' *Gallup* (Web Page) https://news.gallup.com/poll/1597/confidence-institutions.aspx.

[142] Giorgio Barba Navaretti, Giacomo Calzolari and Alberto Franco Pozzolo, 'FinTech and Banks: Friends or Foes?' [2017] (2) *European Economy* 9, 10.

[143] 'B2B Payments Google, Goldman Back X-Border Payments Firm Veem', PYMNTS (Web Page, 27th September 2018) https://www.pymnts.com/news/b2b-payments/2018/veem-gv-goldman-sachs-venture-capital-investments/.

[144] Hou Yunlong, 'Ant Financial Published BASIC Strategy, Focusing on Blockchain, AI, Security, LoT and Cloud Computing', Economic Information Daily (Web Page, 12nd October 2017) http://jjckb.xinhuanet.com/2017-10/12/c_136673870.htm.

[145] AFD China Intellectual Property, 'China: Alibaba Files Patent for Blockchain System That Allows "Administrative Intervention', Mondaq (Web Page, 29th October 2018) https://www.mondaq.com/china/Intellectual-Property/749404/Alibaba-Files-Patent-For-Blockchain-System-That-Allows-Administrative-Intervention.

How much blockchain can achieve is still an open question. Blockchain does present some benefits but whether they will work in practice is still unknown. Blockchain provides some features, namely, decentralization, autonomy and immutability, that potentially bridge the gap of trust. Blockchain facilitates trust in contractual agreements by verifying consensus without a centralised repository of information—instead creating a network of information that cannot be overwritten without consensus within the entire network.[146] The trust afforded to centralised systems is ultimately contingent on the reliability of the central authority, which risks the emergence of predatory and monopolistic platforms.[147] The decentralization allegedly enabled by blockchain avoids powers being concentrated in the hands of a few people. However, it is now apparent that there is a significant concentration of power in the hands of founders or key members.[148] To relieve centralization risks, Pocket Network, for instance, has introduced a network which is comprised of features reminiscent of the 'three branches' in a state, emulating the separation of powers setup.[149]

In blockchain designs, each individual within a digital ecosystem is autonomous and operates their own database which verifies agreed transactions and counteracts tampering.[150] The implementation of smart contracts, for instance, is not derived from a single authority with central power or control.[151] This eliminates suspicion of third-party control and enables greater trust via a decentralised system.[152] Nodes in a network are constantly communicating and synchronised.[153] Blockchain is therefore based on a radical system of trust: based not in trust of other parties, but in a personal copy of a ledger to which each party is accountable.[154] In recognizing that technology has not yet reached a fully self-executory stage, human intervention has been introduced. For example, in order to resolve disputes, Aragon has enabled

---

146 Max Raskin, 'The Law and Legality of Smart Contracts' (2017) 1(2) *Georgetown Law Technology Review* 305, 318.

147 Johan Pouwelse et al., 'Laws for Creating Trust in the Blockchain Age' (2017) 6(3) *European Property Law Journal* 321, 325.

148 Angela Walch, Deconstructing 'Decentralization': Exploring the Core Claim of Crypto Systems in Chris Brummer (ed), *Crypto Assets: Legal and Monetary Perspectives* (Oxford Scholarship Online, 2019) 39.

149 Andrew Nguyen, Michael O'Rourke and Luis C de Leon, *Pocket Network* (White Paper, 2020) https://pokt.network/wp-content/uploads/2020/03/POCKET-NETWORK-WHITEPAPER-V0.3.0.pdf.

150 See, e.g., Johan Pouwelse et al., 'Laws for Creating Trust in the Blockchain Age' (2017) 6(3) *European Property Law Journal* 321, 330.

151 Md Nazmul Islam and Sandip Kundu, 'IoT Security, Privacy and Trust in Home-Sharing Economy via Blockchain' in Kim-Kwang Raymond Choo, Ali Dehghantanha and Reza M Parizi (eds), *Blockchain, Cybersecurity, Trust and Privacy* (Springer, 2020) 33, 34.

152 Md Nazmul Islam and Sandip Kundu, 'IoT Security, Privacy and Trust in Home-Sharing Economy via Blockchain' in Kim-Kwang Raymond Choo, Ali Dehghantanha and Reza M Parizi (eds), *Blockchain, Cybersecurity, Trust and Privacy* (Springer, 2020) 33, 34.

153 Kevin Werbach, *The Blockchain and the New Architecture of Trust* (MIT Press, 2018) 7.

154 Kevin Werbach, *The Blockchain and the New Architecture of Trust* (MIT Press, 2018) 7.

agreements that can be enforced by a decentralized court of jurors.[155] Existing legal vehicles such as corporations are also wedded with technology to protect the rights of investors. Some have been registered in US states such as Delaware and New York as limited liability corporations and limited cooperative associations.[156] In 2020, the LAO (a member-directed venture capital fund based on the initial DAO) was established as a limited liability company in Delaware.[157] In 2021, Wyoming passed a law defining DAOs as limited liability companies[158] and explicitly setting out a process for their formation.[159]

Blockchain further amplifies trust in a system by the feature of immutability. It is challenging for blockchain ledgers to be altered 'in a way not instantly clear to every single user involved'.[160] The main advantage of blockchain is its resilience to data manipulations and its unique level of trust.[161] Blockchain technology therefore guarantees a degree of security and transparency—individuals can trust that the blockchain has not been freely and unilaterally edited in the absence of accountability mechanisms. This is affirmed by a hashing process which is conducted on the block, attributing each iteration or amendment with a unique hash value, timestamp and

---

[155] 'Aragon Agreements', *Aragon* (Web Page) https://aragon.org/agreements.

[156] 'The Era of Legally Compliant DAOs', *OpenLaw* (Blog Post, 27 June 2019) https://medium.com/@OpenLawOfficial/the-era-of-legally-compliant-daos-491edf88fed0.

[157] 'What is the LAO?', *The LAO* (Web Page, 9 March 2021) https://docs.thelao.io/.

[158] Wyo Stat Ann § 17-31-104.

[159] Wyo Stat Ann § 17-31-105. However, CryptoFed, the first DAO created under this law, was recently subject to an order by the Securities and Exchange Commission halting its registration of digital tokens due to a 'materially deficient and misleading registration form'United States Securities and Exchange Commission, 'Registration of Two Digital Tokens Halted' (Press Release, 2021) https://www.sec.gov/news/press-release/2021-231. There are limitations in the current practical operation of DAOs. Firstly, investor rights may be impaired by the risks of fraud and opportunism created by large-scale token issuances Timothy Nielsen, 'Cryptocorporations: A Proposal for Legitimizing Decentralized Autonomous Organizations' [2019] (5) *Utah Law Review* 1105, 1111.. Secondly, issues arise in relation to business structure categorisation. For example, a DAO may be conceptualised in law as a group of persons rather than a legal person in its own right, which would prevent legal action in the absence of joint or unanimous coordination Vincent Mignon, 'Blockchains: Perspectives and Challenges' in Daniel Kraus, Thierry Obrist and Olivier Hari, *Blockchains, Smart Contracts, Decentralised Autonomous Organisations and the Law* (Edward Elgar, 2019) 1, 6.. While it has been argued that a DAO could be considered a limited liability corporation ('LLC') in jurisdictions such as Delaware, certain requirements may complicate this classification: for example, Delaware requires identifying information for each member, which may compromise the pseudonymity of DAOs, and the flexibility of the LLC Agreement in Delaware law may obfuscate investor understandings and expectations of their rights and protections Timothy Nielsen, 'Cryptocorporations: A Proposal for Legitimizing Decentralized Autonomous Organizations' [2019] (5) *Utah Law Review* 1105, 1118..

[160] Reza M Parizi, 'Blockchain in Cybersecurity Realm: An Overview' in Kim-Kwang Raymond Choo, Ali Dehghantanha and Reza M Parizi (eds), *Blockchain, Cybersecurity, Trust and Privacy* (Springer, 2020) 1, 2.

[161] Alexander Savelyev, 'Contract Law 2.0: 'Smart' Contracts as the Beginning of the End of Classic Contract Law' (2017) 26(2) *Information & Communications Technology Law* 116, 133–4.

transaction data.[162] Invalid transactions are not admitted by honest miners and it is virtually impossible to delete transactions once they are in the blockchain.[163]

In particular, contrasting to permissioned blockchains, permissionless blockchains do not require special permission to submit or validate transactions.[164] In permissionless systems, individuals can act autonomously to verify transactions without relying on a central validator.[165] Further, a core benefit of blockchain in a permissionless system is that it is computationally challenging to alter blockchain ledgers due to the hashing process,[166] the chaining of transactions and the inability to delete transactions once they are on the blockchain.[167]

---

162 Ala Ekramifard et al., 'A Systematic Literature Review of Integration of Blockchain and Artificial Intelligence' in Kim-Kwang Raymond Choo, Ali Dehghantanha and Reza M Parizi (eds), *Blockchain, Cybersecurity, Trust and Privacy* (Springer, 2020) 147, 148.

163 Gautam Srivastava, Reza M Parizi and Ali Dehghantanha, 'The Future of Blockchain Technology in Healthcare Internet of Things Security' in Kim-Kwang Raymond Choo, Ali Dehghantanha and Reza M Parizi (eds), *Blockchain, Cybersecurity, Trust and Privacy* (Springer, 2020) 161, 172. Blockchain transactions based on the Unspent Transaction Output model are associated with previous unspent transactions – this makes transactions easily verifiable and trackable.

164 Siamak Solat, Philippe Calvez and Farid Nait-Abdesselam, 'Permissioned vs. Permissionless Blockchain: How and Why There Is Only One Right Choice' (2021) 16(3) *Journal of Software* 95, 97. By requiring additional permissions to send transactions, permissioned blockchains do not allow entirely open participation in the transaction process. Because permissioned blockchains still involve a central third party who both validates transactions and controls the pool of permissioned validators Siamak Solat, Philippe Calvez and Farid Nait-Abdesselam, 'Permissioned vs. Permissionless Blockchain: How and Why There Is Only One Right Choice' (2021) 16(3) *Journal of Software* 95, 103, trust in a permissioned system still requires trust in a coordinating authority.

165 See, e.g., Johan Pouwelse et al., 'Laws for Creating Trust in the Blockchain Age' (2017) 6(3) *European Property Law Journal* 321, 330.

166 Ala Ekramifard et al., 'A Systematic Literature Review of Integration of Blockchain and Artificial Intelligence' in Kim-Kwang Raymond Choo, Ali Dehghantanha and Reza M Parizi (eds), *Blockchain, Cybersecurity, Trust and Privacy* (Springer, 2020) 147, 148.

167 Gautam Srivastava, Reza M Parizi and Ali Dehghantanha, 'The Future of Blockchain Technology in Healthcare Internet of Things Security' in Kim-Kwang Raymond Choo, Ali Dehghantanha and Reza M Parizi (eds), *Blockchain, Cybersecurity, Trust and Privacy* (Springer, 2020) 161, 172. On the other hand, other differences of permissioned blockchains may be more likely to garner trust than permissionless blockchains. Notably, a permissioned network allows for more oversight and regulation of members. In its April 2020 White Paper, the Libra Association proposed a model for membership that required applications to include due diligence, technical information, economic performance information and financial contribution Libra Association, Libra White Paper (White Paper, April 2020) 23.. These restrictions can only be imposed in a permissioned network. In contrast, permissionless blockchains depend on anonymous users subject to governance deficiencies such as the potential for a 'hard fork'—in which a distributed ledger system is splintered when some users update the system code while others do not. These events may subsequently have effects on the stability of the system, as liquidity, exchange and reserves are also divided Dirk A Zetzsche, Ross P Buckley and Douglas W Arner, 'Regulating Libra' (2021) 41(1) Oxford Journal of Legal Studies 80, 90. Consequently, permissionless systems may be seen as less trustworthy and unable to overcome the instability introduced by decentralised users.

In general, blockchain eliminates the need for 'middlemen and data silos across thousands of platforms selling users' personal details'.[168] For instance, companies such as AirBnB act as conduits for transactions conducted between consumers—exposing insecurities in information transfer through their positions as unnecessary middlemen.[169] Technology continues to evolve and continues to challenges the status quo financial markets. In banking, a pertinent question currently is whether stablecoin is capable of performing similar functions as banks. Stablecoins are 'cryptocurrencies that maintain a stable value against a target price' that combine liquid collateral or algorithmic stabilisation with supply.[170] Their development and integration not only demonstrates that they are able to perform similar functions as banks, but also extends upon those functions through mechanisms that traditional banks are unable to access.

This similarity has been recognised by the United States President's Working Group on Financial Markets, Federal Deposit Insurance Corporation, and the Office of the Comptroller of the Currency, who collectively suggested that stablecoins should be subject to a prudential framework.[171] Gerald Corrigan, former president of the Federal Reserve Bank of Minneapolis, argued that banks perform three essential functions: (1) issuing transaction accounts (i.e. liabilities that are 'payable on demand' and 'readily transferable'), (2) providing a backup source of liquidity, and (3) acting as a transmission mechanism for monetary policy.[172] Stablecoins are capable of fulfilling all three of these functions.[173]

---

[168] Md Nazmul Islam and Sandip Kundu, 'IoT Security, Privacy and Trust in Home-Sharing Economy via Blockchain' in Kim-Kwang Raymond Choo, Ali Dehghantanha and Reza M Parizi (eds), *Blockchain, Cybersecurity, Trust and Privacy* (Springer, 2020) 33, 34.

[169] Md Nazmul Islam and Sandip Kundu, 'IoT Security, Privacy and Trust in Home-Sharing Economy via Blockchain' in Kim-Kwang Raymond Choo, Ali Dehghantanha and Reza M Parizi (eds), *Blockchain, Cybersecurity, Trust and Privacy* (Springer, 2020) 33, 36.

[170] Marco Dell'Erba, 'Stablecoins in Cryptoeconomics from Initial Coin Offerings to Central Bank Digital Currencies' (2019) 22(1) *New York University Journal of Legislation and Public Policy* 1, 7.

[171] President's Working Group on Financial Markets, Federal Deposit Insurance Corporation, and the Office of the Comptroller of the Currency, *Report on Stablecoins* (Report, November 2021) 2.

[172] Gerald Corrigan, Federal Reserve Bank of Minneapolis, *Are Banks Special?* (Annual Report, 1982) 2.

[173] Firstly, stablecoins are both payable on request and transferable. Stablecoins are redeemable upon demand, although redemption rights may vary between issuers: some issuers are permitted to postpone or suspend redemptions, or do not provide direct redemption rights President's Working Group on Financial Markets, Federal Deposit Insurance Corporation, and the Office of the Comptroller of the Currency, *Report on Stablecoins* (Report, November 2021) 4.. The stable value of a stablecoin counteracts risks of volatility that confine the use of cryptocurrencies to speculative investment activities, making it a more reliable prospect for transfer Marco Dell'Erba, 'Stablecoins in Cryptoeconomics from Initial Coin Offerings to Central Bank Digital Currencies' (2019) 22(1) *New York University Journal of Legislation and Public Policy* 1, 16.. Distributed ledger systems are also structurally similar to traditional banks, in that they comprise of an initiation of payment, validation of the message, and settlement of the transaction. President's Working Group on Financial Markets, Federal Deposit Insurance Corporation, and the Office of the Comptroller of the Currency, *Report on Stablecoins* (Report, November 2021) 5.

There is also a possibility that smart contracts could replace dispute resolution systems. Smart contracts refer to fully automated contracts that are performed 'without human involvement'.[174] Terms are facilitated by a computerised transaction algorithm—for instance, a trade that is executed by a computer system and not by a trader.[175] This arrangement has been described as a system of 'self-help' where contracts are designed 'to ensure performance without recourse to the courts'.[176] More specifically, smart contracts rely on the implementation of blockchain technology.[177] Human intervention is required at this stage. Decentralized courts of jurors are introduced in an attempt to resolve disputes. Aragon Court is one such example.[178]

Secondly, stablecoins can be used as a liquidity reserve. Unlike other virtual currencies, stablecoins that use collateral—such as a fiat currency—also receive the benefit of a reserve. For example, the stablecoin Tether is backed by the US dollar. This enables it to fulfil the function of providing backup liquidity, which may fulfil the functions of banks in digital spaces—for instance, a stable reserve of liquid assets may help cryptocurrency miners with the costs of computing resources. This capacity to provide funding mirrors the traditional role of banks and contributes to bank disintermediation Marco Dell'Erba, 'Stablecoins in Cryptoeconomics from Initial Coin Offerings to Central Bank Digital Currencies' (2019) 22(1) *New York University Journal of Legislation and Public Policy* 1, 18–19. However, the capacity of stablecoins to act as a reserve still relies on a presumption of convertibility into fiat currency: funding strains may arise if a sudden run on stablecoins requires substantial liquidation of collateral European Central Bank Crypto-Assets Task Force, 'Stablecoins: Implications for Monetary Policy, Financial Stability, Market Infrastructure and Payments, and Banking Supervision in the Euro Area' (Research Paper No 247, September 2020) 20..

Thirdly, stablecoins can be used by monetary policymakers. While monetary policy enacted through banks requires leverage to create liquidity, stablecoins generate liquidity 'without the need for leverage'. Caitlin Long, 'Ten Stablecoin Predictions and Their Monetary Policy Implications' (2021) 41(2) *Cato Journal* 307, 310.However, multi-currency stablecoins may reduce the effectiveness of domestic monetary policy if central banks are unable to control shocks to the value of another currency European Central Bank Crypto-Assets Task Force, 'Stablecoins: Implications for Monetary Policy, Financial Stability, Market Infrastructure and Payments, and Banking Supervision in the Euro Area' (Research Paper No 247, September 2020) 21. This may concentrate power in issuers, who retain the ability to adjust issuances or interest rates for their own profit Dong He, 'Monetary Effects of Global Stablecoins' (2021) 41(2) *Cato Journal* 353, 358.

[174] Alexander Savelyev, 'Contract Law 2.0: 'Smart' Contracts as the Beginning of the End of Classic Contract Law' (2017) 26(2) *Information & Communications Technology Law* 116, 117.

[175] Alexander Savelyev, 'Contract Law 2.0: 'Smart' Contracts as the Beginning of the End of Classic Contract Law' (2017) 26(2) *Information & Communications Technology Law* 116, 120–1.

[176] Max Raskin, 'The Law and Legality of Smart Contracts' (2017) 1(2) *Georgetown Law Technology Review* 305, 306. Raskin (2017) further defines the existence of two subcategories of smart contracts: 'strong' and 'weak' smart contracts, where strong contracts have 'prohibitive costs of revocation and modification' compared to easy alterability of weak contracts by a court; see Max Raskin, 'The Law and Legality of Smart Contracts' (2017) 1(2) *Georgetown Law Technology Review* 305, 310.

[177] Manifesting a contracting environment in which contracts are performed automatically, and where code is stored on a blockchain to be triggered by blockchain transactions. While a self-executing contract is not entirely novel, the emergence of blockchain signals a paradigmatic shift in enabling the automation of contractual performances of not one, but both, parties. Alexander Savelyev, 'Contract Law 2.0: 'Smart' Contracts as the Beginning of the End of Classic Contract Law' (2017) 26(2) *Information and Communications Technology Law* 116, 121.

[178] 'Fast and Fair Dispute Resolution', *Aragon* (Web Page) https://aragon.org/court.

4 Concluding Remarks

Since the Roosevelt Government's introduction of the *Banking Act* of 1933, the *Securities Act* of 1933, and the *Securities Exchange Act* of 1934, states all around the world have regulated financial markets and are an integral part of the financial system. The regulation of financial markets in the US and elsewhere over the past several decades is largely reliant on prudential regulation and information disclosure. Technology led by Bigtechs transforms the way that information is collected, analysed, and utilized. It is apparent that to some extent, technology is able to alleviate the problem of information asymmetry and therefore reduce the costs of financing and make financing more efficient and more accessible. Technology enables the creation of new forms of markets which provide alternatives to traditional markets.

Technology is capable of galvanizing a process of disintermediation of traditional services providers, i.e. banks, which would simplify verification of participants in banking and financial services. In doing so, technology tends to remove or reduce human intervention in the process, thereby filling in the trust void left by governments and banks. It is critical that technology provides an alternative to the *status quo* without eroding public trust.

At the same time, Bigtechs and technology present challenges to *status quo* financial regulation and financial systems. By analysing the case of Libra and the most recent case of the suspension of Ant Finance IPO, it is apparent that the extent of regulatory restraint over new technologies has been decided by a tussle between *status quo* financial regulation and Bigtechs. Technology potentially enables Bigtechs to challenge practices and orders established largely by the Roosevelt Government in the 1930s. As demonstrated in the case of Libra and Ant Finance, it is doubtful that the State will relinquish its power in regulating financial markets.

The future success of Bigtechs is largely dependent on technological advancement and the extent to which Bigtechs are able to harness it. The evolution of financial regulation does not occur in a vacuum. It is a result of a struggle of vested interests in the system. The question remains as to whether technology will be allowed to reshape the role of the State and how the State imposes checks and balances on Bigtechs to protect various interests or to mitigate drawbacks of technology. In any event, it is safe to conclude that technology has changed the way that financial markets operate and the way that financial markets have been regulated. In this light, at least, the functions or the roles of the State in financial markets perhaps should be reconsidered. Arguably, it is possible that technology may provide a means to return us to Adam Smith's night watchman state.

Chapter 8
Revolution of Securities Law in the Internet Age: A Review on Equity Crowd-Funding

Abstract Along with the development and prevalence of Internet technology, a new financing model—equity crowd-funding—has been rising rapidly in recent years. Against this background, it becomes an important global topic in the field of securities law about how to balance both policy agendas of investor protection and capital formation. By referring to the JOBS Act in the US as a typical example, it is suggested in this chapter that modern securities law is making an active response to the demand of equity crowd-funding development. Besides expanding the application space of small issues exemption rules, securities law is also going beyond the traditional conceptual division between public and private offerings by introducing a brand-new system of equity crowd-funding exemption.

1 Introduction

The Internet is changing not only our way of life, but also the way how the law develops. The rise of a new field of law—cyber law or internet law[1]—can be seen as a good example of such an influence. And more importantly, the appearance of the Internet inspires us to review the functioning boundary of all relevant legal systems, and a series of brand-new legal issues and problems. These include but are not limited to digital signatures, cyber-crime, remedies to online invasion of privacy, constitutional protection on freedom of online speech, etc. They lead us, however, to consider how the law may adjust itself to the Internet Age. In this chapter, the authors intend to refer to the prevalence of an innovative financial transaction model—equity crowd-funding—as an example to show the evolutionary influence of the Internet on the legal system of financial markets.[2]

[1] E.g. see Chris Reed, *Making Laws for Cyberspace* (Oxford University Press, 2012); Brian Craig, *Cyberlaw: The Law of the Internet and Information Technology* (Prentice Hall, 2012); Patricia Bellia, Paul Berman & Brett Frischmann, *Cyberlaw: Problems of Policy and Jurisprudence in the Information Age* 4th ed. (West Academic Publishing, 2010).

[2] For some detailed review on the influence of internet on financial law, please see Matthew Kien-Meng Ly, "Coining Bitcoin's 'Legal-Bits': Examining the Regulatory Framework for Bitcoin and Virtual Currencies", *Harvard Journal of Law & Technology*, Vol. 27, No. 2, 2014; Gönenç

T. Huang and W. He, *Politics Meets Markets*, Contemporary Chinese Civil and Commercial Law, https://doi.org/10.1007/978-981-97-9176-7_8

As defined by the International Organization of Securities Commissions (IOSCO), crowd-funding refers to:

> An umbrella term describing the use of small amounts of money, obtained from a large number of individuals or organisations, to fund a project, a business or personal loan, and other needs through an online web-based platform.[3]

In a broad sense, the term "crowd-funding" may embrace four types of fundraising acts: social lending/donation crowd-funding, reward crowd-funding, peer-to-peer lending and equity crowd-funding.[4] However, from a perspective of application of law, only the last two categories, i.e. peer-to-peer lending and equity crowd-funding, are caught by the radar of financial law (particularly securities law) around the world.[5] Furthermore, in some countries like China, since peer-to-peer lending has in practice "mutated" into shadow banking and then become an indirect financing model, it would "escape" the range of securities law which simply regulates direct financing.[6] Thus, this paper only focuses on equity crowd-funding, due to its clear securities law implication.

Since the first platform of equity crowd-funding went online in 2009,[7] we witness such new financing models springing up vigorously in almost all major countries around the world. As the leading country with the most developed financial market and information technology, the US has an industry of equity crowd-funding worth

---

Gürkaynak and Ilay Yilmaz, "Regulating Payment Services and Electronic Money: A comparative regulatory approach with a specific focus on Turkish legislation", *Computer Law & Security Review* 31 (2015); Daniel C. Rowe, "Periodic Reporting in a Continuous World: The Correlating Evolution of Technology and Financial Reporting", 13 *Duke Law & Technology Review* 248 (2015); Kevin C. Taylor, *FinTech Law: A Guide to Technology Law in the Financial Services Industry* (Bloomberg BNA, 2014).

[3] Eleanor Kirby and Shane Worner, "Crowd-funding: An Infant Industry Growing Fast", Staff Working Paper of the IOSCO Research Department, Staff Working Paper: [SWP3/2014], p. 8.

[4] Yannis Pierrakis and Liam Collins, "Banking on Each Other: Peer-to-Peer Lending to Business: Evidence from Funding Circle", (Project Report) London, U.K.: NESTA, 2013, p. 43.

[5] See Ibid., p. 11.

[6] In theory, peer-to-peer lending shall be regarded as a typical kind of direct financing as the person who intends to raise capital is attracting money directly from the public investors without reliance on a credit institution (e.g. a bank). So, in the US, the SEC requires those peer-to-peer lending platform to put their business under the regulatory system of registration of securities issuance. See Andrew Verstein, The Misregulation of Person-to-Person Lending, 45 *UC Davis Law Review* 445 (2011). However, in China, many peer-to-peer lending platforms accept money saving from the public for the purpose of granting loans to borrowers, or provide guarantee to the investors for repayment through itself or its related companies. In other words, in this circumstances, those platform is no longer promoting direct financing, but actually get involved in credit service similar to the one provided by commercial banks. For the review on Chinese peer-to-peer lending market practice, see Bing Peng, "Review on P2P Online Lending Regulation Models" (P2P Wangdai Jianguan Moshi Yanjiu), *Financial Law Forum* [China], Vol.2, 2014; Yuan Zhao, "Review on Legal Issues of P2P Online Lending from the Perspective of Direct Financing", *SJTU Law Review* [China], Vol.4, 2014.

[7] See "Venture Capital 2.0: Grow VC Launches Private Beta (We Have Invites)", available at http://www.arcticstartup.com/article/venture-capital-2-0-grow-vc-launches-private-beta-we-have-invites/.

billions dollars, far exceeding the size of other countries.[8] In addition, China is certainly a "rising star" attracting attention in the global crowd-funding market. By the end of 2015, there had been 121 equity crowd-funding platforms in China. According to a report of the World Bank, it is predicted that in 2025 this industry in China will reach a size of $50 billion dollars.[9]

When the Chinese stock market crashed in 2015, and incidents and scandals plagued the internet finance industry, the policies which were once conducive to financial innovation segued into something much more restrictive, which directly influenced the revising process of the China's securities law.[10]

One manifestation was the controversy over the exemption rules for internet equity crowdfunding. The first draft revision of the *Securities Law* published in 2015 included a provision stating that "securities can be publicly issued through crowdfunding via internet by securities institutions or other institutions approved by the State Council's securities regulatory authority. If the issuer and investors meet the conditions specified by the State Council's securities regulatory authority, registration or approval may be exempted", providing a basis for the legality of equity crowdfunding.

Subsequently, this provision completely disappeared in the second draft revision of the *Securities Law*, indicating the controversy on this issue.[11] It appears that concerns about systemic risks associated with equity crowdfunding have prevailed.

The *Securities Law* (Revised Draft for Third Review solicited public opinions starting from April 26, 2019, reintroducing the relevant provisions. It stipulated that "the issuance of securities may be exempted from approval or registration in the following circumstances: (1) issuing securities through internet platforms approved by the State Council's securities regulatory authority, with relatively small amounts of funds raised and subscribed by individual investors…".

The final version of the new *Securities Law* which came into force in 1st March 2020 does not include the above-mentioned provisions. The legalization of equity crowdfunding in China remains uncertain for now.

---

[8] In 2013, the size of investment of equity crowd-funding in the US has reached 3 billion dollars. See Deloitte, "Let's Get Together: Crowdfunding Portals Bring in the Bucks", 2013, available at http://www.deloitte.com/assets/DcomShared%20Assets/Documents/TMT%20Predictions%202013%20PDFs/dttl_TMT_Predictions2013_LetsGetTogeather.pdf. It is expected that the enactment of JOBS act would further stimulate the development of this new industry.

[9] See the World Bank, "Crowdfunding's Potential for the Developing World", 2013, available at http://www.infodev.org/infodev-files/infodev_crowdfunding_study_0.pdf.

[10] Weiping He, Financial development and de-financializing in China, Capital Markets Law Journal. 17, 4, p. 513–543 31 p.

[11] 《中华人民共和国证券法(修订草案)》(2015年一审稿) Draft Amendment to the Securities Law of the People's Republic of China (First Reading Draft, 2015).

《中华人民共和国证券法(修订草案)》(2017年二审稿) Draft Amendment to the Securities Law of the People's Republic of China (Second Reading Draft, 2017).

《中华人民共和国证券法(修订草案)》(2019年三审稿) Draft Amendment to the Securities Law of the People's Republic of China (Third Reading Draft, 2019).

By reviewing the rise of internet-based equity crowding-funding, we will discuss the revolutionary impact of modern information technology to the system of securities law. Following the introduction at 1, this chapter now divides into four additional parts: Part 2 explains two primary objectives of securities law, i.e. protection of investors and facilitation of financing. Part 3 outlines the necessity of establishing the system of small issues exemption and expanding its application against the background of the Digital Age. Part 4 argues that regulation needs to go beyond the traditional division in the field of securities law between public and private offering, offering new theoretical and practical perspectives to support the introduction of a new category of "crowd-funding exemption".

2 Two Primary Objectives of Securities Law: Investor Protection and Facilitation of Financing

2.1 Investor Protection

It is widely accepted that the sustainable development of capital markets in one nation is to a large extent determined by the strength of investor protection offered by its legal system.[12] And when we talk about such protection, the first thing flashing into our mind is normally the securities law. Before the 1930s, in all jurisdictions, there did not exit any comprehensive legislation and regulatory body to keep an eye on the operation of the stock market, and investors were supposed to defend their interests through traditional litigation strategies—bringing a law suit before the courts on the basis of contract law or tort law. However, after the Securities Act of 1933 and Securities Exchange Act of 1934 came out in the US, the conception of a modern securities law started to take root on a global scale. The appearance of securities law means that the model of "private enforcement"—through court proceedings—is no longer the only way investors may seek to protect themselves. The model of "public enforcement"—through the authority of administrative or regulatory bodies—may open new forms of safeguard.[13] Since then, the securities issue and transactional activity are never purely "free trading" in the sense of *caveat emptor*, but facing more and more requirements or limitations from rules in the domain of public law. Among all these rules, the most typical example is the obligation that securities issuers shall normally register their issue with competent authorities (e.g. Securities Exchange

[12] Rafael La Porta, Florencio Lopez-de-Silanes, Andrei Shleifer and Robert W. Vishny, "Law and Finance", *Journal of Political Economy*, Vol. 106, No. 6, 1998.

[13] As for the comparison between private and public enforcement, see William Landes & Richard Posner, "The Private Enforcement of Law", 4 *Journal of Legal Studies* 1, 1975; Mitchell Polinsky, "Private versus Public Enforcement of Fines", 9 *Journal of Legal Studies* 105, 1980.

Commission (SEC) in the US) and publicly disclose all relevant information so as to reduce so-called "information asymmetry"[14] between issuers and investors.[15]

2.2 *Facilitation of Capital Formation*

However, although the existence of such regulatory rules may promote protection for investors, an inevitable side effect is that they could increase the burdens on issuers, e.g. a listed company must spend more time and money than private firms on releasing all kinds of financial statements and public announcements. Such additional financing costs may scare away some promising investment from financing through the capital market, and thus cause restraint on the development of the financial industry and a negative impact on social welfare. Therefore, during its design, securities law must maintain a reasonable balance between investor protection and capital formation.[16]

Traditionally, in seeking to balance these two objectives, a number of exemption rules have been introduced into securities law for the purpose of creating a "green channel" for certain securities issues without the concern of jeopardizing the interests of public investors. A well-known example is the creation of a conceptual distinction between public and private offerings of securities. By referring to this distinction, the securities law may determine which kinds of securities issues shall be subject to strict regulation (i.e. from the point of value orientation emphasizing investor protection) or be exempted from its application (i.e. preferring the goal of financing facilitation).[17] So, in many jurisdictions, securities issues are divided into these two branches and under different treatments. As a result private offerings are to be released from the requirements of registration and disclosure imposed on the public offerings, so as to avoid putting excessive cost on financing. However, in terms of the price to be paid,

---

[14] In contract theory and economics, "information asymmetry" deals with the study of decisions in transactions where one party has more or better information than the other. This creates an imbalance of power in transactions, which can sometimes cause the transactions to go awry, a kind of market failure in the worst case. For example, in the second-hand car market, the dealers always know more than their customers about the quality of the cars they sell, and thus some dishonest dealers may take this advantage by selling cars of poor quality for high price. At the end, the market order will be destroyed and the whole industry will suffer. See George A. Akerlof, "The Market for 'Lemons': Quality Uncertainty and the Market Mechanism." *The Quarterly Journal of Economics*, Vol. 84, No. 3, 1970, pp. 488–500.

[15] See Troy A. Paredes, Blinded by the Light: Information Overload and Its Consequences for Securities Regulation, 81 *Washington University Law Quarterly* 417, 418 (2003).

[16] See C. Steven Bradford, "Transaction Exemptions in the Securities Act of 1933: An Economic Analysis", *Emory Law Journal*, Vol.45, 1996; David S. Ruder, "Balancing Investor Protection with Capital Formation Needs After the SEC Chamber of Commerce Case", 26 *Pace Law Review 39*, 2005; *The Investor's Advocate: How the SEC Protects Investors, Maintains Market Integrity, and Facilitates Capital Formation,* available at http://www.sec.gov/about/whatwedo.shtml.

[17] For example, in the US, although its securities law sets up exemption for various types of transaction, a common understanding is that, among all of them, the exemption for private issues—provided by s.4(2) of Securities Act of 1933—shall be seen as the most important one. See Louis Loss and Joel Seligman, *Securities Regulation*, 3rd ed. (Little Brown & Co Law & Business, 1991), p. 1350.

issuers of private offerings will only be allowed to offer the securities to a limited number of investors and will be prohibited from engaging in public advertisement or inducement.

The reason for making such a distinction is because of the view accepted by most people that certain investors—e.g. those who have a close relationship with issuers or are wealthy, along with plenty of investment experience—do not need the protection from securities law. In other words, these investors are deemed to be fully capable of protecting themselves in the market, and thus they can take part in private offerings which are exempted from protective measures designed by the securities law for venerable retail investors.

2.3 The Challenge Brought by Internet Technology

Unfortunately, along with the development of a financing model in this Information Age, the invention of equity crowd-funding is now challenging the traditional philosophy of securities law: the line of distinction between public and private becomes more and more inappropriate, and the idea of screening "venerable" investors and then offering special protection through this distinction is losing its efficiency. The failure may be rooted in two factors. Firstly, the Internet may to a large extent reduce the cost of the public to participate in market transactions (including financial transactions); since as its name suggests, equity crowd-funding is from the very beginning designed as a type of financing open to the general public. In fact many ordinary people are given opportunities to step into financial investment and become a member of the group of securities investors.

However, in accordance with traditional arrangements within securities law, any financing transactions "targeting" these individuals shall be subject to strict requirements imposed on public offerings. This will in turn restrict the application of Internet technology on the financial market. Secondly, the problem of "information asymmetry" (between issuers and investors) has long been regarded as the theoretical explanation of the existence of securities law and regulatory bodies. [18] But because Internet technology—on which equity crowd-funding is based—has by itself the potential power of significantly reducing information costs,[19] this may substantially

[18] See, for example, Paul M. Healy & Krishna G. Palepu, "Information Asymmetry, Corporate Disclosure, and the Capital Markets: A Review of the Empirical Disclosure Literature", 31 *Journal of Accounting & Economics* 405 (2001).

[19] It is argued that, compared with traditional model, information proceeding through Internet have three innovative features: (1) some information which individuals and institutions are not obliged to disclose may be exposed or communicated in social networks, and thus information supply may be promoted; (2) the application of search engine may effectively meet the demand of gathering information, so as to ease the problem of Information overload; (3) the introduction of "cloud computing" may guarantee a capability of high-speed information proceeding. See Ping XIE and Chuanwei ZHOU, "Review on Internet Financing Model" (Hulianwang Jinrong Yanjiu), *Journal of Financial Research* [China], Vol. 11, 2012.

weaken or even deny the value of securities law. In this sense, the rise of equity crowdfunding may become a turning point of development of securities law, announcing a revolution within the legal system caused by the change of technology. Against this background, the solutions offered by the securities law in the past is now facing great difficulties about how to balance both objectives of investor protection and facilitation of financing.

3 Small Issues Exemption and the Expansion of Its Application Scope

3.1 The Necessity of Expanding Application of Small Issues Exemption in the Internet Age

Generally speaking, there are two standards in the securities law to distinguish private issues from public offerings. The first test is the number of investors—when in an issue the number of investors subscribing or purchasing the relevant securities is passing a specific threshold, this issue would be determined as a public issue, otherwise it stays as a private one. For example, as provided in China's Securities Act, an issuance of securities to accumulatively more than 200 specific persons shall be deemed as a public offering.[20] Similarly, in the US, the Regulation D—issued by the SEC—introduces a "safe harbor" that an issuer can only sell its securities to no more than 35 purchasers. These must not be "accredited investors" and must arise in circumstance where general solicitation or advertising is not used for marketing the securities. Should this limit be crossed, no exemption can be enjoyed by the issuer and all rules regulating public offerings will follow.[21]

The other dividing line is to the qualification of investors, i.e. whether these investors are capable of protecting themselves or taking substantial investment loss. In judging this status of investors, the securities may refer to the amount of their investment. In China, for example, the Securities Regulatory Commission (CSRC) determines that private investment funds may only accept investment from "accredited investors" and an important standard of "accredited investors" is that they "invest in a single private fund at an amount not less than RMB 1 million",[22] Alternatively they may consider the wealth of investors, e.g. Rule 501 of SEC Regulation D defines as "accredited investors" any natural person whose individual net worth, or joint net worth with that person's spouse, exceeds $1 million dollars.[23]

---

[20] Article 10, Securities Act of 2005.

[21] 17 C.F.R. §§ 230.506(b)(2)(i).

[22] Section 12, Interim Measures for the Supervision and Administration on Private Investment Funds (CSRC, 2014).

[23] 17 C.F.R. § 230.501(a)(5).

However, no matter how they apply such methods to draw a line between public and private offering, this conceptual distinction may not fit the nature of equity crowd-funding. The feature of borderless Internet means that crowd-funding would inevitably be a "feast" of the masses—the success of crowd-funding depends on whether it can solicit millions of Internet users to join the "club" of securities investors. On the other hand, since the Internet emphasizes equality and is wholly opened to the general public, there is no way for an equity crowd-funding—by reliance on the Internet—to set up an overly high threshold of entrance on the basis of family wealth or investment amounts. Internet financing would lose its innovativeness if only rich network users were allowed to participate and "grass-roots" individuals were excluded.

Given such a background, it becomes necessary for us to consider expanding the applicable scope of another exemption system in the securities law, i.e. small issues exemption. The reason for combining equity crowd-funding with the concept of small issues exemption is based on the fact that crowd-funding through the Internet has made traditional financing transactions become more and more democratic and open. In the Information Age, with rapid popularization of communication technology, the cost of using Internet services (either surfing websites or paying online) is quite low for individuals, thus reducing the threshold of the general public (especially those who do not have massive assets) from taking part in online-based financing transactions. The group of securities investors would thus grow—in theory, any network user may simply pay $1 dollar for purchasing stock in an equity crowd-funding scheme and be a member of the investor group.

On the other hand, by attracting more people to securities investment, small- and medium-sized firms (particularly those star-up firms) would be more likely to win an opportunity of raising sufficient capital from the market. However, the amount of capital these firms pretend to raise is relatively small. If we rigidly put them under the treatment of public offering as typically applied to those larger issuers, their financing costs would certainly increase to an intolerable level and thus force them to give up the equity crowd-funding model.

In order to resolve this problem, a feasible solution may be to incorporate equity crowd-funding into the scope of the small issues exemption, i.e. as long as the amount of capital raising within a specific period does not exceed the limit specified by the law, the issuer of equity crowd-funding will be released from regulatory rules in relation to public offering. By offering this benefit, it may helpfully facilitate small- and medium-sized firms to take advantage of this innovative financing route of crowd-funding and reduce their difficulties of raising capital.

3.2 *The Experience of US Securities Law in Expanding Small Issues Exemption*

To be sure, the small issues exemption is actually not strange to legal scholars and market practitioners. For instance, in the US, it's Securities Act of 1933 provides that the SEC may by its rules and regulations exempt an issuer, subject to certain terms and conditions, from the requirement of registration where the aggregate amount at which the issue is offered to the public does not exceed $5 million dollars.[24] Under this authorization, the SEC has issued Regulation A and D respectively in 1936 and 1982,[25] laying down specific rules on such small issues exemption. Although those American law-makers and regulators did not originally intend to design the system of small issues exemption to serve Internet financing transactions as they appear today, it is interesting to find that until this Information Age its unity has not been reflected.

A representative example is the success of Spring Street Brewin Co. launching a public offering of shares through its online platform by reliance on the exemption provided by SEC Regulation A.[26] However, the early version of small issues exemption also had its own problems. Since the law set up a number of additional conditions on issuers and the exemption of Federal securities law cannot exclude the application of "blue sky laws" (i.e. State securities laws),[27] issuers in the past still had to face high costs even though they sought exemption. The result of this problem was that, for a long time, small issues exemption was widely used in the market.[28] From statistics, during the decade of 1995–2004, there were less than 8 cases of Regulation A exempted small issues per year on average[29]; and from 1998 to 2011, the number of Regulation A exempted small issues dropped from its peak—57 cases in 1998—to just one case in 2011.[30] In response, the Jumpstart Our Business Startups (JOBS) Act of 2012 adds, by its section 401, a new provision into the Securities Act of 1933, i.e. section 3(b)(2), authorizing the SEC to issue new rules on exemption, so as to further reduce the burden of firms active in small issues.

---

[24] Section 3(b)(1), Securities Act of 1933.

[25] Securities Act Release 627–632 (1936); Securities Act Release 6389, 24SEC Dock. 1166 (1982).

[26] Stephen Knute Gregg, Regulation A Initial Public Offerings on the Internet: A New Opportunity for Small Business, *Journal of Small and Emerging Business Law* Vol.1, 1997; Jeffrey J. Hass, Small Issue Public Offerings Conducted Over the Internet: Are They "Suitable" for the Retail Investor? *Southern California Law Review*, Vol.72, 1998.

[27] See James D. Cox, Robert W. Hillman and Donald C. Langevoort, *Securities Regulation: Cases and Materials,* 3rd ed. (Aspen Law & Business, 2001), pp.15–16.

[28] For a detailed review on the rare use of small issue exemption, see United States Government Accountability Office, Factors That May Affect Trends in Regulation A Offerings (Report to Congressional Committees), July 2012, available at http://www.gao.gov/assets/600/592113.pdf.

[29] See Rutheford B. Campbell, Jr., Regulation A: Small Business' Search For "A Moderate Capital", *Delaware Journal of Corporate Law*, Vol. 31, No.1, 2005.

[30] See United States Government Accountability Office, Factors That May Affect Trends in Regulation Offerings (Report to Congressional Committees), July 2012, available at http://www.gao.gov/assets/600/592113.pdf.

On 25 May 2015, the SEC released its final draft of amended regulation, i.e. Regulation A+.[31] In addition to increasing the upper-limit amount of exempted issues, Regulation A+ divides the traditional system of small issues exemption into two tiers: Tier 1 refers to offerings of securities of up to $20 million in a 12-month period (with not more than $6 million in offers by selling security-holders that are affiliates of the issuer); Tier 2 provides for offerings of securities of up to $50 million in a 12-month period (with not more than $15 million in offers by selling security-holders that are affiliates of the issuer).

For Tier 2 offerings, issuers are subject to additional requirements, e.g. disclosing audited financial statements, periodic reporting, and the amount of non-accredited investors purchasing the issued securities may not exceed 10% of their annual income or net assets. And in contrast with Regulation A, an important breakthrough of Regulation A+ is that the small issue under Tier 2 offering can also be exempted from the application of State securities law—this is certainly a good news for issuers.[32]

As discussed above, the justification of creating small issues exemption is to facilitate financing of small- and medium-sized firm and thus prevent them from being rejected from entrance into capital market due to unaffordable costs caused by strict regulatory rules. And since the law lays down a "ceiling" of financing amounts, we do not need to worry too much about the order of the market being seriously jeopardized. Even though some bad things can occur during an offering, against the interests of investors, its small size decides that the overall risk to the market and society is manageable. Certainly, any exemption from regulation by public authorities does not exclude investors from seeking judicial remedies through private litigation. All in all, although the small issues exemption is a rule invented by the law from the past, it may still have an obvious positive effect today in the online world of the Information Age provided we can improve its design and enforcement.

4 Going Beyond the Division Between Public and Private Offering

4.1 The Design of Regulatory Rules on the Basis of "Information Asymmetry"

The reason why the securities law and regulatory bodies exist in our community is based on a theoretical presumption that there is an "information asymmetry" between investors (especially retail investors) and issuers/listed companies, and the risk of so-called "market failure" where investors cannot reasonably distinguish honest issuers

[31] See "SEC Adopts Rules to Facilitate Smaller Companies' Access to Capital", available at: http://www.sec.gov/news/pressrelease/2015-49.html.

[32] Securities and Exchange Commission, 17 CFR Parts 200, 230, 232, 239, 240, 249, and 260 [Release Nos. 33-9741; 34-74578; 39-2501; File No. S7-11-13], RIN 3235-AL39, Amendments for Small and Additional Issues Exemptions under the Securities Act (Regulation A).

or companies from fraud and thus the market falls into the trap of "adverse selection".[33] In order to resolve this problem, regulatory interference by reliance on public authorities seems to be necessary. Since the enactment of the 1933 Securities Act and 1934 Securities Exchange Act after the crash of Wall Street in 1929, most jurisdictions around the world have gradually embraced the idea of introducing securities law and assigning specific bodies to enforce the law. Such a development is described by some scholars as "the rise of the regulatory state".[34]

Of course, it is undeniable that the natural advantage of an information source of issuers/listed companies will very likely to create a breeding ground for the moral hazard of criminality, inducing some participants to fraudulent behavior such as misrepresentation in financial statements.[35] In theory, there are four possible solutions to this problem: (1) private orderings on the basis of market competition; (2) private litigation through *ex-post* judicial review; (3) regulation by public authorities enforcing the securities law; and (4) state ownership.[36]

It is thus suggested that, at least from an academic perspective, the reliance on securities law and regulatory bodies may not be the exclusive choice for protecting investors; and given that "government failure" is not uncommon in reality,[37] we have sufficient ground to doubt whether such a reliance on securities law is actually an optimal option. In a 2006 research, Rafael La Porta, Florencio Lopez-de-Silanes, Andrei Shleifer and Robert Vishny—four leading scholars in the field of law and finance—reviewed legal provisions of 49 countries on securities issue, intending to discover through empirical study whether or to what extent the law may play a positive role in promoting the development of the stock market. It was found that, while the standard of information disclosure and tort liability has a visible positive correlation with the development of the stock market, the establishment of regulatory bodies had a rather limited impact. In other words, the conclusion seems to be that, in contrast with public enforcement by regulatory bodies, the strategy of private litigation through the courts is much more important to its growth.

This once again reminds us that the conception of investor protection is a multi-dimensional system in which a number of different measures may be adopted to achieve the same goal. It is not a good idea for us narrowly to put all our faith on the efficiency of public enforcement and regard it as the only safeguard of investor

---

[33] See Joseph E. Stiglitz, "Equilibrium in Product Markets with Imperfect Information", *American Economic Review*, May 1979, 69(2), pp. 339–345.

[34] See Edward Glaeser and Andrei Shleifer, "The Rise of the Regulatory State", *Journal of Economic Literature*, Vol. 41, 2003, pp. 401–425.

[35] See Ronald J. Gilson and Reinier H. Kraakman, The Mechanisms of Market Efficiency, *Virginia Law Review*, Vol. 70, No. 4, 1984.

[36] As for a comparison of these four strategies, see Simeon Djankov, Edward Glaeser, Rafael La Porta, Florencio Lopez-de-Silanes, and Andrei Shleifer, "The New Comparative Economic", *Journal of Comparative Economics*, Vol. 31(4), 2003, pp. 595–619.

[37] See George J. Stigler, "Public Regulation of Securities Market", *Journal of Law and Economics* 37,1964, pp. 117–142; George J. Stigler, "The Theory of Economic Regulation", *Bell Journal of Economics and Management Science*, No. 3, 1971, pp. 3–18; Sam Peltzman,"Towards a More General Theory of Regulation", *Journal of Law and Economics*, Vol. 19, No. 2, 1976.

interests. In fact, the exemption system designed by securities law recognizes this point, i.e. at least there is no need to spread limited regulatory resources on protecting everyone in the market. The focus shall be on taking care of those who are more vulnerable in terms of being under an information disadvantage.

4.2 How Information Technology May Relieve the Anxiety of "Information Asymmetry"

Then there is the question whether investors in equity crowd-funding may be reasonably treated in the same way as sophisticated or wealthy ones and thus be removed from the scope of securities regulation. It may be of concern that these investors are no different from people purchasing stock in a public offering, as equity crowd-funding is by its nature a solicitation on an Internet platform open to all network users. If we consider a public offering deserves to be strictly regulated due to the need for investor protection, equity crowd-funding is no different. However, such a view may not be justified as it underestimates the power of the Internet on information distribution.

It is argued that, by issuing securities through the Internet platform, the cost of collecting and identifying information could be significantly reduced for investors, and issuers would also find it much more difficult to commit fraudulent behaviors. Why so? Let us recall a scenario at the beginning of the last century when the stock market had just begun. At that moment, how might our investors know things relating to an issuer or listed company? Normally, they would buy a newspaper on the street, listen carefully for stories from the radio, or gather together to share with one other rumors either true or false. But nowadays, the world is totally different. Thanks to the invention of the Internet, it is easy to immediately get the information we need by entering key words in a search engine (e.g. Google) and pressing the 'Enter' key.

Such a convenience will probably help investors of equity crowd-funding: on the face of it, the broad availability of the Internet means a large number of small investors can take part in equity crowd-funding, and thus the ownership structure of those companies issuing stocks through this way will be sufficiently dispersed. In terms of economic theory, a dispersed ownership structure may lead to a deterioration of the problem of "information asymmetry"—a shareholder who has little investment in the company would think it too costly to keep an eye on the performance of a corporate controller (senior management or majority shareholder) and thus give up the incentive of monitoring (especially when they can secure a diversified investment portfolio and the public market provides him with an easy exit). As a result of this "rational apathy",[38] a fraudulent controller might find it easier to abuse their information advantage and, while the general public realizes such a risk exists, they may be reluctant to invest in the stock market. In the end all companies must pay the price; however, the appearance of online platforms offer those investors an opportunity to

[38] See Lucian A. Bebchuk, "Limiting Contractual Freedom in Corporate Law: The Desirable Constraints on Charter Amendments", *Harvard Law Review* Vol. 102, 1989, pp. 1820–1860.

create a relationship of information sharing, as they may rely on the acts of others as a reference to judge the quality of a potential investment project. This is called by some economists "rational herding".[39] For example, in China's industry of equity crowd-funding, it is common that many people will only invest in a project after some well-known individuals or institutions come in as "angel investors".

On the other hand, the development of Web 2.0 also provides network users with an opportunity to take part in the construction of a website.[40] This means that, through the online platform, equity crowd-funding investors can create a virtual community in which they are able to obtain updated information about their project, post their opinions and communicate with fund-raisers or other investors in a more efficient way.[41] Thus, any member of such a community may post anything they know on the social network, and then by gathering all this information, people may piece together a full picture of the investment project's perspective and earnings outlook.[42] In other words, the establishment of a social network may largely reduce the cost of collecting, filtering and assessing information, which for a long time has been the serious obstacle for investors in making their decisions. Such a "wisdom of the crowd"[43] is helpful for investors to overcome the problem of "information asymmetry" in financial markets.

For instance, there was a case in which two investors in Kickstarter, a well-known equity crowd-funding platform, found evidence of the fraudulent behaviour of fund-raisers, and immediately shared this with other investors so as to avoid further loss.[44] Also, it is noteworthy that, under the pressure of market competition, the operators of those equity crowd-funding platforms may have incentives to better monitor fund-raisers and protect their investors, as otherwise disappointed users will leave their platforms (and turn to other platforms which can offer such protection) and their market share as well as earnings will fall. As a result of this dynamics, the platforms will voluntarily play the role of "gatekeeper" to defend the market order.[45]

Obviously, the success of investor protection mechanisms as discussed above is not achieved by promoting public enforcement of securities law, but relies on a

---

[39] See Gordon Burtch, Anindya Ghose, and Sunil Wattal, "An Empirical Examination of the Antecedents and Consequences of Contribution Patterns in Crowd-Funded Markets", *Information Systems Research*, Vol. 24, Issue 3, 2013.

[40] Wikipedia, as a free Internet encyclopedia, is a typical example as almost all of its contents are contributed and edited by its users. See Clay Shirky, "Here Comes Everybody: The Power of Organizing Without Organizations" (Penguin Press, 2008).

[41] See Michal Herzenstein, Scott Sonenshein, and Utpal M. Dholakia, "Tell Me a Good Story and I May Lend You My Money: The Role of Narratives in Peer-to-Peer Lending Decisions", 2011, available at SSRN: http://ssrn.com/abstract=1840668.

[42] See Ping XIE and Chuanwei ZHOU, "Review on Internet Financing Model" (Hulianwang Jinrong Yanjiu), *Journal of Financial Research* [China], Vol. 11, 2012.

[43] James Surowiecki, *The Wisdom of Crowds: Why the Many Are Smarter Than the Few and How Collective Wisdom Shapes Business, Economics, Societies and Nations*, Anchor Press 2004.

[44] See Ajay K. Agrawal, Christian Catalini, and Avi Goldfarb, "Some Simple Economics of Crowdfunding", NBER Working Paper No. 19133, June 2013.

[45] Traditionally, the word "gatekeeper" has been referred to investment bankers, accountants, analysts, lawyers and credit-rating agencies. See John C. Coffee, Gatekeepers: *The Role of the*

strengthened reputation strategy in the Information Age, in which frauds are more easily detected and condemned. Indeed, economists have long claimed that reputation is much more relevant than law in shaping market actors' behavior. In accordance with an empirical study based on 132 samples, it was found that, compared with the monetary loss due to SEC penalty, listed companies suffered greater damage to their reputation.[46] In the Information Age, this reputation strategy is likely to be further strengthened so as to become an important foundation of the equity crowd-funding industry and a feasible alternative to public enforcement. Let us imagine a scene in the eighteenth century, if Internet equity crowd-funding had been invented at the time, when the South Sea Company in the UK lied about its discovery of gold in South America. The scam would quickly be exposed as investors could easily communicate with a local resident to confirm whether there were really a mine—if so, there would be no South Sea Bubble, and the notorious Bubble Act which led to a closure of stock market for almost one hundred years would never have happened![47]

4.3 The Response of Securities Law in Major Jurisdictions

While realizing the importance of balancing the enforcement of securities law and the rapid development of information technology, the law-makers and regulators did take some steps to improve the legal system. For example, in the US, when in the middle of 1990s some fund-raisers started to use online platforms for information disclosure, the SEC initially took a negative opinion by announcing that online disclosure was in breach of the rules of Regulation D (i.e. prohibiting issuers who seek exemption of private offering from public solicitation and advertisement).[48] But later the SEC softened its attitude and allowed Internet companies to provide information services for issuers, as long as they made sure these information sources were only accessible to accredited investors.[49]

Nevertheless, such a progress of regulatory practice is not enough: it still fails to fully understand the public features of Internet technology, and neither can it effectively coordinate both policies of investor protection and facilitation of financing. Along with the prevalence of the Internet, issuers are more likely to use online platforms, as a low-cost medium of information, to advertise their projects and solicit

---

Professions and Corporate Governance, Oxford University Press, 2006. As for the role of "gatekeeper" in equity crowd-funding industry, see Lars Hornuf & Armin Schwienbacher, *Which Securities Regulation Promotes Crowdinvesting?* 17 (2014), *available at* http://ssrn.com/abstract=2412124.

[46] See Jonathan M. Karpoff and John R. Lott, Jr., The Reputational Penalty Firms Bear from Committing Criminal Fraud, *Journal of Law & Economics*, Vol. 36, No. 2 (Oct., 1993), pp. 757–802.

[47] See Ron Harris, "The Bubble Act: Its Passage and Its Effects on Business Organization", *The Journal of Economic History*, Vol. 54, No. 3. (Sep., 1994), pp. 610–627.

[48] See "Use of Electronic Media for Delivery Purposes", Release NO. 33–7233, Oct. 6, 1995.

[49] See Staff no-action letters, IPONET (available July 26, 1996); Lamp Technologies, Inc. (available May 29, 1997).

investors. However, the private offering exemption rules in the securities law (e.g. Rule 506 of Regulation D) normally prohibit companies from "general solicitation or advertising" in the process of securities offering; otherwise, they will no longer be allowed to remain exempt from registration requirements. In other words, Internet financing transactions cannot benefit from the "safe harbor" created by the law for private offering.

This disappointing arrangement has been in some ways improved since 2012 as the JOBS Act relaxed the restriction. In Title II of the Act, it is required that the SEC shall revise Rule 506 to allow "general solicitation or advertising" being used in private offering.[50] It may possibly create more legal space for Internet technology to be applied in fund-raising transactions of small- and medium-sized firms. However, unfortunately, in its final version of the rules issued in 2013, the SEC decided that such a relaxation may only be available in the situation where securities are exclusively offered to accredited investors.[51] Thus, the result of the JOBS Act turns out to be simply a slight adjustment of the current system, rather than a prospective reform to meet the demands of public investors on equity crowd-funding.

Of course, it would be too pessimistic to say that the JOBS Act of 2012 did not bring any good news to the equity crowd-funding industry. The most impressive breakthrough is the inclusion of Title III titled "crowd-funding" in which the Act authorizes the SEC to make rules to offer exemption to equity crowd-funding transactions based on online platforms. Under this authorization, the SEC officially issued its rules in October 2015, exempting issuers in equity crowd-funding from the registration requirement of federal securities law, if the following conditions are satisfied: (1) the amount of the securities that may be sold by an issuer during the 12-month period preceding the date of such transaction cannot exceed $1 million dollars; (2) in a 12-month period, an individual investor is limited to investing in securities sold by an issuer "(i) the greater of $2,000 or 5 percent of the lesser of the investor's annual income or net worth if either annual income or net worth is less than $100,000; or (ii) 10 percent of the lesser of the investor's annual income or net worth, not to exceed an amount sold of $100,000, if both annual income and net worth are $100,000 or more".[52] In addition, the JOBS Act and the SEC Rules also allows equity crowd-funding transactions to be conducted through a "funding portal"[53] so that those Internet-based platforms which are not registered brokers, may be recognized as eligible.

Outside the US, faced with the rise of equity crowd-funding, other jurisdictions have also introduced similar rules to cope with such a new financial phenomenon. For

[50] Pub. L. No. 112-106, 126 Stat. 306 § 201(a)(1).

[51] See Eliminating the Prohibition Against General Solicitation and General Advertising in Rule 506 and Rule 144A Offerings, Release No. 33-9415 (July 10, 2013).

[52] See Crowdfunding, Release Nos. 33-9974; 34-76324 (October 30, 2015).

[53] For the difference between conceptions of "funding portal" and "securities intermediary" (a definition distinct from the traditional idea of "securities broker"), please see Joan M. Heminway, The New Intermediary on the Block: Funding Portals under the CROWDFUND Act (June 18, 2013), *UC Davis Business Law Journal*, Vol. 13, p. 177 (2013).

example, in the UK, the Financial Conduct Authority (FCA) exempts equity crowd-funding on the conditions that those crowd-funding platforms limit their clients to sophisticated investors, high net-worth individuals or investors who are capable of being advised by professional institutions. For other clients not included in the above group, the platforms must ensure that these clients certify not to invest more than 10% of their net investible financial assets (excluding their primary residence, pensions and life cover). And the FCA requires that the platforms must apply an appropriateness test before sending investment materials to clients not otherwise provided.[54]

Similarly, in January 2016, a legal instrument entered into force in several provisions of Canada (including Quebec and Ontario) creating an exemptions rule for Internet-based equity crowd-funding. It provides that the exemption will only be available if: (1) the amount raised by the issuer does not exceed $1.5 million Canadian dollars within the 12–month period; (2) an accredited investor does not invest more than $25,000 Canadian dollars for a single investment (not exceeding $50,000 Canadian dollars for all crowd-funding transactions in reliance on the exemption in the same calendar year), or an individual who is not an accredited investor does not break the upper-limit of investment amount of $2500 Canadian dollars (maximum of 10,000 Canadian dollars for aggregated investment amounts over one year).[55]

In Germany, such kinds of exemption have been explicitly recognized under new legislation—e.g. Kleinanlegerschutzgesetz (Small Investor Protection Act)—which came into force in July 10 of 2015. Subsection 1 of Section 2a makes it clear that, as long as the financing amount did not exceed €2.5 million EURO, there is no disclosure requirement for the issuer to publish a prospectus. Along with the exemption, the Act sets up a limit on maximum investment amounts by an individual to equity crowd-funding. The platforms have a duty to make sure that each investor is only investing, on one investment project, up to €1000 EURO[56] (or up to €10,000 EURO once the investor proves he or she has more than €100,000 EURO financial assets[57]), or his or her investment amount will not be more than twice average monthly net income.[58]

All in sum, from the legislative experience of most jurisdictions, it is not difficult to find that, in the process of designing an exemption system for equity crowd-funding, law-makers are taking every effort to break through the traditional distinction between public and private offerings. The logic of such an old-fashioned classification is based on an understanding that: for offerings open to the venerable public, a strict

[54] See "The FCA's regulatory approach to crowdfunding over the internet, and the promotion of non-readily realisable securities by other media: Feedback to CP13/13 and final rules", Financial Conduct Authority Policy Statement PS14/4, March 2014.

[55] See "Multilateral Instrument 45-108 Crowdfunding", available at http://www.osc.gov.on.ca/documents/en/Securities-Category4/mi_20160114_45-108_crowdfunding.pdf.

[56] Paragraph 1, Subsection 3, Section 2a, Kleinanlegerschutzgesetz. See http://dipbt.bundestag.de/doc/btd/18/047/1804708.pdf; http://www.friedfrank.com/siteFiles/Publications/FINAL%20v6%20English%20-%206-12-2015%20-%20TOC%20Memo%20-%20Investment%20Law%20%20The%20German%20Small%20Investor%20Protection.pdf.

[57] Paragraph 2, Subsection 3, Section 2a.

[58] Paragraph 3, Subsection 3, Section 2a.

enforcement of securities law is necessary to protect investors; but if the size of the offering is small (e.g. the maximum number of investors are restricted to 200 persons similar to that which Chinese securities law provides) or investors are sophisticated or wealthy enough to protect themselves (e.g. the concept of "accredited investors" as US federal securities law requires), then it may be exempted from some regulatory requirements of securities law (e.g. registration of offering) so as to serve the policy agenda of facilitation of financing.

However, in the online world of the Information Age, such a classification has its limitations. The inherent features of equity crowd-funding are to the largest extent taking advantage of the rapid communication function of the Internet, making the offering known to as many people as possible in a short time. However, if we determine that this kind of public offering must unconditionally follow all the requirements of securities law, it would certainly make equity crowd-funding unworkable and thus destroy this innovative financing channel for start-up firms. Consequently, in order to resolve this dilemma, it is noted that many countries are reforming their law or regulatory practice to create an easier way for those firms who are interested in using the Internet to raise funds, i.e. for financing transactions in reliance on Internet-based equity crowd-funding. There is no longer a requirement that they shall comply with all strict rules applicable to public offering, but instead may enjoy an exemption treatment on the condition that the size of fund raising and the amount of an individual's investment do not exceed certain limits.

5 Final Remarks

The coming of the Internet Age makes legal scholars wonder: what changes are brought to the legal institution of securities markets due to the prevalence of information technology? Besides lowering the cost of securities issuance and transactions, at issue is whether the new technology has changed or is about to change the foundation of our securities law and its rule structure? The purpose of this chapter is just to answer these questions and reveal a phenomenon in the legal field: the appearance of equity crowd-funding by reliance on Internet technology not only introduces a new business model to the securities market, but also has a fundamental impact on securities law and its legislative philosophy.

Direct evidence of this phenomenon is that many jurisdictions (US as a typical example) have expanded the exemption system in their securities legislation to cover online equity crowd-funding and created some specific exemption rules for equity crowd-funding. And, of course, such a development as we all can see, is just a beginning. It is not simply some minor modification of one or two rules in the law; predictably, the inherent meaning of this change is to promote a rethink of the internal philosophy of securities law making. In fact, as discussed in this chapter, law-makers and regulatory agencies around the world have realized this structural influence of the internet on the legal system of the securities market and have started to take action to embrace this revolution.

Correction to: Redistribution of Powers in the Case of Asset Management Product Regulation in China

Correction to:
Chapter 3 in: T. Huang and W. He, *Politics Meets Markets*, Contemporary Chinese Civil and Commercial Law, https://doi.org/10.1007/978-981-97-9176-7_3

The original version of the book was inadvertently published with significant typographical error in Chapter 3 which has now been corrected. The book and the chapter have been updated with the changes.

The updated version of this chapter can be found at
https://doi.org/10.1007/978-981-97-9176-7_3

T. Huang and W. He, *Politics Meets Markets*, Contemporary Chinese Civil and Commercial Law, https://doi.org/10.1007/978-981-97-9176-7_9

Conclusion

The genesis of our work stems from the belief that understanding the formation and operation of China's financial markets and its legal system cannot be separated from its unique political system and environment. This key distinction sets China's financial markets legal system apart from those of most other countries, especially developed financial markets. With this "key," we can unlock the essence of the interplay between China's financial markets and its political framework.

It is important to clarify that our observations of China's financial markets legal system from a political perspective is not intended to draw any ultimate conclusions. Instead, the aim is to invoke academic debates as to the relationship between financial markets, law, and political systems. It is crucial to move beyond a naive understanding of financial markets legal systems as merely black-and-white rules or abstract legal framework.

Moreover, as we complete this work, the influence of political factors on China's financial markets legal system appears to be becoming more intense and explicit. At the Central Financial Work Conference held in 2023, Xi Jinping emphasized the "deep understanding of the political and people-oriented nature of financial work", which will determine the direction of financial markets legislation and enforcement in China for a long time. This includes the anti-corruption storms in the financial sector initiated by the Party in recent years, the establishment of the highest de facto financial regulatory authority within the Party system. These policies, though not formally documented in law, continually remind us of the political determinants underlying China's financial markets laws.

Recently, an official publication revealed that Xi Jinping, in an internal speech in 2019, quoted a passage from Vladimir Lenin's *Imperialism, the Highest Stage of Capitalism*:

> Capital has reached an extreme degree of separation from production. Although commodity production is still regarded as the foundation of the entire economy, it has actually been undermined, with most profits being taken by the 'geniuses' engaged in financial dealings.

This may help us better understand the "new era" of China's financial markets.

T. Huang and W. He, *Politics Meets Markets*, Contemporary Chinese Civil and Commercial Law, https://doi.org/10.1007/978-981-97-9176-7

The manufacturer's authorised representative in the EU is Springer Nature Customer Service Centre GmbH, Europaplatz 3, 69115 Heidelberg, Germany. If you have any concerns regarding our products, please contact ProductSafety@springernature.com

Printed and bound by CPI Group (UK) Ltd, Croydon, CR0 4YY
01/10/2026
02225859-0001